How to Get Your Share of Government Treasure

A Guide to Valuable
Benefits and Services

How to Get Your Share of Government Treasure

A Guide to Valuable Benefits and Services

by Gaylord Shaw
and the Editors
of U.S.News &
World Report Books

U.S.NEWS & WORLD REPORT BOOKS

A division of U.S.News & World Report, Inc.

WASHINGTON, D.C.

U.S.NEWS & WORLD REPORT BOOKS

Directing Editor: Joseph Newman

MONEY MANAGEMENT LIBRARY

Editor: Roslyn Grant

First Printing, 1975
Second Printing, Revised, 1976
Third Printing, Revised, 1978

Trade Distribution by Simon and Schuster
New York, New York 10020

ISBN 0-89193-417-0

Library of Congress Catalog Card Number 75-7857

Printed in the United States of America

Contents

Illustrations

Acknowledgments

Gaylord Shaw and the Editors of *U.S. News & World Report Books* are grateful for the assistance of scores of federal officials in gathering material for this book. The helpful officials include those at the Departments of Agriculture, Commerce, Defense, Health, Education, and Welfare, Housing and Urban Development, Interior, Justice, Labor, Transportation, and Treasury, and those at such agencies as ACTION, the Civil Service Commission, Consumer Product Safety Commission, Federal Trade Commission, General Services Administration, Government Printing Office, Library of Congress, National Foundation of the Arts and the Humanities, National Science Foundation, Small Business Administration, Social Security Administration, and the Veterans Administration.

CHAPTER 1

Getting
Your
Fair
Share

Every year you pay your fair share of federal taxes. But you may
not be receiving in return your fair share of government benefits
and services.

Like most Americans, you probably enjoy some government
benefits and services without consciously realizing it—the interstate highway you drive on, the delivery of your mail, the water
that comes to your home from a federally-built reservoir. Then
there are the intangible benefits: a secure, well-defended nation;
an economy that, despite its troubles, is still the strongest in the
world.

Even so, chances are that you are not receiving your full, fair
share of what the government offers. This is because our government offers many benefits and services you may not know about,
including some that you may never have even thought possible.

Each year the government, in effect, bills you for your share of
the benefits and services it is providing. It is up to you to make

certain that you are receiving all that your payments of those bills—your tax payments—entitle you to claim.

The payments made by individual Americans to their government is substantial. In a recent year, individual income taxes accounted for 39 cents of every dollar collected by the government. The employees' share of Social Security taxes amounted to another 14 cents. So income and Social Security taxes paid by individuals made up 53 cents of every dollar in federal revenue.

In return for each dollar received from the taxpayers, the government paid out 38 cents in benefits to individuals, spent 26 cents for national defense, 16 cents in grants to states and localities, 7 cents for net interest, and 13 cents for other federal operations.

Looking at it another way, of the more than $400 billion collected annually in taxes, payments by individuals amount to about $210 billion. On the other side of the ledger, the government expends about $175 billion annually in what economists call "domestic transfer payments"—direct payments to individual Americans.

Since you are paying taxes to your government, and the government is offering benefits and services in return, the question then is: How can you be certain that you are getting your fair share of those benefits and services?

This guide is designed to help you answer that question. It gives details on hundreds of government programs, telling you whether you qualify and, if so, how and where you can apply.

You may say, "It's not worth the trouble. There's so much red tape."

True, there are procedures that must be followed in applying for government benefits and services, but you should not let impatience with red tape deter you. Here are some pointers to guide you through the bureaucratic maze:

• *Make sure that you are dealing with the right office.* Each government agency is divided into many bureaus, divisions, or offices. You will save time and trouble if you begin with the right one.

• *Do not hesitate to ask questions or seek advice.* Government employees are there to serve you—after all, your tax dollars pay their salaries—and you will find that they are experts in their field.

The Federal Budget Dollar

(Fiscal Year 1978 Estimate)

Where it comes from . . .

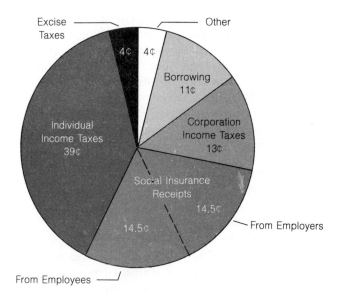

Where it goes . . .

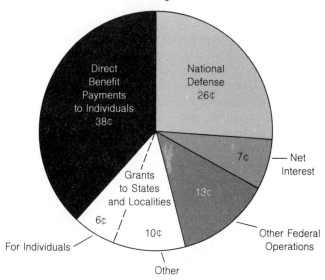

Source: Office of Management and Budget

• *If you are dissatisfied, go to a higher level.* If a local office fails to give you what you think you are entitled to, contact the district or regional office. And if this does not suffice, bring your case to the attention of the national headquarters office.

• *Do not get discouraged and do not give up.* If your request for benefits is turned down, find out why—most agencies are required to explain their decisions to you. Then perhaps you can make the necessary adjustments to win approval of your request.

• *If all else fails, write to your congressional representatives.* Members of Congress are in Washington to serve you, and you will find that their staffs are masters in unclogging the bureaucratic pipeline.

Wide variety of assistance

As you will find in the chapters that follow, government benefits and services come in a remarkably wide variety of forms. There are, for example:

• *Direct Cash Payments.* Perhaps the best known direct payments are Social Security retirement benefits, but there also are Social Security disability and death payments, veterans' education aid and pensions, and a host of other programs such as unemployment compensation.

• *Indirect Payments.* Payments under the Medicare program sometimes go directly to doctors and hospitals for your benefit, and in some educational fellowship programs, the funds go directly to colleges to pay tuition and other expenses.

• *Grants.* In some instances, the government is willing to pick up the tab for your overseas travel expenses if you participate in exchanges and other programs. The government also makes grants to artists, authors, and others.

• *Loans.* Through scores of the programs, loans are made under the auspices of the federal government at a rate of about $30 billion a year. These direct and guaranteed loans offer more favorable terms than are otherwise available to unassisted borrowers. Besides the well-known housing loans, aid is available to business people, farmers, students, and almost anyone else with a good credit rating.

• *Services.* No matter what your field of interest, the government probably can offer you free or low-cost services. There are consumer services, for instance, as well as advice and counseling

Federal Spending Rises...

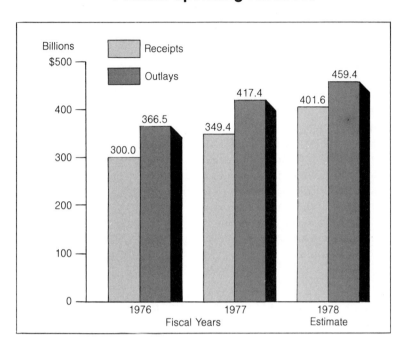

... And the Individual Gets a Bigger Share

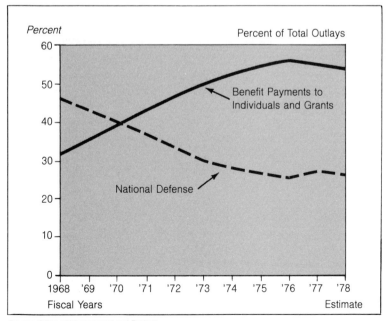

Source: Office of Management and Budget

on employment opportunities and almost countless other subjects.

• *Other Opportunities.* Under other programs, the government makes it possible for you to buy isolated tracts of public
land or surplus government equipment and supplies. It also lets
you stake a mining claim. And it provides opportunities for you to
invest in such government securities as bonds and notes.

All these types of government benefits and services available to
you are just the tip of the iceberg. In the chapters that follow, you
will find scores of programs that can mean cash in your pocket, a
more comfortable standard of living, and perhaps a realization of
long-held ambitions and dreams.

As you read on, remember that any benefits and services you
receive from the government are simply a fair return for the
money you pay in taxes.

CHAPTER 2

If
You
Are in
Business

Government aid for business dates back to the nation's founding fathers. The first Congress in 1789 set up a shipping system that serves as a pattern for today's maritime subsidies. In the nearly 200 years since then, the forms and amounts of aid have grown by leaps and bounds.

The growth of aid to business has been so dramatic that the Commerce Department set up a special section especially to help the business community make fullest use of government resources. But a year after it began operation, the office had not been able to compile a listing of all the types of assistance available to private enterprise. "It's so big," a spokesman said, "that it's just beyond the comprehension of anyone."

One study several years ago by the Associated Press estimated that private enterprise in America collects roughly $30 billion annually from the federal government in all types of aid. The study found that the aid came in many forms: cash payments, tax breaks, loans at bargain rates, technical guidance, and low-cost services.

In this chapter many of the major types of aid for business will be examined to help you determine if you can qualify for assistance in setting up your own business or in expanding your present one.

Some related programs are discussed in subsequent chapters. For example, loans for business people who are veterans are detailed in chapter 7 and loans for business people interested in real estate investment are outlined in chapter 9.

Doing business with the government

The federal government is big business. It awards billions of dollars in contracts each year—and this can mean business for companies large and small. To promote the interest and participation of business concerns in government contracts, the General Services Administration operates a nationwide chain of Business Service Centers.

These centers provide information and counseling—free of charge—to assist business firms in developing the government market potential for their products and services. The centers also aid in obtaining contracting opportunities and in purchasing surplus property. About 150,000 businessmen receive free advice and counseling from the centers each year.

Business opportunities with the government are countless. There are, for example, concession contracts on military bases ranging from bowling alleys to barber shops. There are recurring needs for contractors to repair and renovate government facilities. And there is a vast market in meeting the government's supply and service needs.

If you wish to cash in on these opportunities, your first step should be to contact the GSA Business Service Center nearest you. Their addresses and telephone numbers are listed on page 19. You can obtain a copy of the publication *Doing Business With the Federal Government* from any of these centers.

Small business loans

The Small Business Administration (SBA) makes direct loans and also participates with banks and other lending institutions in providing loans to small manufacturers, wholesalers, retailers, ser-

Locations of Business Service Centers
Operated by the General Services Administration

California
300 North Los Angeles
Los Angeles, CA 90012
(213) 688-3210

525 Market Street
San Francisco, CA 94105
(415) 556-2122

Colorado
Building 41,
Denver Federal Center
Denver, CO 80225
(303) 234-2216

District of Columbia
Seventh and D Streets, S.W.
Washington, DC 20407
(202) 472-1804

Georgia
1776 Peachtree Street, N.W.
Atlanta, GA 30309
(404) 881-3934

Illinois
230 South Dearborn Street
Chicago, IL 60604
(312) 353-5383

Massachusetts
John W. McCormack
   Federal Building
Boston, MA 02109
(617) 223-2868

Missouri
1500 East Bannister Road
Kansas City, MO 64131
(816) 926-7203

New York
26 Federal Plaza
New York, NY 10007
(212) 264-1234

Pennsylvania
600 Arch Street
Philadelphia, PA 19106
(215) 597-9613

Texas
819 Taylor Street
Fort Worth, TX 76102
(817) 334-3284

515 Rusk Street
Houston, TX 77002
(713) 226-5787

Washington
440 Federal Building
915 Second Avenue
Seattle, WA 98174
(206) 442-5556

vice establishments, and other businesses when financing is not otherwise available to them on reasonable terms.

Loans are made for the following purposes:

• To finance business construction, expansion, or conversion.

• To finance the purchase of equipment, facilities, machinery, supplies, or materials.

• To supply working capital.

• To finance special projects under certain circumstances.

SBA prefers not to get involved in debt refinancing and will not do so unless it results in the orderly growth of the business and is not merely a means of substituting an SBA loan for private financing.

In most cases, loans are restricted to small businesses which are independently owned and operated and which are not dominant in their fields. Specific criteria will be explained to you at any SBA office, but generally manufacturers cannot have average employment of more than 250 persons; wholesalers cannot have annual sales of more than $9.5 million; and retail and service concerns cannot have revenues of more than $2 million. There are many exceptions, however, that should be checked out.

In addition to the "small business" criteria, a loan applicant must meet certain credit and policy requirements. Some of the requirements are:

• An applicant must be of good character.

• There must be evidence that the applicant has the ability to operate the business successfully.

• The applicant must have enough capital in the business so that, with loan assistance, it will be possible for him or her to operate on a sound financial basis.

• As required by the Small Business Act, the proposed loan must be "of such sound value or so secured as reasonably to assure repayment."

• The past earnings record and future prospects of the applicant must indicate ability to repay a loan out of earnings from the business.

Since it is a public agency, using taxpayers' funds, the SBA must meet the requirements set by Congress. Thus it will not make regular business loans under certain circumstances. Loans will *not* be granted:

• If the funds are otherwise available on reasonable terms from a private financial institution; or from the disposal at a fair price of assets not required by the applicant in the conduct of the business or not reasonably necessary to its potential growth; or through the use of personal credit and/or resources of the owner, partners, or principal stockholders; or from other government agencies which provide credit specifically for the applicant's type of business; or from other known sources of credit.

• If the loan would be used to pay off creditors who are inadequately secured and are in a position to sustain a loss; or to provide funds for distribution or payment to the owner, partners, or shareholders of an applicant; or to refinance a debt owed to a small business investment company; or to replenish working capital funds previously used for any of these purposes.

• If the loan will provide or will free funds for speculation in any kind of property, real or personal, tangible or intangible.

• If the applicant is a charitable institution or nonprofit enterprise, except for cooperatives that carry on a business activity for the purpose of obtaining monetary benefit for their members in the operations of their otherwise eligible small business concerns.

• If the applicant is a newspaper, book publishing company, magazine, radio or television broadcasting company, or similar enterprise.

• If any of the gross income of the business (or any of its principal owners) is derived from gambling activities, except for those small firms which obtain less than one-third of their gross income from the sale of official state lottery tickets under a state license.

• If the loan is to provide funds to an enterprise primarily engaged in the business of lending or investments or to an otherwise eligible enterprise for the purpose of financing investments not related or essential to the enterprise.

• If the purpose of the loan is to finance the acquisition, construction, improvement, or operation of real property that is, or is to be, held for sale or investment.

• If the effect of the granting of the financial assistance will be to encourage monopoly or will be inconsistent with the accepted standards of the American system of free competitive enterprise.

• If the proceeds of the loan will be used for moving an eligible business when the move is for other than a sound business purpose.

In recent years, the SBA has been approving over 20,000 loans annually, totaling about $2.5 billion in direct and guaranteed loans. The direct loans have averaged about $30,000 and the guaranteed loans have averaged about $75,000.

Most loans carry a ten-year repayment period, but a fifteen-year period is allowed for the portion of the loan required for construction. The interest rate is subject to change, but generally is more favorable than that available in the open market.

How to apply: Applications are filed in the field office serving the area in which the applicant's business is located. When the participating bank is in another area, applications may be filed with the field office serving that area if the two field offices involved agree to this procedure.

Rural business loans

The Farmers Home Administration makes loans to establish business enterprises in any area outside the boundary of a city with a population of 50,000 or more and its adjacent urbanized areas with a density of more than 100 persons per square mile. Priority is given to applications for projects in open country, rural communities, and towns with no more than 25,000 population.

This type of credit is provided through two channels. For individuals and private organizations, the Farmers Home Administration guarantees loans made by private lenders. Application is made to a private lender and the agency contracts to reimburse the lender for up to 90 percent of any loss sustained on such a loan. For public bodies, the agency makes and services the loans, and applicants apply directly to the Farmers Home Administration.

Economic Opportunity Loans

The SBA operates a special loan program for low-income or socially disadvantaged persons who need assistance in starting or operating a small business. Known as Economic Opportunity Loans, the funds are intended for individuals who have been denied the opportunity to acquire adequate business financing on reasonable terms through normal lending channels.

Except for the socially or economically disadvantaged criteria, the requirements for the loans generally are the same as for the regular SBA loan program. Direct or guaranteed loans may be made up to a maximum of $100,000, with a fifteen-year maxi-

Small Business Administration
District Office Locations

Albuquerque, N.M.
Anchorage, Alaska
Atlanta, Ga.
Augusta, Maine

Birmingham, Ala.
Boise, Idaho
Boston, Mass.

Casper, Wyo.
Charlotte, N.C.
Chicago, Ill.
Cincinnati, Ohio
Clarksburg, W.Va.
Cleveland, Ohio
Columbia, S.C.
Columbus, Ohio
Concord, N.H.

Dallas, Tex.
Denver, Colo.
Des Moines, Iowa
Detroit, Mich.

Fairbanks, Alaska
Fargo, N.Dak.

Harlingen, Tex.

Hartford, Conn.
Hato Rey, P.R.
Helena, Mont.
Holyoke, Mass.
Honolulu, Hawaii
Houston, Tex.

Indianapolis, Ind.

Jackson, Miss.
Jacksonville, Fla.

Kansas City, Mo.
Knoxville, Tenn.

Little Rock, Ark.
Los Angeles, Calif.
Louisville, Ky.
Lubbock, Tex.

Madison, Wis.
Marshall, Tex.
Miami, Fla.
Minneapolis, Minn.
Montpelier, Vt.

Nashville, Tenn.
Newark, N.J.

New Orleans, La.
New York, N.Y.

Oklahoma City, Okla.
Omaha, Nebr.

Philadelphia, Pa.
Phoenix, Ariz.
Pittsburgh, Pa.
Portland, Oreg.
Providence, R.I.

Richmond, Va.
Rochester, N.Y.

St. Louis, Mo.
Salt Lake City, Utah
San Antonio, Tex.
San Diego, Calif.
San Francisco, Calif.
Seattle, Wash.
Sioux Falls, S.Dak.
Spokane, Wash.
Springfield, Ill.
Syracuse, N.Y.

Washington, D.C.
Wichita, Kans.

mum maturity. Again, interest rates generally are less than those asked by regular lenders.

In recent years, the SBA has made or guaranteed about $120 million in Economic Opportunity Loans annually. The direct loans have averaged about $20,000 and the guaranteed loans have averaged about $22,000.

How to apply: Applications are made to and processed by the SBA field office serving the area in which the business is located.

Small Business Investment Companies

In an effort to increase the flow of financial assistance to small business concerns, the SBA licenses and provides some financial aid for Small Business Investment Companies, known as SBICs.

An SBIC can be either publicly or privately owned and can qualify for SBA assistance at the rate of three or four dollars for every dollar obtained from private sources. The SBA funds are made available either through the purchase of an SBIC's debentures, through SBA guarantee of the firm's debentures sold to institutional lenders or to the public, or through the purchase by SBA of the firm's preferred stock.

Each SBIC in turn provides financial assistance to small business concerns either by making long-term loans or by purchasing securities of the debt or equity type issued by the small business firms.

According to the SBA, the emphasis is on providing assistance to pioneering concerns which are developing new products, processes, and markets.

How to apply: Further information and appropriate forms can be obtained from any SBA office. Applications should be submitted to the SBA headquarters office, 1441 L Street, N.W., Washington, D.C. 20416.

Energy crisis loans

With the energy crisis of the 1970s, the SBA initiated a program of direct or guaranteed loans to assist small business concerns seriously and adversely affected by a shortage of fuel, electrical energy, energy-producing resources, or by a lack of materials resulting from such energy shortages.

The funds may be used for working capital, to convert operations to a different fuel source, or to handle exceptional expenses caused by the energy shortage. Except for Vietnam-era veterans, the business must have been in operation for the preceding three years.

Applications are made to SBA field offices.

Management assistance

To help prospective as well as present small business people improve their skills in operating a business, the SBA offers a wide-ranging program of management assistance, counseling, and training. This assistance includes the following:

• *Workshops, Management Courses, Conferences, and Clinics.* In recent years, the SBA has arranged about 4,000 of these sessions annually, with attendance by about 150,000 current or future business owners.

• *Volunteer Management Counselors.* The Service Corps of Retired Executives (SCORE) and the Active Corps of Executives (ACE) are the backbone of this volunteer program. SCORE has 6,200 retired successful business people who offer lifetimes of practical experience to new business people, and ACE has 2,700 men and women still active in all fields of business who do counseling on a volunteer basis.

• *Small Business Institutes.* More than 350 colleges and universities participate in this program in which senior and graduate students majoring in business administration help small firms develop improved business practices. During one recent year, about 8,600 students handled more than 4,300 cases, providing small business firms with the needed management counseling and at the same time gaining academic credits.

• *Publications.* During a typical year the SBA distributes more than five million publications, most of which offer practical advice to small business people. One of the most popular recent publications is *Business Plan for Retailers,* a combination of narrative and worksheets to help owners and prospective owners of retail businesses to prepare a feasible plan.

How to apply: To obtain management assistance, written or personal applications should be made to any Small Business Administration field office.

Procurement assistance

The SBA also makes extensive efforts to assure that small businesses receive a fair share of contracts and subcontracts for federal government supplies and services and a fair share of property sold by the government.

This assistance takes varied forms. For example, the SBA maintains a nationwide roster of some 20,000 small firms—manufacturing, services, supply, construction, research, and minority—for referral to government purchasing agents and the nation's largest prime contractors.

In addition, the agency presses for small business set-asides on federal contracts, restricting the bidding and awards to small business only. It also issues certificates of competency to small businesses that are low bidders on contracts and need to have their ability to perform, credit, and production capacity verified.

A measure of the success of this program is that in a recent year, out of a total of $50 billion in federal contracts, small businesses received $13 billion, more than one-fourth of the total.

How to apply: Contact any SBA field office.

Aid for minority business people

Members of minority groups who are business people or potential business people are eligible for a range of special programs as well as the government's regular aid programs.

The Office of Minority Business Enterprise within the Commerce Department coordinates federal assistance programs for minorities to establish or expand businesses. It does not make loans and grants directly to minority business people, but it does channel funds to nonprofit, community-based organizations which in turn help individual business people. This office also offers a number of publications, such as the *Special Catalog of Federal Programs Assisting Minority Enterprise.* This and other publications can be obtained by writing OMBE Service Information Center, Department of Commerce, Washington, D.C. 20230.

The SBA has been the principal source of minority financing among all federal departments, making 90 percent of all loans and guarantees. In recent years, about 25 percent of all SBA loans and 15 percent of its total loan dollars went to minority enterprises.

In addition to the loans, the SBA has special programs of procurement assistance, management counseling, and technical assistance for minority or disadvantaged business people, plus a pro-

Increase in Loans to Minority Businesses
By Small Business Administration
(Direct and Guaranteed Loans)

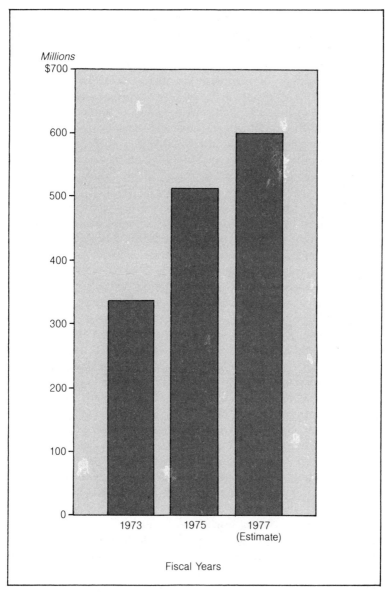

Source: Office of Management and Budget

gram to help minority firms supply goods and services to major corporations. In explaining eligibility requirements for these special programs, the SBA says:

"A principal factor in eligibility is qualification as a disadvantaged person. These are persons who, because of reasons beyond their control, have been deprived of the opportunity to develop and maintain a position in the competitive economy because of social or economic disadvantage. In many cases, persons in the following minority groups have been so deprived: Black Americans, American Indians, Spanish Americans, Oriental Americans, Eskimos, and Aleuts. However, the class of socially or economically disadvantaged is not limited to members of these groups."

How to apply: Contact any SBA field office or the Office of Minority Business Enterprise.

Special types of loans

For business people facing hardships because of such circumstances as required compliance with federal safety and inspection standards, the government has several specialized loan programs. There also is a program for small firms that are unable to obtain surety bonds, and aid for business people who cannot market their products because of disease or toxicity resulting from natural or undetermined causes. Here are the details:

• *Meat and Poultry Inspection Loans.* The SBA makes direct and guaranteed loans to assist small business concerns which suffer substantial economic injury caused by compliance with standards of federal egg, poultry, and meat inspection laws. The loans are to make additions to or alteration in equipment, facilities, or methods of operations to meet federal requirements. Loans generally are limited to $500,000, with a maximum thirty-year repayment period unless substantial hardship is proven. Prior to filing a loan application with the SBA, the business must be inspected by the Department of Agriculture or a state agency which provides a written list of changes that are necessary to meet established requirements.

• *Occupational Safety and Health Loans.* Another SBA program offers direct and guaranteed loans to help small businesses that are likely to suffer substantial economic injury because of compliance with standards under the Occupational Safety and Health Act (OSHA) of 1970. Loans usually are limited to

$500,000, with a maximum thirty-year maturity. An applicant must submit a report from a licensed engineer or an architect covering work required to comply with OSHA standards.

• *Coal Mine Health and Safety Loans.* To assist small coal mine operators in complying with federal health and safety standards, the SBA makes direct and guaranteed loans to improve equipment, facilities, or method of operation. Although there is no statutory dollar limitation, the loans generally do not exceed $500,000. The applicant must have fewer than 250 employees and must have received a notice of deficiency from the Mining Enforcement and Safety Administration.

• *Product Disaster Loans.* The SBA makes direct loans of varying amounts to small business firms suffering economic injury resulting from inability to market a product for human consumption because of a finding of toxicity from natural or unknown causes. The loans, which have a maximum repayment period of thirty years, can be used to pay current liabilities the business could otherwise have paid if the disaster had not occurred. Funds also can be used for working capital and, to some extent, to acquire equipment or facilities to make a marketable product.

• *Air and Water Pollution Control Loans.* To aid small business people likely to suffer economic injury because of having to meet air and water pollution control requirements, the SBA offers both direct and guaranteed loans. There usually is a $500,000 limit for these loans, but in recent years some have exceeded that amount.

• *Displaced Business Loans.* Small business firms suffering economic injury caused by federally-assisted construction projects are eligible for direct and insured loans with repayment periods of up to thirty years. The loans have usually been in the $100,000 to $150,000 range. In a similar category are loans for economic injury resulting from the closing of military bases or installations.

• *Handicapped Assistance Loans.* Direct, insured, and guaranteed loans are available to organizations and businesses owned by or employing the handicapped. These loans have a fifteen-year repayment period. The loans can range up to $350,000, but in recent years they have averaged about $77,000.

• *Surety Bond Guarantees.* Small construction contractors who, for various reasons, are unable to obtain surety bonds may be eligible for aid from the SBA. The agency guarantees up to 90 percent of the losses on bonds for contracts of $1,000,000 or less on which bonding is a requirement. Guarantees are available on a case-by-case basis for contractors whose gross annual receipts average less than $2,000,000 a year. The contractor applies directly to an insurance company or broker, which in turn contacts a surety company to process the application. The surety company deals directly with the SBA. Local SBA offices provide information and help to contractors in the preparation of applications.

Aid for businesses overseas

Business people interested in expanding or launching overseas operations may be eligible for technical assistance, loans, guarantees, and investment insurance from the federal government.

The Commerce Department's Domestic and International Business Administration, for example, handles about 70,000 inquiries a year from firms seeking information on overseas opportunities, foreign economics, trade openings abroad, aid to exporters, and export quotas and tariffs. The agency also provides guidance to American business people through the use of foreign marketing journals and statistical reports.

To encourage business people to initiate or expand export trade, the agency offers advice and counseling as well as assistance in such sales promotion efforts as trade fairs.

Business people seeking this type of information or assistance should contact their nearest Commerce Department field office or the headquarters office, Washington, D.C. 20230.

The Overseas Private Investment Corporation (OPIC) administers programs of financial assistance for American investors interested in foreign operations. Here are details of OPIC programs:

• *Foreign Investment Guarantees.* To encourage private American investment in developing countries, OPIC will guarantee loans to U.S. citizens, corporations, partnerships, or wholly-owned foreign subsidiaries of such corporations. The guaranteed loans may not exceed 75 percent of the total investment in the project. These are not small projects—the assistance ranged from $500,000 to $12.5 million in recent years and averaged nearly $6 million.

• *Foreign Investment Insurance.* Another OPIC program insures investments of eligible American investors in less-developed friendly countries and areas against the risks of inconvertibility, expropriation, war, revolution, and insurrection. Foreign government approval is required before the insurance can be approved by the OPIC. Again, the insurance is for major projects. In recent years, the insured investments have ranged up to nearly $25 million and have averaged more than $2 million.

• *Pre-Investment Assistance.* The objective of this OPIC program is to initiate and support—through financial participation, incentive grant, or other methods—the identification, assessment, surveying, and promotion of private investment opportunities overseas. The funds advanced normally are subject to repayment with interest. Applicants must be U.S. firms capable of carrying out the project if the survey indicates feasibility. The assistance has averaged about $10,000 per project.

• *Direct Investment Loans.* The OPIC makes a few direct dollar loans for projects in less-developed countries where other financing services are inadequate. Applicants must be privately-owned firms or firms of mixed private and public ownership. Loans for mining and other extractive industry projects are prohibited by statute. The loans, which are repayable in seven to fifteen years, have averaged about $800,000.

How to apply: With most of these programs, the OPIC encourages prospective applicants to contact the agency via letter as the first step. This will be followed by discussions with the OPIC staff. If it is decided the project can be encouraged, application instructions will be provided. Write to the Overseas Private Investment Corporation, Washington, D.C. 20527.

Trade adjustment assistance

American firms seriously injured or threatened by increased imports resulting from trade agreement concessions may be eligible for trade adjustment assistance.

After the International Trade Commission or the President makes a finding of eligibility for such firms, the Commerce Department provides aid to implement recovery. This is in the form of technical, financial, and tax assistance, furnished separately or in any combination required.

Financial assistance may consist of direct or guaranteed loans for capital equipment, buildings, land, and, in exceptional circumstances, working capital. This aid is not provided if funds are available from private sources.

Technical assistance, in the form of contracts for consulting services, may be used to help develop and implement the firm's recovery proposal.

Tax assistance is available by allowing five-year operating loss carrybacks.

How to apply: The initial contact of a prospective applicant should be with the International Trade Commission, 701 E Street, N.W., Washington, D.C. 20436.

Copyright service

If you are the creator of "original works of authorship fixed in any tangible medium of expression," the government provides protection for your work through the copyright law. The copyright law, in brief, gives the copyright owner exclusive rights (with certain limitations) to copy, adapt, record, and perform the work. Anyone who makes such a use of the copyrighted material without the permission of the copyright owner may be subject to legal proceedings. The law covers literary works, musical works, dramatic works, pictorial, graphic and sculptural works, motion pictures and other audio-visual works, sound recordings, and similar works.

Under recent extensive revisions in the law, the copyright duration beginning in 1976 was fixed as the life of the author plus fifty years. For works copyrighted prior to 1976, the duration was extended to a total of seventy-five years. Previously, the statutory copyright lasted for twenty-eight years and could be extended for another twenty-eight years.

Copyright is relatively easy and inexpensive to obtain. Detailed information and application forms may be obtained by writing the Copyright Office, Library of Congress, Washington, D.C. 20559.

Obtaining a patent

If you are an inventor or discoverer of "any new and useful process, machines, manufacture, or composition of matter, or any new and useful improvement thereof," you can obtain a patent from the U.S. government. The patent normally is granted for a period of seventeen years and gives the inventor the right to exclude all others from making, using, or selling his or her invention within the United States.

Unlike a copyright, which can be easily and quickly obtained, it can be a complex, time-consuming process to obtain a patent. The Patent and Trademark Office advises inventors to employ a patent attorney or agent. But the inventor should first have a preliminary search conducted to make certain that his idea or product has not already been patented. This search can be made at Patent and Trademark Office Headquarters, 2021 Jefferson Davis Highway, Arlington, Virginia, where information is available on more than 3.9 million U.S. patents. In addition, many public libraries have information on patents. If you want copies of previous patents, they can be obtained from the patent office at 5 cents each.

An inventor needing general information about patents should write to the Patent and Trademark Office, Department of Commerce, Washington, D.C. 20231.

3

If
You
Need a
Job

Periodic economic recessions have vividly demonstrated that even reliable workers of long standing can lose their jobs through no fault of their own.

The unemployed are not just the lazy, the unskilled, the restless, or the disagreeable. Hard economic times can bring abrupt cutbacks in industries like automobile manufacturing and can ripple quickly to the small businessman or shopkeeper whose customers suddenly have less money to spend.

Even in good times, jobs can disappear because of corporate mergers, relocation of a firm to another part of the country, loss of a major contract, or failure of a company to keep up with the competition.

If you should fall victim to unemployment, there are two things you would want quickly: financial assistance to tide you through the jobless period, and a new job. The government can help you to fill both of these needs.

Unemployment insurance

The unemployment insurance program is a cooperative federal-state undertaking which will pay you benefits if you are involuntarily unemployed and looking for work.

The amount you receive is based on how much you were earning while you had a job. These benefits run only for a set period of time. The object is to help you to keep your financial head above water until you can get another job for which you are suited by your experience and training.

Specific details of the program vary from state to state. State regulations cover such matters as who is eligible for benefits, how long you can collect benefits, how much you will be paid, and how long you must be out of work before you can qualify.

More than 80 percent of the wage earners and salaried workers in the United States are covered by unemployment insurance. Most of the group which is not covered are either employees of state or local governments, work in agriculture, or are domestic workers.

The money to pay your unemployment benefits comes from employers. They pay a specific tax on the wages of their employees. Most of that tax goes into a fund which is used strictly to pay benefits to eligible persons. The rest of the money is handled by the federal government. Much of it is used to finance administrative costs of the program at the federal and state levels.

The federal government also provides advice and technical help to the states so that their programs can run more efficiently and effectively. Each year the federal government reviews each state's unemployment program to make sure it is conforming with federal law.

Claiming a benefit

If you lose your job, you can file a claim for unemployment insurance benefits at your local unemployment insurance office. You can also register for work at this office.

If you live in one state and worked in another, you can usually file your benefit claim in the state where you live. Your home state will act as your agent and take care of the necessary paper work with the state where you were last employed.

If you had jobs in several states, you may be able to combine your wage and employment records from the various locations

Aid to the Unemployed

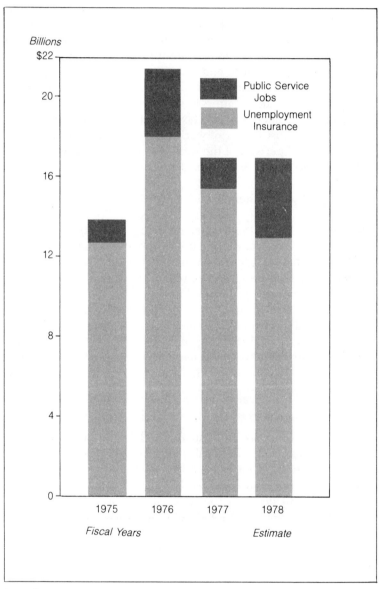

Source: Office of Management and Budget

and have your benefits claim processed under the laws of one state.

After you file your claim, the unemployment office will examine your wage records and figure what benefit you are entitled to receive. The reason you give for losing your job will also be checked. Your reason for leaving might not allow you to collect benefits.

There are three major causes for disqualification from benefits:
• Voluntarily leaving work without good cause, such as quitting because you did not get a promotion you wanted.
• Being discharged for misconduct, such as for dishonesty.
• Refusing to accept suitable work without good cause.

If you are refused benefits, you will be told the reason. If you disagree with the determination made by unemployment officials, you can appeal. Then an impartial referee will examine the facts in your case. In most states, there is also a second stage of appeal. If you are still unsatisfied, you can take your case to court. Most decisions on qualification are clear-cut, so there is little chance that you would have to go to court to settle the matter.

Rules differ from state to state on how long you must have worked in order to qualify for benefits. But in every state you must have had a certain amount of wages in a recent one-year period in order to receive benefits.

Some states have a flat annual-wage requirement. In California, for example, you must have earned $750. Other states require you to have worked a certain number of weeks in the year: forty in Connecticut and thirty in Louisiana, as examples. Others tie qualification to some multiple of your potential benefit or to wage minimums in specific quarters of the year.

Most states require you to be unemployed for one week before you can file for benefits, and you will not receive any benefits for that first week. Exceptions to this rule are Alabama, Connecticut, Delaware, Kentucky, Maine, Maryland, Michigan, Nevada, New Hampshire, Pennsylvania, and Wisconsin, in any of which you can collect benefits for that first week. In some other states, you may eventually be paid for that first week if your unemployment continues for specified time periods.

Collecting a benefit

Unemployment insurance is paid every week. In some states

you must come to the unemployment office every week. In other states continuing claims can be handled by mail. In any case you must certify every week that you are able to work and available for work. Some states also require that you actively seek work.

The benefits you receive through your state from the federal unemployment trust fund are not subject to income tax. You should keep a separate record of these benefits, since some other kinds of financial aid you might receive while out of work, such as union benefits, are subject to income tax.

Amount of benefits

States have various methods of calculating your unemployment benefit. Generally, formulas are designed to give you about half the amount of your previous weekly wages, up to some specific maximum. In eleven states, you can receive extra benefits depending on the number of your dependents.

Here are some examples of weekly benefits that were available in late 1977 and how they were calculated:

Connecticut: one-twenty-sixth of your wages for the highest recent calendar quarter, up to a maximum of 60 percent of the average weekly wage in the state, plus $5 per dependent up to a ceiling of one-half of your basic weekly benefit.

Florida: half of your average weekly wage.

New Jersey: two-thirds of your average weekly wage up to a ceiling of half the average weekly wage in the state.

Translating these benefit formulas into actual dollars meant your weekly benefit could range from $15 to $174 in Connecticut, $10 to $82 in Florida, and $20 to $104 in New Jersey.

If you are able to get part-time work while you are unemployed, states will disregard certain amounts of such earnings while you collect your benefit. The amount disregarded varies from as little as $2 per week in Hawaii up to half the amount of your unemployment benefit in several states.

In most states you can draw unemployment benefits for twenty-six weeks. A few states permit payment of benefits for a few weeks longer, up to a maximum of thirty-six weeks in Utah.

Unemployment assistance is a program particularly susceptible to quick changes when economic conditions cause large numbers of people to lose their jobs. States may change their laws and regulations to meet severe problems.

Maximum Weekly Unemployment Benefits

Some of these benefits are contingent on the number of personal dependents.

Alabama	$90	Montana	$104
Alaska	$120	Nebraska	$90
Arizona	$85	Nevada	$94
Arkansas	$100	New Hampshire	$95
California	$104	New Jersey	$104
Colorado	$121	New Mexico	$83
Connecticut	$174	New York	$95
Delaware	$140	North Carolina	$105
District of Columbia	$148	North Dakota	$115
Florida	$82	Ohio	$161
Georgia	$90	Oklahoma	$101
Hawaii	$120	Oregon	$112
Idaho	$110	Pennsylvania	$141
Illinois	$138	Rhode Island	$126
Indiana	$124	South Carolina	$111
Iowa	$124	South Dakota	$96
Kansas	$109	Tennessee	$95
Kentucky	$94	Texas	$63
Louisiana	$120	Utah	$119
Maine	$129	Vermont	$102
Maryland	$89	Virginia	$110
Massachusetts	$162	Washington	$119
Michigan	$136	West Virginia	$139
Minnesota	$122	Wisconsin	$133
Mississippi	$80	Wyoming	$111
Missouri	$85		

For these reasons you should contact your local unemployment insurance office for information on the latest standards and levels of benefits.

You also should be aware that Congress periodically enacts special unemployment assistance programs. One example was a program adopted during the 1974-75 recession which provided up to an additional twenty-six weeks of unemployment benefits for persons who had used all of their jobless entitlements.

Still another emergency program provided up to thirty-nine weeks of benefits for workers not normally covered by unemployment compensation—principally agricultural and domestic workers and government employees.

In both of these programs the emergency benefits were keyed to job conditions. If the conditions improved in a state, the program expired ahead of schedule.

The job search

Unemployment benefits obviously are not a long-term substitute for a paycheck. So even as you begin drawing these emergency funds, you will be starting your hunt for a new job.

Newspaper advertisements, private employment agencies, personnel offices of major employers in your area, and contacts through your friends and associates each might lead to a job. And so might the help of the government.

State employment services operated in cooperation with the U.S. Department of Labor's Employment and Training Administration have counseled job-hunters for more than forty years. These offices have placed individuals in more than 400 million jobs during that period, and have administered over forty million aptitude and proficiency tests and over fifty million counseling interviews for jobseekers.

Getting in touch with a government employment service office is easy since there are more than 2,400 around the country, an average of almost one office for every county in the nation. These offices are listed under the "State of---" listing in telephone directories. Titles vary from state to state, so check such entries as "Labor Department," "Employment Division," and so forth.

The employment office can offer you a number of services suited to your job-hunting needs:

• *Specific job information.* The office will have on hand requests from area employers for individuals to fill specific vacancies. You can be referred quickly to the employer if your skills match the requirements.

• *Orientation and counseling.* An employment officer can analyze your particular situation and advise you as to the best way to proceed about your job-hunting. If you have worked for a number of years without interruption you may feel totally adrift in the seas of unemployment. An experienced counselor can help you get your bearings and put you to work at the job of finding a job. Early orientation and counseling can help you avoid an attitude of helplessness and despair which can keep you from taking steps toward getting a new job.

• *Testing.* Although a natural inclination is to seek a job doing the same thing you had been doing, you might be able to perform other kinds of work as well. Competent aptitude testing can measure your chances for success in other fields.

• *Referral for training.* Tests may show that you are suited for a new kind of work but that some training is needed before you will be ready to go to work. Employment officials can help you locate the training you need and advise you whether a job is likely to be waiting when you finish the training.

Comprehensive Employment and Training

In addition to the general services provided by the government through state employment services, a number of more specifically targeted programs have been spawned in Washington in recent years. Because some of these program regulations seemed too strict and inflexible, Congress decided to change the structure of employment and training aid beginning in 1974.

Congress passed the Comprehensive Employment and Training Act (CETA) so that communities could better structure job programs for their particular populations and requirements.

The emphasis of this program is to help the disadvantaged get jobs. Funds spent under this program "will be spent to serve those people in our society who cannot make it without public help," according to the Department of Labor's Employment and Training Administration.

The usual image of a disadvantaged person includes lack of education or bad family situation or trouble with the law or a physical handicap or perhaps all of those.

What Federal Employment and Training Activities Cost

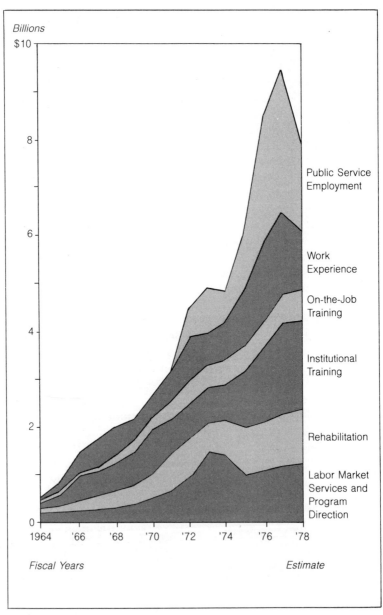

Billions

Public Service Employment

Work Experience

On-the-Job Training

Institutional Training

Rehabilitation

Labor Market Services and Program Direction

1964 '66 '68 '70 '72 '74 '76 '78

Fiscal Years

Estimate

Source: Office of Management and Budget

New Enrollees in Employment and Training Activities

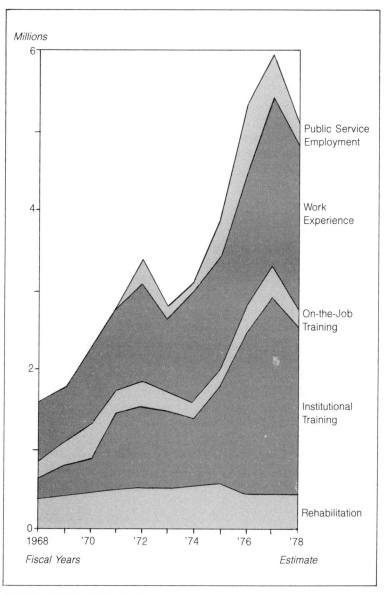

Source: Office of Management and Budget

It may be that you do not qualify for these programs even if you are out of work. But requirements for participation vary from community to community and you should check to see what is available.

You may also be able to help another member of your family or a friend take advantage of these programs if they have employment problems.

Comprehensive Employment and Training Act programs are carried out through government units called prime.sponsors. If you live in a city or a county of 100,000 population or more, it may be the prime sponsor for your area. Smaller cities and towns may join with nearby larger cities. If you live in a more sparsely populated area, the state may be the prime sponsor for you.

The state employment service or the mayor's or city manager's office in your community should be able to direct you to the prime sponsor of these programs.

Prime sponsors are free to develop their own specialized employment and training programs, and they vary from location to location.

Here are some of the services you may find:

• Active recruiting of persons to participate in these programs. You may see announcements telling where to go for help or you might even be contacted directly by mail.

• Assessment of a participant's employability, aptitudes, abilities, and interests through interviews and testing.

• Orientation on job-related topics ranging from the CETA program itself to guidance on how to conduct oneself at a job interview.

• Counseling to help individuals decide what kind of job or training they should pursue and to continue supporting them through their job and training development.

• Assistance in transportation, health care, child care, legal matters, or emergencies, without which individuals might have to drop out of the program.

• Classroom training in specific job skills or for more general educational attainment.

• On-the-job training under contract with an employer. In these cases, the individual is hired and learns the necessary skills as he or she works. The employer receives financial help from the government to meet his or her training costs.

Other job assistance

Although recent legislation has shifted the emphasis in job program development to local communities, some specific kinds of assistance are still operated uniformly from the federal level. They include:

• *Job Corps.* This program is designed to provide intensive training for low-income and disadvantaged young men and women in residential centers so that they can become more employable and productive citizens.

Those who work with youth groups, at church or elsewhere, may know young people who could benefit from this program. Enrollees must be between fourteen and twenty-two years old, come from a low-income family and currently live "in an environment so characterized by cultural deprivation, a disruptive homelife, or other disorienting conditions as to substantially impair his prospects for successful participation in any other program providing needed training, education, or assistance."

Enrollees may spend up to two years in the Job Corps, often at a residential center where they are counseled, trained, and gain work experience designed to start them on a successful career.

• *Apprenticeship.* In cooperation with industry and labor, the U.S. Department of Labor encourages and assists in development and improvement of apprenticeship and training programs in which young people learn a skilled trade through one to five years of supervised on-the-job training.

Standards for these programs ensure that the apprentice will receive proper training and periodic evaluation and not simply be left to fend for himself or herself.

Apprenticeship Information Centers at the larger employment service offices help young people to apply for these programs. Application can also be made to an employer, labor union, or joint apprenticeship and training committee.

Among the more than 500 occupations for which training through apprenticeship is available are those of airplane mechanic, baker, boilermaker, cabinetmaker, butcher, draftsman, electrical worker, engraver, glass worker, iron worker, machinist, operating engineer, patternmaker, plumber, and telephone worker.

• *Veterans' services.* If you are a Vietnam veteran, you will find at many state employment service offices a full-time veterans

Assistant Regional Directors
For Employment and Training

If you are unable to get the job assistance you want through federally-funded state and local employment and training offices, you can contact an assistant regional director for employment and training at one of these locations:

Connecticut
Maine — John F. Kennedy Building
Massachusetts — Boston, Massachusetts 02203
New Hampshire — (617) 223-6439
Rhode Island
Vermont

New Jersey
New York — 1515 Broadway
Canal Zone — New York, New York 10036
Puerto Rico — (212) 399-5445
Virgin Islands

Delaware
Maryland — 3535 Market Place
Pennsylvania — Philadelphia, Pennsylvania 19101
Virginia — (215) 596-6346
West Virginia

Alabama
Florida
Georgia — 1371 Peachtree Street, N.E.
Kentucky — Atlanta, Georgia 30309
Mississippi — (404) 881-4411
North Carolina
South Carolina
Tennessee

Illinois	
Indiana	230 South Dearborn Street
Michigan	Chicago, Illinois 60604
Minnesota	(312) 353-0313
Ohio	
Wisconsin	
Iowa	
Kansas	911 Walnut Street
Missouri	Kansas City, Missouri 64106
Nebraska	(816) 374-3796
Arkansas	
Louisiana	555 Griffin Square Building
New Mexico	Dallas, Texas 75202
Oklahoma	(214) 749-2841
Texas	
Colorado	
Montana	1961 Stout Street
North Dakota	Denver, Colorado 80202
South Dakota	(303) 837-3031
Utah	
Wyoming	
Arizona	
California	
Hawaii	450 Golden Gate Avenue
Nevada	San Francisco, California 94102
American Samoa	(415) 556-7414
Guam	
Trust Territory	
Alaska	
Idaho	909 First Avenue
Oregon	Seattle, Washington 98174
Washington	(206) 442-5570

employment representative. These representatives were mandated by Congress in 1973 to provide employment help particularly suited to veterans.

Federal government jobs

The federal government employs more than two million persons on a career basis in the United States and around the world. Nearly all of these positions are filled through the civil service, a program designed to ensure that jobs are held on a basis of merit rather than political patronage or other unfair standards. Jobs range from clerical and custodial up to high-level professional and managerial positions.

The personnel office of any federal agency you may be interested in working for can tell you what jobs are open, what requirements must be met, and what your chances are of being employed.

The U.S. Civil Service Commission, 1900 E Street, N.W., Washington, D.C. 20415, can provide general information about working for the federal government.

CHAPTER 4

If
You Want
Help
as a
Consumer

The federal government can help you as a consumer in many ways. Two of the major forms of assistance are:

• Providing information about products and services you are considering purchasing.

• Standing up for you when you think that you have been cheated or mistreated in the marketplace.

It requires effort and knowledge on your part to take advantage of this government assistance, but the task is becoming easier because of the rapid growth in consumer consciousness during the past few years. Politicians and bureaucrats have responded with new programs to help the consumer. They have a growing realization that the consumer has rights which the government cannot ignore.

Almost all public officials agree that the federal government has an obligation to share its vast amount of information on products, services, and other subjects of consumer concern. But there have been continuing questions within the government over how best to accomplish this task. Late in 1977, Congress was considering a proposal to consolidate many federal consumer functions into a new agency, but the fate of the proposal was uncertain.

Published information

Armed with facts before you buy, you are more likely to make wise decisions as a consumer and less likely to need government help in trying to correct the wrongs or disappointments of faulty products or bad service. Most of the government information that you will find useful is in printed form.

Your handiest tool for finding this information is the *Consumer Information Index.* This is a listing of about 250 consumer-oriented federal publications which is updated and reissued every three months. It lists publications that are helpful anytime, such as *Budgeting for the Family,* and spotlights those dealing with concerns of a particular time, as *Tips for Energy Savers.*

The Consumer Information Index is compiled by the Consumer Information Center of the General Services Administration. The center was established in 1970 to encourage federal agencies to develop and release information which would help consumers.

This philosophy is a turnaround for the government. In the recent past, for example, the Veterans Administration had fought through administrative channels and the courts against having to release results of hearing-aid tests it had conducted. Finally, a private consumer group, Consumers Union, won access to the test results which could help thousands of persons who have hearing problems.

In a few cases, the *Consumer Information Index* and other federal sources offer information on a brand-name basis. For example, test results of automobile gasoline consumption are available for each year's auto models since 1973, listing how many miles per gallon each car achieved during a standardized test.

More often, however, government information will offer guidelines on what qualities to look for in a product without mentioning specific brands. A 1976 edition of the *Consumer Information Index,* for example, listed such publications as *Automobile Batteries: Their Selection and Care, Soaps and Detergents for Home Laundering, Fish at the Market,* and *Portable Dehumidifiers.*

Categories of publications listed in a recent edition of the *Con-*

sumer Information Index included automobiles, budget, children, clothing, food, health, housing, landscaping and recreation.

About half of these publications are free. Others, principally the longer and more detailed, are sold for a modest price, seldom more than $1.

You should be able to find a copy of the latest *Consumer Information Index* at federal facilities in your area, such as Social Security offices, agricultural extension offices, large federal buildings, and even national parks and monuments. More than twenty million copies are made available every year, but if you cannot find one, write to Consumer Information, Public Documents Distribution Center, Pueblo, Colorado 81009.

Pursuing your complaint

Consumer tips are fine for staying away from careless purchases and unfavorable agreements. But if you find yourself victimized by anything from a faulty product to a fraudulent contract, you want more help than a pamphlet telling you how you might have avoided the problem.

You want somebody to go to bat for you, and you do not want to spend more money rectifying the situation than it would have cost to resign yourself to it.

In many cases, the federal government will stand up for your rights. But an agency cannot act in your behalf unless it knows that you have a problem. You must make the complaint and then you must maintain a followup alert so that your complaint will not fade for lack of attention.

You should, of course, try to resolve a consumer complaint first with the source of your problem. Suppose that you have purchased a refrigerator and it stops working while it is still under warranty. First, contact the dealer from whom you purchased the refrigerator. If he will not fix it satisfactorily, then contact the manufacturer. If the manufacturer brushes you off, seek help from a local consumer agency. If all these steps fail to solve the problem, contact the federal government.

Some kinds of specific complaints are dealt with by agencies directly responsible for a particular area. For example, if you think that an airline overcharged you, complain to the Civil Aeronautics Board. If a moving company mistreated you, protest to the Interstate Commerce Commission.

The place to go with a complaint if you do not know of a specific agency that handles your kind of problem is the Office of Consumer Affairs, New Executive Office Building, Washington, D.C. 20506.

Virginia H. Knauer, special assistant for consumer affairs under Presidents Richard Nixon and Gerald Ford, told consumers: "If all your efforts on the local level fail, write to us. While we can't guarantee 100 percent satisfaction in every individual case, we can guarantee that we will do our best to help you."

Problems and questions pour into the Office of Consumer Affairs every day. Annoying telephone solicitations, repairmen who do not repair things, warranties that are not honored, products that do not work—all these are subjects of the complaints.

The Office of Consumer Affairs sometimes intervenes directly with a manufacturer. Sometimes complaints are forwarded to appropriate government agencies for action. Or sometimes the consumer is sent information on what steps he or she can take personally to resolve the difficulty.

The Office of Consumer Affairs keeps track of what kinds of problems are most frequent or seem most pressing and as a result recommends new policies to an industry or asks other federal agencies to consider new regulations.

Whether you are contacting the Office of Consumer Affairs or some other government agency with a complaint, follow this procedure so that your problem can be handled efficiently and with the best possible opportunity for action in your favor:

1. *Write it down.* A written complaint gives officials something tangible to work with. A telephoned complaint can be forgotten and is easily misunderstood. Even if you complain by telephone on an emergency basis, follow up immediately with a letter.

2. *Be specific.* Do not say that you bought a kitchen range about a year ago and now it will not work. Say that you bought it on August 10, 1976; the warranty still has three months to go; and the problem is that two of the burners will not heat up any warmer than low.

3. *Tell what you have already done to solve the problem.* Give the dates on which you called the dealer and what he did or did not do in response. List in order other steps taken regarding your complaint, along with the response or lack of response to each.

4. *Include documentation, within reason.* If your complaint

concerns the terms of a warranty, send along a photocopy of the warranty. If you think an advertisement was false and misleading, send a copy of it if at all possible.

5. *Be calm and rational.* A diatribe telling what a thief you think your appliance dealer is or calling a salesperson names does not accomplish anything except letting off steam. Exaggeration can hurt your case by giving your adversary an opportunity to show that you are not telling the strict truth. So if, for example, you called the repairman three times and he would not come, say it was three times, not "I must have called him a hundred times" or "I was on the phone morning, noon, and night for a week." If some response was made in good faith to your complaint, tell about this, too, then explain why it was nevertheless unsatisfactory.

6. *Tell the agency what you want it to do.* This can affect what action is taken. Do you want a refund? A replacement? Or do you think a product is unsafe and should be taken off the market?

7. *Identify yourself fully and include how you can be reached.* This sounds basic, but public agencies often receive letters in which the sender forgets to include his or her address and telephone number.

8. *Send copies of your letter to the individual or firm against whom you are complaining.* The mere fact that they know you are serious about your complaint may result in a remedy for the situation. And your own knowledge that a copy of the letter is going to your antagonist will help to keep you from exaggerating your side of the story.

9. *Follow up.* If you have not received an acknowledgment of your letter after about four weeks, write again and ask what has been done about your complaint. The resolution of your problem may take longer, but you should at least be told that your letter is under study. If, after complaining, you are able to resolve your problem, let the agency know so that it will not do needless work on your behalf.

Agency specialties

Following are thirteen principal areas involving consumers that are handled by specific federal agencies. If you have consumer questions or problems in their areas, the officials listed here may be able to help you.

• *Food.* The U.S. Department of Agriculture has broad responsibilities for developing better food and fibers, inspecting food and food products, and making practical research findings available to families and individuals.

Agriculture extension offices located in virtually every county of the nation can provide information on family finance, credit, shopping, nutrition, housing, health, clothing, child care, and other topics related to family living. These offices also can help with information on growing food or landscape and decorative crops and plants. Extension agents are usually located at the courthouse, post office, or other government building at the county seat.

For problems related to agriculture, contact Special Assistant to the Secretary for Consumer Affairs, Department of Agriculture, Washington, D.C. 20250.

• *Business.* The Commerce Department promotes American business and is therefore concerned with problems consumers have with business. A unit of the department, the National Bureau of Standards, sets voluntary and mandatory standards for certain consumer goods.

Problems can be brought to the attention of the Office of the Ombudsman for Business, Department of Commerce, Washington, D.C. 20230.

• *Product Safety.* The Consumer Product Safety Commission was established to find and call attention to products that are unsafe. This agency went so far as to recall its own promotional pin-buttons in 1974 when it determined that they were hazardous.

Complaints about unsafe products used in and around the home can be voiced by using the commission's toll-free hotline, 800-638-2666 (in Maryland, 800-492-2937), or by writing to Consumer Product Safety Commission, Washington, D.C. 20207.

• *Energy.* Since the energy crisis began to make itself felt in the form of scarce supplies and steep prices, consumers have become more conscious of their energy costs. Complex formulas and complicated regulations make it difficult for consumers to know if they are being properly charged.

Complaints about energy costs can be sent to two places: Director for Consumer Affairs and Special Impact, Department of Energy, Washington, D.C. 20461, and to the Director of Public

How Consumers Rate Value Received For Money Spent

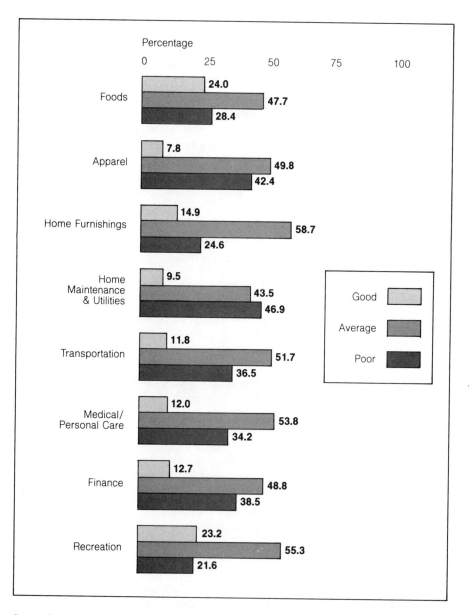

Percentage

| | 0 | 25 | 50 | 75 | 100 |

Foods
- 24.0
- 47.7
- 28.4

Apparel
- 7.8
- 49.8
- 42.4

Home Furnishings
- 14.9
- 58.7
- 24.6

Home Maintenance & Utilities
- 9.5
- 43.5
- 46.9

Transportation
- 11.8
- 51.7
- 36.5

Medical/Personal Care
- 12.0
- 53.8
- 34.2

Finance
- 12.7
- 48.8
- 38.5

Recreation
- 23.2
- 55.3
- 21.6

Good
Average
Poor

Sources: The Conference Board, National Consumer Finance Association

Information, Federal Power Commission, Washington, D.C. 20426.

• *Food, Drugs, Cosmetics.* The Food and Drug Administration is responsible for protecting consumers from adulterated or mislabeled foods, drugs, medical devices, cosmetics, and veterinary products. It tries to assure that foods are safe, pure, and wholesome; that drugs and devices are safe and effective; that cosmetics are safe; and that all of these products are honestly and informatively labeled and packaged.

Consumer complaints can be directed to: Senior Educational Director, Office of Consumer Affairs, Food and Drug Administration, 5600 Fishers Lane, Rockville, Maryland 20856.

• *Advertising, Credit, Fraud.* The Federal Trade Commission has responsibility to prevent deceptive advertising, packaging, and selling. It requires proper disclosures in credit transactions, and in general is charged with fostering a more responsive, competitive, and economically fair market-place. It has been particularly active recently in requiring advertisers to document their product claims.

Problems can be addressed to the Secretary, Federal Trade Commission, Washington, D.C. 20580.

• *Mail.* The mail problems of many consumers are caused by the U.S. Postal Service itself. But the Postal Service also can step in to protect consumers against mail fraud and can help them cut off certain types of objectionable mail.

Send your complaints to Consumer Advocate, U.S. Postal Service, Washington, D.C. 20260.

• *Banking, Alcohol, Guns, Taxes, Foreign Travel, Imports.* Various agencies of the Department of the Treasury are involved in widely divergent consumer interests. Complaints about banking matters should be sent to Comptroller of the Currency, Department of the Treasury, 490 L'Enfant Plaza East, S.W., Washington, D.C 20219. Complaints about alcohol and firearms are handled by the Office of the Director, Bureau of Alcohol, Tobacco, and Firearms, 1200 Pennsylvania Avenue, N.W., Washington, D.C. 20226. Tax complaints should be directed to the Associate Director, Office of Tax Analysis, Department of the Treasury, Washington, D.C. 20220. Complaints about foreign travel and imports should be sent to the Office of the Commissioner, U.S. Customs Service, Department of the Treasury, 2100

K Street, N.W., Washington, D.C. 20229. For general inquiries, write to: Special Assistant for Consumer Affairs, Department of the Treasury, Washington, D.C. 20220.

• *Stocks, Bonds.* The Securities and Exchange Commission regulates the sellers and issuers of securities. The commission requires companies selling their stock to the public to file voluminous material which is available for your inspection. The commission seeks to ferret out fraud, and regularly takes action against swindlers.

The Director, Office of Public Information, Securities and Exchange Commission, Washington, D.C. 20549, will receive your complaints.

• *Antitrust.* The antitrust division of the Department of Justice tries to end monopolistic practices in business that can drive up costs to the consumer. By moving against monopolies, this division attempts to foster competition that will give the consumer a broader choice of products.

Complaints about monopolistic practices should go to the Chief, Consumer Affairs Section, Antitrust Division, Department of Justice, Washington, D.C. 20530.

• *Housing and Urban Development.* A broad range of programs in the Department of Housing and Urban Development can affect your housing. If you have bought a new home with a Federal Housing Administration (FHA) mortgage, the builder had to meet certain FHA standards for materials and construction. The department's Office of Interstate Land Sales can protect you against swindles in the purchase of land, particularly second-home or retirement property. Chapter 9 discusses government housing assistance in detail, but if you have a consumer problem in this field, you can contact the Consumer Affairs Coordinator, Department of Housing and Urban Development, Washington, D.C. 20410.

• *Environment, Resources, Parks.* The Department of the Interior provides numerous recreation opportunities which are discussed in chapter 11. If as a consumer you encounter a problem in this area, contact Departmental Consumer Liaison, Department of the Interior, Washington, D.C. 20240.

• *Transportation.* The Civil Aeronautics Board (CAB) regulates commercial airlines and charter flights. Contact this agency if you think you have been overcharged for a flight, if your baggage has been lost and you have not received compensation, or if you have other complaints about airline service. The CAB's Office of Consumer Affairs not only handles complaints about airline service but seeks to represent the consumer viewpoint in CAB proceedings. Complaints should go to the Director, Office of the Consumer Advocate, Civil Aeronautics Board, Washington, D.C. 20428.

The Interstate Commerce Commission has authority over elements of interstate bus and train travel and motor and rail freight. It sets standards which must be met by household moving firms. If you have a complaint, contact Consumer Affairs Office, Interstate Commerce Commission, Washington, D.C. 20423.

The Department of Transportation can assist in consumer matters related to auto safety, highways, and mass rapid transit. Contact Office of Consumer Affairs, Department of Transportation, Washington, D.C. 20590.

Organizing the consumer fight

If you want to go beyond your personal struggle as a consumer and become a marketplace watchdog either on your own or with friends, the government can help you.

To keep you informed on consumer developments, the Office of Consumer Affairs publishes a newsletter, *Consumer News,* twice a month. It costs $4 a year and may be ordered from Consumer Information, Pueblo, Colorado 81009.

Recent issues reported on such topics as:

• The recall of faulty lids used in home canning.

• How to make your views known on proposed ways to reduce the costs of prescription drugs.

• Latest government test results on the tar and nicotine content of 130 brands of cigarettes.

• How to get a free copy of *A Shopper's Guide to Health Insurance.*

• Tips on buying a used car.

The Office of Consumer Affairs has also developed detailed instructions on how to form a consumer organization in your town or neighborhood. The guidelines contained in *Forming Consumer Organizations* extend from the first informal meeting of a few interested people to the formation of committees, drafting of bylaws, and preparation of press releases to let the public know what you are doing.

If you are not sure whom to deal with on the state and local level about consumer problems, check the directory of state, county, and city government consumer offices compiled by the Office of Consumer Affairs.

If you think your youngsters and their schoolmates should be receiving consumer education, you might wish to obtain the detailed publication entitled *Suggested Guidelines for Consumer Education, Grades K-12.* A companion publication discusses *An Approach to Consumer Education for Adults.*

All of these publications are available from the Office of Consumer Affairs, Washington, D.C. 20201.

CHAPTER 5

If
You
Want Student
Financial Aid

As all college students and their parents know, the cost of higher education has gone through the roof. A private university that cost $3,000 a year to attend in 1970 is predicted to cost at least $6,000 a year by 1980. With college expenses rising at such a rapid clip, students and their parents need all the financial help they can get.

The federal government is a major source of financial assistance. Some of the loan, grant, and fellowship programs administered or financed by the federal government are open to virtually all students; others are specialized. As you might expect, competition for some of the aid is intense. But do not hesitate to apply if you think you are qualified.

Federal programs described in other chapters also can be of assistance in paying for a college education. Veterans' education benefits, for example, are outlined in chapter 7, and some grant programs discussed in chapter 6 are open to college applicants.

Do not overlook, either, the many forms of aid that are available from states and private organizations. There are literally thousands of loan, grant, and scholarship programs offered by these sources. Careful research could pay off in cash.

Now let us see how you can get help from the federal government in paying for the spiraling costs of higher education.

Guaranteed Student Loans

About one million college students obtain loans every year under the Guaranteed Student Loan Program administered by the U.S. Office of Education. The loans do not actually come from the government. Rather, they are made by such lenders as banks, credit unions, savings and loan associations, pension funds, insurance companies, and schools. The government guarantees, or insures, the lender against loss.

Eligibility requirements may vary from state to state, but generally any U.S. citizen, national, or person in the United States for other than a temporary purpose may apply for a loan if he or she is enrolled or accepted for enrollment on at least a part-time basis at an eligible institution.

The maximum loan for undergraduate or vocational students is $2,500 per academic year, and total loans outstanding may not exceed $7,500. For graduate and professional students the limits are $5,000 a year and $15,000 total outstanding. Repayments generally are made during a five-to-ten-year period after the student leaves school, but can be deferred for up to three years under certain conditions, such as when the loan recipient is serving in the U.S. armed forces. Excluding periods of authorized deferments, the entire period from the date of the original loan until the date it is repaid cannot exceed fifteen years.

How to apply: Loan applications can be obtained from lenders, such as banks. The completed application should be returned to the lender. The educational institution must certify that the student is enrolled or accepted for enrollment, and may recommend a loan amount. The lender disburses proceeds of the loans to the applicant after a commitment is received from the insuring or guaranteeing agency.

National Direct Student Loans

Under the National Direct Student Loan Program, formerly

known as the National Defense Student Loan Program, the federal government supplies funds to an estimated 3,400 institutions which in turn make loans to undergraduate and graduate students so that they can complete their education.

To qualify, students must demonstrate need for the assistance, must maintain good academic standing, and must be enrolled or accepted for enrollment as at least half-time students.

Under this program, you may borrow up to a total of $2,500 if you are enrolled in a vocational program or if you have completed less than two years of a program leading to a bachelor's degree; $5,000 if you are an undergraduate student who has completed two years of study toward a bachelor's degree; or $10,000 for graduate study. (The $5,000 and $10,000 maximums include any amount you borrowed under this program for your undergraduate study.)

The loans can be repaid over a ten-year period beginning nine months after either graduation or termination of at least half-time study. No payments are required for up to three years while you serve in the armed forces in an area of hostilities. There also is a special feature of interest to prospective teachers. The loans can be canceled over a period of several years for service in any of the following capacities: as a full-time teacher in an officially listed low-income school, as a full-time teacher of handicapped children, or as a full-time member of a Head Start preschool program.

How to apply: Application forms are available from participating educational institutions. A borrower who becomes a teacher or member of the armed forces should inform the institution that granted the loan.

Work-study programs

The College Work-Study Program is intended to promote the part-time employment of students, particularly those with great financial need, who require assistance to pursue their studies at institutions of higher education.

The program is administered by the U.S. Office of Education, but the government does not make payments directly to students. Instead, it supplies funds to participating institutions to pay 80 percent of the earning of qualified students in eligible jobs.

The jobs are at educational institutions or at public and private nonprofit organizations that have made arrangements with the institutions. The students work part time while attending classes.

To be eligible, students must be enrolled at least half-time. Their resources, including parental contributions, must be inadequate to allow them to continue their education without the job assistance.

A similar program is operated for vocational education students. To be eligible, the students must be between the ages of fifteen and twenty and must need the jobs to remain in school.

Under a related program, the federal government provides project grants to colleges and universities to operate cooperative education programs. Students participating in these programs alternate periods of full-time academic study with periods of full-time public or private employment. State boards of vocational education can obtain formula grants to foster similar cooperative work-study arrangements.

How to apply: For application forms and further information, students should contact the financial aid office of the educational institution they are attending or plan to attend.

Educational Opportunity Grants

To help undergraduate students who lack funds to meet their educational expenses, the government finances two Educational Opportunity Grant programs.

Under the basic program, schools decide the amount of financial aid students are to receive. The amount of each award is based on the student's eligibility, the cost of attendance at the school, and a payment schedule issued to approved educational institutions by the U.S. Office of Education.

Under the supplemental program, grants range from $200 to $1,500 a year and are intended for students with exceptional financial need. The program is restricted to undergraduate students attending school at least half-time, and the total that may be awarded is $4,000 for a four-year course of study or $5,000 for a five-year course.

If you are selected for a supplemental grant, your school must provide you with additional financial aid at least equal to the amount of the grant.

Unlike loans, the grants under these two programs do not have to be repaid.

Aid for Students

Agency	Outlays (millions)			Students (thousands)		
	1976	*1977 (estimates)*	*1978*	*1976*	*1977 (estimates)*	*1978*
Undergraduate						
Health, Education, and Welfare:						
Office of Education	$2,030	$2,680	$2,236	2,750	3,290	2,510
Social Security						
Administration	967	1,144	1,035	535	637	697
Health agencies and other	28	26	21	43	39	26
Veterans Administration	3,806	2,820	2,277	1,810	1,418	1,242
Defense	183	183	192	36	34	33
Justice	39	46	41	22	93	79
Other	46	45	60	22	24	24
Subtotal, undergraduate	$7,099	$6,944	$5,862	5,218	5,535	4,611
Graduate						
Health, Education, and Welfare:						
National Institutes of Health	$ 122	$ 85	$ 96	10	10	9
Office of Education	158	172	168	450	375	400
Other HEW	169	169	135	100	81	60
Veterans Administration	495	367	296	203	163	143
National Science Foundation	19	16	14	2	2	2
Defense	117	126	125	434	588	613
Other	9	7	8	9	9	8
Subtotal, graduate	$1,079	$ 942	$ 842	1,208	1,228	1,235
TOTAL *	$8,178	$7,886	$6,704			

* Student totals not shown because some students receive awards under more than one program.
Source: Office of Management and Budget

How to apply: Students may obtain application forms and further information from the financial aid office of the school they are attending or wish to attend.

Grants for Indian students

The Bureau of Indian Affairs administers a grant program to encourage Indian students to continue their education and training beyond high school.

To qualify, a student must be at least one-fourth Indian, Eskimo, or Aleut, and a member of a tribe served by the bureau. He or she must be enrolled or accepted for enrollment in an accredited college and have a financial need as determined by the institution's financial aid office.

The grants range from $150 to $7,000 and may be continued through the graduate level if the student maintains an acceptable academic standing.

How to apply: A student must be accepted by a college or university before applying. Application forms are available from the agency or area office having jurisdiction over the applicant's tribal group. Completed forms are submitted to the agency superintendent or the bureau's area director for approval.

Aid for specialized studies

Through a variety of programs, the federal government underwrites loans, scholarships, and other assistance for students pursuing certain specialized studies. The following programs are for undergraduates or, in some cases, for both undergraduate and graduate students. Aid intended solely for graduate students is discussed later in this chapter.

• *Nursing.* Long-term, low-interest loans are available for students in need of financial assistance to pursue studies in professional nursing education. As with other programs, the federal funds are divided up among nursing schools, which then make loans to full- or half-time students in good standing.

Loans may be up to $2,500 a year and are limited to a total of $10,000. The repayment period is ten years. Up to 85 percent of the loan can be canceled at the rate of 15 percent per year for the first three years and 20 percent per year for the fourth and fifth year of full-time employment as a professional nurse for a public or private nonprofit agency or institution. For nurses who agree to work in an area having a shortage of nurses, up to 85 percent of the loan can be canceled at the rate of 30 percent per year for the first and second years and 25 percent for the third year.

Loan applications can be obtained from participating nursing schools.

• *Health professions.* Students needing financial aid to pursue studies in medicine, dentistry, osteopathy, optometry, podiatry, pharmacy, or veterinary medicine are eligible for low-interest, long-term loans.

The program is similar to that offered to student nurses, except that the maximum loan for any academic year is $3,500. Up to 85 percent of the loan may be canceled at the rate of 30 percent for the first two years and 25 percent for the third year of practice in an area having a manpower shortage in the particular health field. Up to 100 percent of the loan may be canceled at a rate of 15 percent a year for practice in rural, low-income areas.

Applications should be made to the institution the student is attending or wishes to attend.

• *Law Enforcement.* Employees of a public law-enforcement agency, including police, courts, and corrections personnel, are eligible for grants of up to $250 a quarter or $400 a semester for study at a participating institution of higher education. Full-time students who enroll in a course of study related to law enforcement are eligible for loans of up to $2,200 per academic year.

Individuals receiving grants must agree to remain in full-time criminal justice employment for at least two years. The student loans are canceled at the rate of 25 percent for each full year of employment in a public law enforcement agency following completion of school.

The program is administered by the Justice Department's Law Enforcement Assistance Administration, but applications are submitted through participating institutions of higher education.

• *Teachers of the Handicapped.* Financial assistance is available for qualified undergraduate, graduate, and professional personnel for training in the education of handicapped children and children with specific learning disabilities.

Undergraduate applicants must be juniors or seniors enrolled full-time in a program with primary emphasis on working with the handicapped.

Application forms and further information can be obtained from participating institutions of higher education.

• *Teacher Corps.* College graduates or those who have attended college for at least two years may be eligible for the Teacher Corps, a federally-assisted program intended to improve educational opportunities in low-income areas. Project grants go to colleges, universities, and local education agencies, which in turn employ teacher-interns to work in schools while continuing their education at nearby colleges or universities.

Application may be made to the participating colleges or school districts or to Teacher Corps, Washington, D.C. 20202.

Cash for graduate studies

While some of the major loan and grant programs are aimed at undergraduate and graduate students alike, there are other aid programs for graduate students only. Here are the details:

• *Science Fellowships.* To encourage excellence in the training of scientists and to promote progress in science and technology, the National Science Foundation makes grants for fellowships to graduate students and postdoctoral scholars. The recipient must be a full-time student for the duration of the grant. In recent years the fellowships have averaged more than $7,000, including stipends and an allowance for fees such as tuition.

Application forms are available from the National Science Foundation, 1800 G Street, N.W., Washington, D.C. 20550.

• *Doctoral Dissertation in Employment and Training.* Graduate students who have completed all requirements for a doctoral degree except the dissertation are eligible for dissertation research grants in the field of employment and training. The grants range from $2,500 to $13,500, and have averaged about $11,000.

Guidelines for proposals are available from the Office of Research and Development, Employment and Training Administration, Department of Labor, Washington, D.C. 20213.

• *Law Enforcement Research Fellowships.* Doctoral candidates engaged in dissertation research on a problem related to the criminal justice system are eligible for fellowships from the Law Enforcement Assistance Administration (LEAA). The stipend for a twelve-month fellowship is $4,000, plus a dependency allowance of up to $1,600. Tuition and other fees are paid directly to the university.

Application forms can be obtained from the Office of Criminal Justice, Education, and Training, LEAA, Washington, D.C. 20531.

• *Health Research Fellowships.* Research fellowships are awarded by the National Institutes of Health in such fields as allergies and infectious diseases, arthritis, cancer, child health, dental research, environmental health services, eye research, heart and lung research, neurological diseases and strokes, and nursing research. Most of the fellowships are for postdoctoral or special research, but a few predoctoral fellowships are awarded.

For further information and application forms, contact the Career Development Review Branch, Division of Research Grants, National Institutes of Health, Bethesda, Maryland 20013.

CHAPTER 6

If You Want a Grant for Study or Work

Would you like to travel abroad while you study, teach, or do research—at government expense?

Would you like to compose a musical work—at government expense?

Or would you like to attend a summer seminar—at government expense?

These are just a few of the many grant programs under which the federal government offers cash assistance to individuals in a wide variety of fields.

For those with a desire to travel abroad, the government has several research and fellowship programs. Perhaps the best-known is the Fulbright-Hays program, named after its congressional sponsors.

Faculty research abroad

Every year dozens of professors and scholars at U.S. colleges and universities receive grants for research and study abroad in foreign languages and area studies. The program is intended to help keep them current in their specialties.

Candidates for these faculty research awards must be U.S. citizens who have engaged in at least half-time teaching or research relevant to their specialties during the two years prior to receiving the award.

The awards include: a stipend in lieu of salary; cost of round-trip jet economy air fare; an allowance of $250 for materials and supplies; and a local travel allowance. In recent years the financial assistance has ranged from $5,000 to $17,000, and has averaged about $10,600.

Awards are not available for projects focusing primarily on Western Europe, nor in countries where the United States has no diplomatic representation.

How to apply: Candidates for awards should apply directly to their employing institution. The institutions screen the applications and forward those selected to the Office of Education's division of international education. The division makes the initial selection, subject to the review and final approval of the Board of Foreign Scholarships.

Teacher exchange

Under the Mutual Educational and Cultural Exchange Act of 1961, the government offers an opportunity for qualified American teachers to work in elementary and secondary schools abroad. In some instances teacher-training institutions and technical institutes participate in the program.

To be eligible, an applicant must be an elementary or secondary school teacher, college instructor, or assistant professor. He or she must have at least a bachelor's degree, be a U.S. citizen at the time of application, and have at least three years of successful full-time teaching experience. Two years of experience are required for participation in summer seminars. Evidence of good health and emotional maturity and stability also is required.

The government provides round-trip transportation to most countries for those selected to participate, but no transportation is provided for dependents of teachers, such as a spouse or children. A maintenance allowance, paid in the currency of the host country, is based on that country's cost of living. For teachers going to Canada or Great Britain, the successful applicant's U.S salary is continued by his or her own school.

This program also offers opportunities for American teachers to participate in selected short-term seminars abroad. Grants for these seminars usually include round-trip transportation and tuition costs, but for some seminars the participants are responsible for their own maintenance expenses.

How to apply: Application forms can be obtained from and then submitted to the Teacher Exchange Section, Division of International Education, U.S. Office of Education, ROB-3, Seventh and D Streets, S.W., Washington, D.C. 20202. Regional interviewing committees conduct preliminary screening of applicants before the grants are awarded.

Foreign language and area studies fellowships

Graduate students and qualified individual researchers are among those eligible for two programs intended to meet the need for experts in foreign languages, area studies, and world affairs.

Under the National Defense Foreign Language Fellowship Program (NDFL), approximately 1,000 graduate fellowships have been awarded annually for the study of over 90 modern foreign languages and related area studies. The flat rate for assistance per academic year is $4,900; the applications are made directly to institutions having quotas for NDFL fellowships.

Under a separate program, qualified individual researchers as well as institutions of higher education can obtain contracts intended to improve foreign language and area studies training in the United States through the support of research, experimentation, development of specialized instructional materials, and studies. These contracts range upward from $2,500, and generally are for periods of not more than 18 months. Awards are made by the U.S. Office of Education.

Group projects

Groups of teachers of foreign languages, area studies, and world affairs, as well as graduate students or upperclassmen who plan teaching careers in those fields, can participate in a program of training grants for work and study abroad.

Funds for group projects are available primarily in those coun-

tries where U.S.-owned foreign currencies are available for educational purposes—India, Pakistan, Tunisia, and Egypt. A limited
amount of U.S. dollar funds is available for a few high-priority
projects in other parts of the world. These include centers for
intensive advanced language instruction and selected summer
seminars and workshops.

The grants go to universities and colleges, state departments of
education, and nonprofit educational organizations, which in turn
select participants for group projects.

Grant funds can be used for round-trip air fare, maintenance
allowances, project-related travel in the overseas area, clerical
and professional services in the country of study, and purchases of
artifacts, books, and other teaching materials. Duration of the
projects ranges from six weeks to twelve months, and assistance
has ranged from $15,000 to $180,000, with an average of about
$50,000.

How to apply: Applications are made by an institution or organization, which must give assurances that the individuals it nomi-
nates to undertake the project are fully qualified. Guidelines for
the preparation of proposals are available from the Division of
International Education, U.S. Office of Education, ROB-3, Seventh and D Streets, S.W., Washington, D.C. 20202.

Doctoral dissertation research abroad

Fellowships are available to allow advanced graduate students
to engage in full-time dissertation research abroad in modern
foreign language and area studies.

Candidates must be citizens or nationals of the United States,
plan to teach in a U.S. institution of higher education, be working
toward a doctoral degree in foreign language, area studies, or
world affairs, and provide evidence of adequate language skills to
carry out the proposed project.

Project grants range from $2,660 to $17,400 and in recent
years have averaged about $9,670 for a period of at least six
months but not more than one year. The grant includes a stipend
based on the cost of living in the country where research is to be
conducted, round-trip air fare for the award recipient only,
allowance for a maximum of four dependents, project allowance
of up to $500 to purchase expendable materials and supplies, and
local travel allowance for project-related transportation.

Awards have not been available in recent years for projects focusing on Western Europe, or in countries where the U.S. has no diplomatic representation.

How to apply: The graduate dean of a college or university accepts, screens, and forwards to the Division of International Education those applications which meet the institution's technical and academic criteria. Individual candidates for these fellowships apply directly to their institutions, not to the Office of Education in Washington.

Grants for the arts

The National Endowment for the Arts has a dozen programs of project grants to promote the arts in America. Some general rules apply to these programs. For example, grants can be made only to nonprofit organizations or to individuals who are U.S. citizens of exceptional talent. None of the funds can be used for construction of facilities. With few exceptions, grants to organizations must be matched at least dollar-for-dollar by nonfederal funds.

With those general rules in mind, let us examine details of the specific programs:

• *Architecture and Environmental Arts.* These grants are for projects, including research, professional education, and public awareness in architecture, landscape architecture, and environmental design. In recent years the grants to individuals have ranged from $4,000 to $26,000 and those to organizations have been in the range of $1,750 to $50,000.

• *Dance.* Grants may be used to assist dancers, choreographers, and dance organizations in the creation of new works, touring, workshops, criticism, management improvement, national services, regional development, and dance films. Generally, funds cannot be used for study abroad, scholarships, publications, or research. The size of grants has ranged from $1,000 to $27,500 for individuals and from $1,200 to $223,000 for organizations, with the latter averaging about $30,000.

• *Education.* These grants, for special innovative projects in arts education, may be used for placement of professional artists in elementary and secondary schools and for projects which bring professional artists and young people together in arts activities beyond the traditional school environment. Most of these grants have gone to organizations and have ranged from $2,000 to

$80,000, with the average grant amounting to about $15,000.

• *Literature.* These grants provide fellowships for creative writers and support organizations devoted to the development of the literary arts in America. Grants are awarded for the creation of new works, for bringing creative writers into elementary and secondary schools and colleges, for support of small literary magazines and presses, and for international conferences of writers hosted in the United States. Grants to individuals have averaged about $7,500 and grants to organizations have ranged from $500 to $300,000, averaging about $8,000.

• *Museums.* Grants in this category can go to individuals as well as nonprofit organizations and can be used for mounting special exhibitions, utilizing collections, visiting specialists, conservation, training museum professionals, and such museum renovation as climate control, security, and storage. Grants awarded to individuals have ranged from $1,200 to $17,800 and organizations have received up to $500,000.

• *Music.* Grants are intended to assist symphony orchestras, opera companies, national audience development projects, contemporary music groups, composers, and organizations which serve the field of music. The grants may be used for new works, touring, concert series expansion, special music education projects, forums, and institutes. Grants also are available for jazz, folk, and ethnic musicians and organizations. In recent years individual grants have ranged from $300 to $10,000 and those for organizations have reached $600,000 with an average of about $50,000.

• *Public Media.* These grants are intended to support innovative programming for film, television, and radio. A portion of the funds also goes to the American Film Institute, which carries out a number of assistance programs for film. The grants usually are received for public media arts programming and experimental projects in film, videotape, and sound recording. Assistance to individuals has ranged from $2,500 to more than $10,000 while organizations have received an average of $15,000.

• *Theater.* Grants have gone to professional theater companies, professional experimental theater companies, new play producing groups, playwright development programs, and professional theater for children and youths. As a general rule, grants in this category have not gone to individual artists. Aid to organizations has ranged from $1,000 to $200,000, with the average grant about $20,000.

• *Visual Arts.* Grants under this program have gone to individual painters, sculptors, printmakers, art critics, craftsmen, and photographers of exceptional talent. They also have been used for commissioning and installing art work in public areas, for short-term residencies of artists, critics, craftsmen, and photographers in educational and cultural institutions, and for workshops and artists' services. Grants to individuals have been in the $1,000 to $10,000 range and the average for organizations has been about $10,000.

How to apply: Applications for these grants should be directed to the director of the program in which you are interested (such as Director of Music Program) at the National Endowment for the Arts, 2401 E Street, N.W., Washington, D.C. 20506. Standard application forms (NEA-2 for individuals and NEA-3 for organizations) are available from the same address.

Grants for the humanities

The National Endowment for the Humanities, like its twin in the arts field, offers a variety of grants for the promotion of the humanities. There are several general rules for these grants. Applicants generally must be U.S. citizens. Foreign institutions or organizations are not eligible. Foreign nationals are also ineligible unless affiliated with a U.S. institution or organization. Cost sharing usually is required for grants to organizations, with the government providing no more than 80 or 90 percent of the total project funds.

Here are details of the specific programs:

• *Fellowships for the Professions.* Under this program, grants go to persons in the nonteaching professions, such as journalism, law, and medicine, to give them an extended period in which to examine in historical, social, cultural, and philosophical perspective the bodies of knowledge on which their professions draw. Fellowships have been awarded to journalists for study at Stanford University and the University of Michigan. Stipends have been made available to lawyers for attendance at one-month summer seminars at Columbia University and the University of Wisconsin, and to members of the medical professions to attend one-month seminars at the University of Pennsylvania, the University of Texas Medical Branch at Galveston, and Williams College. Applicants should be, or show promise of becoming, leaders in their professions. Fellowships usually equal a participant's current salary, up to a monthly maximum of $1,666. Seminar stipends are set at $1,500.

• *Media Grants.* This program is intended to encourage and support the production of fine films in such humanistic disciplines as history, jurisprudence, literature, and philosophy. The films are for nationwide broadcast or distribution to the general adult population in the United States. Only nonprofit agencies, institutions, organizations, or groups are eligible. However, each proposal should involve direct collaboration between outstanding scholars and producers, screenwriters, directors, and actors of top professional stature. The grants cover personnel and other costs of production or presentation. They are not to be used for the purchase of permanent equipment or for training of personnel. Grants have ranged from $10,000 to $1.5 million and have averaged about $200,000.

• *Research Grants.* Under this program, grants are used to fund, wholly or partially, research projects that contribute to knowledge and understanding of the humanities. The grants, which can cover a period of up to thirty-six months, usually support the basic costs of research and editing projects—often collaborative—including travel, per diem payments, supplies, and appropriate research assistance. Funds cannot be used to purchase equipment nor to pay for released time of academic persons. In recent years these grants have ranged from $5,000 to $500,000, with the average about $35,000.

• *Independent Study and Research Fellowships.* These grants are intended to provide time for uninterrupted study and research by scholars, teachers, writers and others who have produced or demonstrated promise of producing significant contributions to humanistic knowledge. The funds may be used for a project of study or research within the applicant's special interest, or for a program of general study in some other field that will help the applicant better understand his or her own field and become more broadly informed. In the past the grants have averaged about $17,000, and usually have been for a period of six to twelve months.

• *Summer Seminars for College Teachers.* These grants are intended to provide opportunities for teachers at small private and state colleges and junior and community colleges to work during the summer in their areas of interest under the direction of distinguished scholars at institutions with first-rate libraries. The grants go to scholars who agree to serve as directors of summer projects. The directors in turn select the teacher participants. In recent years the seminars have been in such fields as history, philosophy, and English and American literature. The grants have averaged about $40,000 per seminar.

• *Youth Grants.* These grants, normally awarded only to persons under the age of thirty, are intended for research, education, film, and community projects in one or more of the fields included in the humanities: history, philosophy, language, linguistics, literature, archeology, jurisprudence, art history and criticism, and the humanistic social sciences. Funds may be used to cover participants' stipends, adviser honoraria, clerical support, travel, supplies and materials, and rental of space and equipment. The grants cannot be used for the general educational or training expenses of individuals. Grants range up to $10,000 but have averaged about $2,000 for individual projects.

How to apply: Application forms and further information on these grants can be obtained by writing to the National Endowment for the Humanities, Washington, D.C. 20506. In some cases the endowment encourages preliminary draft proposals prior to formal applications.

Scientific research

Millions of dollars in federal funds are available in the form of grants for scientific research. This research covers a broad spectrum of fields, from the search for the secrets of the polar ice cap to the quest for clues to the causes of cancer.

The National Science Foundation (NSF) offers some of the major programs for scientific research. Much of the money goes to colleges, universities, and non-profit organizations, but some grants are made to individuals and profit-making organizations. Here are details of NSF grant programs:

Science Fellowships. In an effort to create a more effective supply of scientific manpower, the NSF offers fellowship and traineeship grants to students to pursue their studies at the institutions of their choice. The typical grant is for a nine-to-twelve-month period, and the recipient must remain a full-time student for the duration of the grant. The fellowship stipend has averaged about $3,900, and the cost-of-education allowance, $3,400. These payments are paid through the institution, rather than directly to the recipient.

• *International Cooperative Scientific Activities.* Grants are provided by NSF for U.S. scholars to carry out studies abroad, to conduct research, to travel to special scientific meetings, to engage in joint research projects with foreign organizations, and to support scientific conferences. Recent participants include Australia, New Zealand, Argentina, Brazil, Mexico, the Republic of China, France, India, Italy, Japan, Romania, Czechoslovakia, Bulgaria, the Soviet Union, Poland, Yugoslavia, and Hungary. The financial assistance has ranged upward from $1,000.

• *National Needs.* The NSF supports scientific research focusing on selected problems of national importance, including such areas as the environment, productivity, exploratory research, technology assessments, and research and development incentives. The grants and contracts are for research projects, exploratory studies, symposia, and conferences. Most of the money goes to academic institutions, but grants to individuals are occasionally made. The grants have ranged from $1,000 to $2 million.

• *Scientific Research.* Through a variety of programs, the NSF supports research to increase the store of scientific knowledge and thus to enhance the understanding of basic problems confronting the nation. For instance, there is a program to support work in the disciplines of physics, chemistry, mathematical sciences, engineering, materials research, and computer research. Another program supports work in astronomical, atmospheric, earth and ocean sciences; and a third program supports research in physiology, cellular and molecular biology, behavioral and neural sciences, environmental biology, and the social sciences. In general, most of the research supported is basic in character, although work of an applied nature may be supported. The funding is provided for research workshops, symposia, and conferences, and for the purchase of scientific equipment. Most of the grants go to academic institutions and nonprofit research institutions but some may be made to unaffiliated scientists.

How to apply: Generally, applications are made by such institutions as colleges and universities on behalf of their staff members, although individual scientists can apply directly in some cases. Specific guidelines are contained in the publications *Grants for Scientific Research* (NSF 73-12) and *Guide to Programs* (NSF 74-42). These publications can be obtained free of charge by writing to the National Science Foundation, Washington, D.C. 20550.

Medical research

The government, through the National Institutes of Health and similar agencies, makes grants for research into the causes and treatment of diseases. In most cases, the grants go to universities, hospitals, or nonprofit research institutions for support of research by a specified principal investigator. Applications usually are made by the institutions, rather than the individual researchers.

There also are specific research programs in such areas as mental health, alcoholism, and drug abuse. For application forms and information on the mental health research grants, contact the National Institute of Mental Health, 5600 Fishers Lane, Rockville, Maryland 20852. For application forms for the drug-abuse research grants, contact the National Institute on Drug Abuse, 11400 Rockville Pike, Rockville, Maryland 20852. For application forms for the alcoholism research grants, contact the National Institute on Alcohol Abuse and Alcoholism, 5600 Fishers Lane, Rockville, Maryland 20852.

Oceanic research

Private agencies and laboratories are among those eligible for project grants for marine research, education, and training services under the Sea Grant program.

Selections for the grants are made on a competitive basis, and the applicant must have demonstrated capacity to serve the state or region in marine affairs. At least one-third of the total cost of the project must be obtained from nonfederal sources. The grant money cannot be used to rent, purchase, or construct ships or facilities, but can be used for personnel salaries, travel, and instrumentation.

In recent years the grants have ranged from $25,000 to $1.3 million, with the larger grants going to major universities.

How to apply: Informal proposals are welcomed. The formal proposal must fully document the need for the grant and the proposed amount. Obtain further information from the Director, National Sea Grant Program, National Oceanic and Atmospheric Administration, 2001 Wisconsin Avenue, N.W., Washington, D.C. 20235.

Forestry research

The U.S. Forest Service makes grants under a pair of programs for research in such fields as timber management, forest recreation and fire protection, forest insect and disease control, forest products utilization, and forest products marketing.

Under both programs, individuals are eligible, along with colleges and other research institutions.

The first program requires cooperative research agreements between the Forest Service and other institutions, such as colleges. The grants usually range from $1,000 to $100,000, with the average about $10,000.

The second program calls for direct grants. They ranged in a recent year from $2,000 to $100,000 and averaged about $20,000.

How to apply: In both programs, initial contact should be with the director of the regional Forest Service experiment station nearest you. If you cannot locate the office's address in your telephone book, write the Deputy Chief for Research, Forest Service, U.S. Department of Agriculture, P.O. Box 2417, Washington, D.C. 20013.

CHAPTER 7

If You Are a Veteran

Veterans of U.S. military service are the beneficiaries of more specific programs than perhaps any other group in America. These programs range from educational assistance to housing aid, from pension and death benefits to free medical care, from insurance to employment assistance.

The special programs are the government's way of saying thanks to veterans for their service to the country. Veterans who make full use of the benefits can find the programs a way to keep pace with a rising cost of living.

Educational aid

Over the past several decades, millions of veterans have helped finance their education or training through what is commonly known as the GI Bill.

Veterans are eligible for this aid if they served on active duty for at least 181 continuous days, any part of which occurred after

Eligibility Requirements

All Veterans Administration benefits, with the exception of insurance, require a particular period of military service and that the service be terminated under conditions other than dishonorable.

Veterans with *honorable* and *general* discharges are eligible for benefits. *Dishonorable* discharges are a bar to VA benefits. Veterans with *undesirable* and *bad conduct* discharges may or may not qualify, depending upon a special determination made by the VA, based on the facts of each case, as to whether the veteran was separated from service under "dishonorable conditions" or "other than dishonorable conditions." A veteran may apply for a review of such a discharge by submitting Department of Defense Form DD-293, which may be obtained at any VA office.

January 31, 1955, but before January 1, 1977, and were either discharged under conditions other than dishonorable or were discharged for a service-connected disability. Service personnel who are currently on active duty and have been for 181 continuous days also are eligible.

The 181 days of required active duty cannot include any period when assigned full time by the armed forces to a civilian institution for a course substantially the same as a course offered to civilians. Nor can it include time served as a cadet or midshipman at a service academy. Also excluded are periods of active-duty training in the Army or Air Force National Guard or in the Army, Navy, Air Force, Marine Corps, or Coast Guard Reserve, unless the guardsman or reservist later serves on active duty for a consecutive period of at least one year's duration. Before benefits can be paid, the educational institution being attended by the veteran must be approved by the Veterans Administration (VA). Most educational institutions already have obtained such approval, but a veteran should make certain before enrolling.

The approved institutions include public or private elementary, high, vocational, correspondence, or business schools; junior or teachers colleges; normal schools; colleges and universities; and professional, scientific, and technical institutions within the United States.

Veterans' Monthly Education Benefits

| | Number of Dependents | | | Each Additional |
	None	One	Two	Dependent
Full-Time	$292	$347	$396	$24
Three-Quarter	219	260	297	18
Half-Time	146	174	198	12
Cooperative (work-study)	235	276	313	18

For study overseas, only college-level institutions are eligible for VA approval. The VA administrator, at his discretion, may deny or discontinue the educational assistance of any veteran in a foreign educational institution if he finds that such enrollment is not in the best interest of the veteran or the government.

Each eligible veteran is entitled to educational assistance for a period of one and one-half months or the equivalent in part-time training for each month or fraction of a month served on active duty after January 31, 1955, but not to exceed forty-five months. If the veteran served for eighteen months or more after that date and has been released under conditions satisfying the active-duty obligation, he or she qualifies for the full entitlement of forty-five months.

There is a ten-year time limit for using educational assistance. For example, a veteran released from active duty on August 1, 1970, has until August 1, 1980, to use the entitlement. However, the entitlement of all veterans is scheduled to expire on December 31, 1989.

Benefits can be paid for a wide variety of educational or training courses. The Veterans Administration has this broad guideline: "Each eligible person may select a program of training at any educational institution or training establishment which will accept and retain him as a student trainee in any field or branch

Outlays for Veterans' Benefits and Services

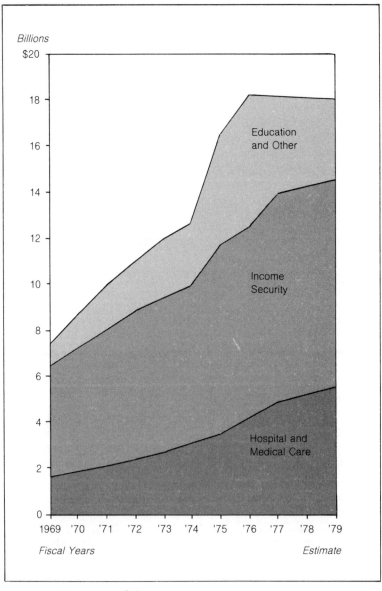

Billions

Source: Office of Management and Budget

of knowledge which the institution finds him qualified to undertake."

A veteran who must complete high school training or pass an equivalency examination to qualify for higher education may receive the educational assistance allowance without a charge against his or her basic entitlement. This provision also permits additional secondary school training such as refresher courses or deficiency courses needed to qualify for admission to an appropriate educational institution.

In addition, payment for tutorial assistance is allowed for veterans or service personnel who are in postsecondary (above high school) training on a half-time or more basis. Tutorial payments may not exceed $65 a month up to a maximum amount of $780 with no charge against the basic entitlement.

How to apply: Recently discharged veterans will receive at their home address a computer-generated VA Form 22-1990v, which consists of a notice of eligibility, an application, and enrollment certification. Application forms also are available from any VA office (VA Form 22-1990 for veterans, Form 22-1990a for service personnel). The completed applications can be submitted to the nearest VA office.

Educational aid for dependents

The VA also provides educational assistance for the dependents of deceased or totally disabled veterans. These monthly payments can go to the wives or husbands of disabled veterans, the widows or widowers of deceased veterans, and to children between eighteen and twenty-six years old if death or disability of a parent was the result of service in the armed forces.

The payments can be made for up to forty-five months of schooling, or the equivalent of forty-five months if enrolled part-time.

Generally, the period of eligibility for wives, husbands, widows, and widowers is ten years from the time of death or permanent disability of the veteran. For wives and husbands of service personnel missing in action, eligibility extends to December 24, 1980, or ten years from the date the spouse was listed as missing, whichever is later. A child remains eligible for benefits even if he or she marries, but a spouse's remarriage terminates entitlement.

Monthly payments under this program are the same as those that are made to veterans with no dependents under the GI Bill.

Application forms for this educational aid can be obtained from any VA office.

Vocational rehabilitation

Veterans with a service-connected disability are eligible for vocational rehabilitation intended to restore their ability to obtain employment. The program provides for the entire cost of tuition, books, fees, and training supplies.

During training and for two months following rehabilitation, a veteran is paid a subsistence allowance in addition to disability compensation. The full-time monthly subsistence allowances range from $226 for a veteran with no dependents to $329 for a veteran with two dependents, plus $24 for each additional dependent. The allowances are scaled down if the veteran receives training on a part-time basis.

In most cases, the vocational rehabilitation training period is four years. This training generally must be completed within nine years following the date of discharge from the service. Extensions are possible in some instances.

Application forms can be obtained from any VA office. Awards are authorized at regional VA offices.

GI home loans

Eligible veterans and service personnel may obtain so-called GI loans from private lenders for the following purposes:

• To purchase, construct, refinance, or improve a home.

• To purchase a farm on which there is a residence which will be occupied by the veteran as a home.

• To purchase a mobile home and/or lot.

• To purchase and improve a mobile home lot on which to place a unit owned and occupied by the veteran.

• To purchase a one-family residential unit in certain condominium projects.

Eligibility requirements vary according to the time of service. World War II veterans must have had at least ninety days of active duty between September 16, 1940, and July 25, 1947, unless they were discharged sooner for service-connected disability.

Korean War veterans must have had at least ninety days of

VA-Guaranteed Home Mortgage Loans

Year	Number	Amount (in millions)
1955	649,000	$7,271
1960	145,000	1,985
1961	135,000	1,829
1962	188,000	2,652
1963	211,000	3,045
1964	186,000	2,846
1965	164,000	2,652
1966	157,000	2,600
1967	201,000	3,405
1968	211,000	3,774
1969	214,000	4,072
1970	168,000	3,440
1971	282,000	5,961
1972	370,000	8,293
1973	365,000	8,357
1974	311,000	7,709
1975	310,000	8,072
1976	325,365	9,900
1977 (est.)	335,600	10,400
1978 (est.)	354,600	12,100

Source: Veterans Administration

active duty between June 27, 1950, and January 31, 1955, or have been discharged for a service-connected disability.

Veterans of the post-Korean or Vietnam War eras must have served on active duty for at least 181 continuous days, any part of which occurred after January 31, 1955, or have been released from active duty since that date for a service-connected disability.

(So-called six-month enlistees—those who joined reserve units and received full-time training for six months—are not eligible since their service does not constitute "active duty" as defined by law.)

Also eligible for GI home loans are the unmarried widows and widowers of service personnel who died as the result of service-connected disabilities, and the spouses of service personnel who have been listed officially as missing in action or prisoners of war and who have been so listed for more than ninety days.

In addition to the service requirements, to qualify for a home loan the veteran must be a satisfactory credit risk and be able to show that his or her income is sufficient to meet mortgage payments, take care of other obligations and expenses, and leave the veteran with an adequate amount for family support.

Under the program as amended in early 1975 the VA can guarantee a home loan by a private lender up to $17,500, or 60 percent of the loan, whichever is less. Besides the purchase of a home, the loans may be used for alterations, repairs, or improvements on homes already owned and occupied. The VA no longer has authority to guarantee farm and business loans.

Loans to purchase individual residence units in qualified condominium projects may be guaranteed up to 60 percent but not for more than $17,500.

If the veteran has not used any of the entitlement for home loans, he or she may obtain a VA guarantee of 50 percent to purchase a single-width mobile home for an amount not to exceed $12,500 or up to $27,500 for a double-width mobile home. Extra aid is available for the purchase of a mobile home and a developed lot and/or the cost of site preparation. Use of the mobile home loan benefit precludes the use of any other home loan benefit until the mobile home loan has been repaid in full.

Interest rates on GI loans cannot exceed the maximum set by the VA. Like the FHA maximum, it varies from time to time, according to mortgage market conditions. Your nearest VA office can tell you the current maximum rate.

Home loans can be made for a maximum of thirty years. Loans for the purchase of a single-width mobile home are made for a maximum of twelve years and thirty-two days; if a lot is also purchased, the maximum term is fifteen years and thirty-two days. All loans for double-width mobile homes with or without lots have maximum terms of twenty years and thirty-two days.

As with FHA-insured loans, arrangements for GI home loans are made through the usual lending channels, such as banks, savings and loan associations, and mortgage loan companies. Veterans should obtain a certificate of eligibility from the nearest VA office and present it to the lender. Application for loan guaranty is then made by the lender to the VA regional office.

Veterans who used their entitlement before 1975 may have additional entitlement available for GI home loan purposes. In 1950, the maximum loan entitlement was raised from $4,000 to $7,500. In 1968, it was increased to $12,500. In 1975, it went to $17,500. The amount of such additional entitlement is the difference between the maximum and the amount of entitlement used on prior home loans. In addition, certain veterans may meet the

Veterans Administration Offices

For information and assistance in applying for veterans' benefits, write, telephone, or visit one of the offices listed.

Alabama
474 S. Court St.
Montgomery, AL 36104
(205) 265-5611

Alaska
Federal Bldg., U.S. Post
  Office & Courthouse
P.O. Box 1288
709 W. 9th St.
Juneau, AK 99801
(907) 586-7472

Rm. 214, Loussac-Sogn Bldg.
429 D St.
Anchorage, AK 99501
Zenith 2500

Arizona
Federal Bldg.
3225 N. Central Ave.
Phoenix, AZ 85025
(602) 263-5411

Arkansas
Federal Bldg.
700 W. Capitol Ave.
Little Rock, AR 72201
(501) 378-5971

California
Old Post Office Bldg.
101 S. Willowbrook Ave.
Compton, CA 90220
(213) 537-3203

11000 Wilshire Blvd.
Los Angeles, CA 90024
(213) 479-4011

2022 Camino del Rio North
San Diego, CA 92108
(714) 293-5724

211 Main Street
San Francisco, CA 94105
(415) 495-8900

Colorado
Denver Federal Center
Denver, CO 80225
(303) 233-6300

Connecticut
450 Main St.
Hartford, CT 06103
(203) 244-3740

Delaware
1601 Kirkwood Highway
Wilmington, DE 19805
(302) 998-0191

District of Columbia
941 N. Capitol St., N.E.
Washington, DC 20421
(202) 872-1151

Florida
Post Office & Courthouse
  Bldg.
311 W. Monroe St.
Jacksonville, FL 32201
(904) 356-1581

Rm. 100, 51 S.W. 1st Ave.
Miami, FL 33130
(305) 358-0669

Post Office Bldg.
Pensacola, FL 32576
(904) 434-3537

P.O. Box 1437
144 1st Ave., South
St. Petersburg, FL 33731
(813) 898-2121

Georgia
730 Peachtree St., N.E.
Atlanta, GA 30308
(404) 881-1776

Hawaii
P.O. Box 3198
680 Ala Moana Blvd.
Honolulu, HI 96801
(808) 546-8949

Idaho
Federal Bldg. &
  U.S. Courthouse
550 West Fort St. - Box 044
Boise, ID 83724
(205) 345-7491

Illinois
536 S. Clark St.
Chicago, IL 60680
(312) 663-5510

Indiana
575 N. Pennsylvania St.
Indianapolis, IN 46204
(317) 635-5221

Iowa
210 Walnut St.
Des Moines, IA 50309
(515) 280-7220

Kansas
5500 E. Kellogg
Wichita, KS 67218
(316) 685-2221

Kentucky
600 Federal Pl.
Louisville, KY 40202
(502) 582-5811

Louisiana
701 Loyola Ave.
New Orleans, LA 70113
(504) 561-0121

510 E. Stoner Ave.
Shreveport, LA 71101
(318) 493-6249

Maine
Togus, ME 04330
(207) 623-8411

76 Pearl St.
Portland, ME 04111
(207) 833-3223

Maryland
31 Hopkins Plaza
Baltimore, MD 21201
(301) 962-4686

Massachusetts
John Fitzgerald Kennedy
  Federal Bldg.
Government Center
Boston, MA 02203
(617) 227-4600

1200 Main St.
Springfield, MA 01103
(413) 836-9301

Michigan
P.O. Box 1117A
477 W. Michigan Ave.
Detroit, MI 48226
(313) 964-5110

Minnesota
Federal Bldg., Ft. Snelling
St. Paul, MN 55111
(612) 726-1454

Mississippi
2350 Highway 80 West
Jackson, MS 39024
(601) 969-4873

Missouri
Federal Office Bldg.
601 E. 12th St.
Kansas City, MO 64106
(816) 861-3761

Rm. 4705, Federal Bldg.
1520 Market St.
St. Louis, MO 63103
(314) 342-1171

Montana
Fort Harrison, MT 59636
(406) 442-6410

Nebraska
100 Centennial Mall North
Lincoln, NB 68508
(402) 475-3413

Nevada
1201 Terminal Way
Reno, NV 89502
(702) 329-9244

New Hampshire
497 Silver St.
Manchester, NH 03103
(603) 669-8448

New Jersey
20 Washington Pl.
Newark, NJ 07102
(201) 645-2150

New Mexico
500 Gold Ave., S.W.
Albuquerque, NM 87101
(505) 766-3361

New York
O'Brien Federal Bldg.
Clifton Ave. & N.
  Pearl St.
Albany, NY 12207
(518) 562-4206

Federal Bldg.
35 Tillary St.
Brooklyn, NY 11201
(212) 330-4737

Federal Bldg.
111 W. Huron St.
Buffalo, NY 14202
(716) 842-2285

252 7th Ave.
New York, NY 10001
(212) 660-6261

100 South State St.
Rochester, NY 14614
(716) 473-5780

Gateway Bldg.
809 S. Salina St.
Syracuse, NY 13202
(315) 951-2680

North Carolina
251 N. Main St.
Winston-Salem, NC 27102
(919) 748-1800

North Dakota
21st Ave. & Elm St.
Fargo, ND 58102
(701) 232-3241

Ohio
Rm. 1024, Federal Off. Blc
550 Main St.
Cincinnati, OH 45202
(513) 684-2200

Federal Office Bldg.
1240 E. 9th St.
Cleveland, OH 44199
(216) 621-5050

Bryson Bldg.
360 S. Third St.
Columbus, OH 43215
(614) 469-7334

Oklahoma
2nd & Court Sts.
Muskogee, OK 74401
(918) 683-3161

200 N.W. 4th St.
Oklahoma City, OK 73102
(405) 231-4115

Oregon
1220 S.W. 3rd Ave.
Portland, OR 97204
(503) 221-2431

Pennsylvania
P.O. Box 8079
5000 Wissahickon Ave.
Philadelphia, PA 19101
(215) 438-5225

1000 Liberty Ave.
Pittsburgh, PA 15222
(412) 281-4233

19-27 N. Main St.
Wilkes-Barre, PA 18703
(717) 592-7261

Philippines
1131 Roxas Blvd.
APO San Francisco
Manila, PI 96528

Puerto Rico
U.S. Courthouse
Carlos G. Chardon St.
Hato Rey
San Juan, PR 00918
(809) 753-4490

Rhode Island
321 S. Main St.
Providence, RI 02903
(401) 528-4431

South Carolina
1801 Assembly St.
Columbia, SC 29201
(803) 765-5861

South Dakota
300 N. Dakota Ave.
Sioux Falls, SD 57101
(605) 336-3496

Tennessee
110 9th Ave. South
Nashville, TN 37203
(615) 254-5411

Texas
U.S. Courthouse & Federal
Office Bldg.
1100 Commerce St.
Dallas, TX 75202
(214) 749-3201

2515 Murworth Dr.
Houston, TX 77054
(713) 664-4664

Federal Bldg.
1205 Texas Ave.
Lubbock, TX 79401
(806) 762-7011

410 S. Main Ave.
San Antonio, TX 78285
(512) 225-4841

1400 N. Valley Mills Dr.
Waco, TX 76710
(817) 772-3060

Utah
125 S. State St.
Salt Lake City, UT 84138
(801) 524-5960

Vermont
White River Jct., VT 05001
(802) 295-9363

Virginia
210 Franklin Rd., S.W.
Roanoke, VA 24011
(703) 981-9337

Washington
Federal Office Bldg.
915 Second Ave.
Seattle, WA 98174
(206) 624-7200

West Virginia
502 8th St.
Huntington, WV 25701
(304) 522-8294

Wisconsin
342 N. Water St.
Milwaukee, WI 53202
(414) 278-8680

Wyoming
2360 E. Pershing Blvd.
Cheyenne, WY 82001
(307) 778-7550

requirements for having their entitlement restored. This restoration can occur if the property which secured the loan has been disposed of by the veteran or has been destroyed by fire or other natural hazard; and the loan has been repaid in full, or the VA has been relieved of liability on the loan.

Since April 1, 1975, veterans selling homes purchased with GI loans have been able to regain the use of their home loan benefits for another GI loan, provided that the purchaser is an eligible veteran who has agreed to substitute his or her entitlement for that of the veteran-seller, and the veteran-buyer and the property meet VA's criteria.

In some rural or small community areas where the VA determines that private mortgage financing is not generally available, the agency can make direct loans to qualified veterans. Application forms can be obtained from the nearest VA office.

There also is a special grant program for "wheelchair homes" especially adapted for certain disabled veterans. The grants can cover up to 50 percent of the cost of building, buying, or remodeling such homes, or repaying debts on such homes already acquired, up to a maximum of $25,000. To qualify for this grant program, the veteran must have a service-connected permanent and total disability such as the loss of use of both legs. Applications for this grant program can be obtained from any VA office.

Inpatient care

Veterans are eligible for inpatient care at VA hospitals across the country. The hospital care includes transportation and incidental expenses for veterans who are unable to defray transportation costs. The hospitals have these general admission priorities:

First—Veterans needing hospitalization because of injuries or disease incurred or aggravated in the line of duty in active service have top priority for admission for treatment of the disability.

Second—Veterans who were discharged or retired for disability incurred or aggravated in the line of duty, or who are receiving a veteran's pension, or who would be eligible for a pension except for receipt of retirement pay, will be admitted as beds are available for treatment of an ailment not connected with their military service.

Third—Veterans who were not discharged or retired due to

disability may be admitted for treatment of a nonservice-connected disability if three conditions are met: First, that hospitalization is deemed necessary; second, that they state under oath that they are unable to defray the cost of necessary hospital charges elsewhere; and third, if beds are available. (The "ability to pay" requirement does not apply to any veteran who has been awarded the Medal of Honor, or who is sixty-five years of age or older, or who receives a VA pension.)

Under certain circumstances, medical care is available for the spouse or child of a veteran who has a total and permanent service-connected disability, and for the widow, widower, or child of a veteran who died of a service-connected disability.

How to apply: Application may be made personally at a VA hospital, outpatient clinic, or regional office; through any veterans' service organization; or by mailing VA Form 10-10 to the nearest VA hospital. A ruling is made the same day if a veteran applies in person; generally within a week if he or she applies by mail.

Outpatient care

Medical and dental services, medicines, and medical supplies may be provided to eligible veterans on an outpatient basis.

The following are eligible for medical outpatient services: veterans suffering from a disease or injury incurred or aggravated in service, veterans suffering from a nonservice-connected illness which has aggravated a service-connected illness, veterans with established eligibility for pre- and posthospital care, Spanish-American War veterans, veterans entitled to vocational rehabilitation, military retirees, veterans with a service-related disability rated at 50 percent or more, veterans who receive increased allowances and aid because they are permanently housebound, veterans who require outpatient treatment to obviate the need for hospitalization, and wives, husbands, widows, widowers, and children of veterans who were totally disabled by a service-connected condition or who died from service-connected injury or illness.

Eligibility requirements for outpatient dental treatment generally are the same as for outpatient medical treatment but there are some special rules. Veterans who have a service-connected, compensable dental disability or condition may apply at any

Loans to Veterans

Program	1976	1977 (est.)	1978 (est.)
Housing:	(in millions of dollars)		
Direct loan disbursements	$ 399	$ 418	$ 451
Direct loan repayments	459	688	448
Direct loans outstanding, end of period	1,681	1,331	1,293
Guaranteed loans outstanding, end of period	64,116	70,822	77,369
Education:			
Direct loan disbursements	6	15	1
Direct loan repayments	1	1	2
Direct loans outstanding, end of period	7	22	22
Income Security:			
Insurance policy loans:			
Direct loan disbursements	132	118	118
Direct loan repayments	120	108	105
Direct loans outstanding, end of period	1,142	1,159	1,172

Source: Office of Management and Budget

time. Veterans whose dental conditions are service-connected but noncompensable must apply within one year after discharge or release from active duty.

The outpatient care may be administered at VA hospitals and clinics or by private physicians on a fee basis. Eligible veterans may be furnished drugs or medicine ordered by prescription.

How to apply: Applications (VA Form 10-10) may be obtained from any VA office or hospital.

Nursing homes

Veterans who are not acutely ill and not in need of hospital care but who require skilled nursing care and related medical services can qualify for the VA's nursing home program.

Eligibility requirements for admission or transfer to VA nursing home care units are essentially the same as for hospitalization.

Direct admission to private nursing homes at VA expense is limited to veterans who require nursing care for a service-connected disability after medical determination by the VA, and any person in an armed forces hospital who requires a protracted period of nursing care and who will become a veteran upon discharge from the armed forces.

The VA may transfer hospitalized veterans who need a protracted period of nursing care to a private nursing home at VA expense. Normally, VA authorized care may not be provided for longer than six months except for veterans who require such care for a service-connected or adjunct disability.

How to apply: If a veteran is in a VA hospital, transfer to a nursing home is made on the determination of his or her VA physician. Veterans not under care at VA expense should submit VA Form 10-10 to the nearest VA medical facility.

Domiciliary care

The VA domiciliary care program is intended to provide ambulatory self-care for veterans disabled by age or disease who are not in need of hospitalization or the skilled nursing services provided in nursing homes.

Eligible applicants include veterans discharged from active duty for a disability incurred in or aggravated by military service, veterans receiving compensation for a permanent disability, and war veterans unable to defray the expenses of necessary domiciliary care.

In addition to federal domiciliaries, the VA provides financial-support for states to operate domiciliaries for veterans. Eligibility requirements are basically the same for both types of institutions.

How to apply: Application should be made on VA Form 10-10 available at any VA office. This application must be approved prior to admission.

Special medical programs

The VA also offers special medical programs. Among them are:

• *Drug and Alcoholism Treatment.* Any veteran who requires treatment for alcohol or drug dependence is eligible if he or she served on active duty and was discharged or released under conditions other than dishonorable. Special treatment units are located at VA hospitals.

• *Prosthetic Appliances.* Prosthetic and related appliances and services are provided to disabled veterans. The program also includes the replacement and repair of appliances as well as training in the use of artificial limbs, artificial eyes, aids for the blind, hearing aids, braces, orthopedic shoes, eyeglasses, crutches, and canes.

• *Aid for the Blind.* A blinded veteran may be eligible to receive electronic and mechanical aids or a guide dog, including the expense of training the veteran to use the dog and the cost of the dog's medical care.

• *Clothing Allowance.* An annual clothing allowance payment of $203 may be made to any veteran who is entitled to receive compensation for a service-connected disability for which he or she wears or uses prosthetic or orthopedic appliances, including a wheelchair which the VA determines wears out or tears the veteran's clothing.

Automobiles for the disabled

The VA provides financial assistance to certain disabled veterans for the purchase of an automobile and special equipment necessary for the veteran to operate it. The one-time payment cannot exceed $3,300 toward the purchase price of the automobile. The VA, however, will pay the costs of repairing, reinstalling, or replacing the special equipment.

To qualify, veterans of World War II and thereafter must have sustained the service-connected permanent loss of use of one or both hands or feet, or permanent impairment of vision of both eyes to a prescribed degree.

How to apply: An application (VA Form 21-4502) may be obtained from any VA office and submitted to the nearest regional office.

Life insurance

During World Wars I and II and the Korean War, the government offered low-cost life insurance—commonly called GI insurance—to millions of men and women in the armed forces. Upon leaving the service, these veterans could maintain the insurance protection by paying the premiums. All of these older programs are closed for new issues, but under certain circumstances a veteran so insured can convert a term policy to a permanent policy.

He or she also can borrow against the cash value of a permanent policy.

Two more recent programs are still open for new issues. They are the Service Disabled Veterans Insurance (SDVI), mainly for disabled veterans of the Korean and Vietnam wars, and Veterans Mortgage Life Insurance (VMLI), which offers mortgage protection life insurance to veterans who have received a VA grant to secure specially-adapted housing.

A veteran separated from service on or after April 25, 1951, with a service-connected disability but otherwise in good health may apply to the VA for an SDVI policy within one year from the date of notification by the VA that the disability has been rated as service-connected.

A veteran who has been given a VA grant for specially-adapted housing will be notified that he or she is automatically insured for mortgage protection unless the veteran elects in writing not to be so insured or fails to respond within sixty days after a final request for information on which the premium can be based. There must be a mortgage in existence at the time the veteran applies. This type of insurance is handled only by the VA Center in Saint Paul, Minnesota.

How to apply: Applications for new policies, as well as requests involving policies already issued, are handled by two VA centers. Veterans living east of the Mississippi River should contact the Veterans Administration Center, P.O. Box 8079, Philadelphia, Pennsylvania 19101. Veterans living west of the Mississippi should contact the Veterans Administration Center, Federal Building, Fort Snelling, Saint Paul, Minnesota 55111.

Pensions and compensation

The Veterans Administration supervises a massive and complex system of pensions and compensation for veterans and their dependents and survivors. The major programs include:

• *Compensation for Service-Connected Disabilities.* Monthly compensation is paid to veterans who are disabled by injury or illness incurred in or aggravated by active service in the line of duty during wartime or peacetime. The pensions are scaled according to the average impairment in earning capacity the disability causes in civilian occupations. The table on page 98 shows the monthly payments according to the degree of disability.

Compensation for Service-Connected Disability

Degree of Disability	Monthly Rate
10 percent	$ 41
20 percent	75
30 percent	113
40 percent	155
50 percent	216
60 percent	277
70 percent	322
80 percent	373
90 percent	419
Total disability	754

Higher rates than those listed above—up to $1,759 a month—are paid for disabilities such as blindness or the loss of arms or legs. Veterans whose service-connected disabilities are rated at 50 percent or more are entitled to additional allowances for dependents.

• *Pensions for Nonservice-Connected Disabilities.* The VA has a pension system to assist wartime veterans whose nonservice-connected disabilities are permanent and total and prevent them from following a substantially gainful occupation. To qualify, a veteran must have had ninety days or more of honorable wartime service or, if less than ninety days, must have been discharged because of a service-connected disability. The veteran must be permanently and totally disabled, but not necessarily due to service. Also eligible are wartime veterans sixty-five years of age or older who are considered permanently and totally disabled.

There are income limitations, with the amount of the pension scaled to the amount of income. To qualify, the annual income of a veteran with no dependents cannot exceed $3,540, and the income of a veteran with one or more dependents cannot exceed $4,760. The monthly pension rates are shown in the table on page 99.

• *Pensions for Widows, Widowers, and Children.* A separate

Pensions for Nonservice-Connected Disability

When Annual Income Is Not More Than:	Monthly Pension for Veteran Alone Is:	Monthly Pension for Veteran With One Dependent Is:
$ 300	$185	$199
1,000	155	186
1,500	125	167
2,000	88	147
2,500	48	126
3,000	8	101
3,500	5	72
4,000	—	34
4,500	—	5

Veterans who are within the income limits and in need of regular aid and attendance receive an additional $155 a month and veterans who are housebound receive an additional $57 a month.

Veterans are entitled to an additional $5 for each dependent up to a maximum of three.

VA pension system provides a partial means of support for needy widows, widowers, and children of wartime veterans whose deaths were not due to service. To qualify, the veteran must have had at least ninety days of honorable active wartime service or, if less than ninety days, must have been discharged for a service-connected disability. A widow or widower must have been married to the veteran for at least one year prior to the death unless a child resulted from the union. A widow or widower of a Vietnam era veteran is eligible regardless of when the marriage took place. If a widow or widower remarries, she or he loses eligibility for the pension. Children must be unmarried and under eighteen or under twenty-three if still attending school. Children remain eligible after age eighteen if they are disabled.

Again, there are income limitations, with the size of the pension scaled to the amount of income. The maximum income cannot exceed $3,540 for a widow or widower without a child, and $4,760 for a widow or widower with a child. The table on page 100 shows examples of the pension rates.

Pensions for Veterans' Widows, Widowers, and Children

When Annual Income Is Not More Than:	Monthly Pension for Widow or Widower Alone Is:	Monthly Pension for Widow or Widower And One Child Is:
$ 300	$125	$149
1,000	109	146
1,500	86	137
2,000	61	124
2,500	34	109
3,000	5	89
4,000	—	57
4,500	—	57

The monthly pension is increased by $24 for each additional child.

• *Compensation for Service-Connected Deaths.* There are two systems of compensation for dependents of veterans whose deaths are service-connected. The first is known as Dependency and Indemnity Compensation (DIC) and the second is called Death Compensation.

DIC payments go to widows, widowers, unmarried children under eighteen (or under twenty-three if still in school), and certain parents of service personnel or veterans who died on or after January 1, 1957, from a disease or injury incurred or aggravated in the line of duty while on active duty, active duty for training, or inactive duty training, or from a disability otherwise compensable under laws administered by the VA.

Payments to widows and widowers under DIC depend on the rank of the service personnel or veterans. For parents to qualify for payments, their income must be under $3,540 annually for one parent or $4,760 for two parents.

Under the other program, Death Compensation is payable to widows, widowers, children, and dependent parents of veterans who died before January 1, 1957, because of a service-connected disability. Those who qualify under this program have the option of taking payments instead under the previously described DIC program. Death Compensation does not vary according to the veteran's rank. Thus, in some cases, the DIC program is more advantageous.

How to apply: Both programs use the same application forms (VA Form 21-534 and 21-535). These can be obtained from any local VA office. They must be submitted to the nearest regional office.

Burial expenses

The VA pays up to $250 toward the funeral and burial expenses of a qualified veteran, plus $150 for a plot or interment expenses if the veteran is not buried in a national cemetery. If the death is service-connected, $800 is payable for funeral and burial expenses. This is in lieu of the $250 and $150 allowances. In addition to these payments, the VA pays the costs of transporting the remains to the burial site if the death occurred in a VA hospital or facility.

For the family or funeral director to qualify for the payments, the veteran must have served during wartime or, if a peacetime veteran, must have been entitled to service-connected compensation at the time of death.

Burial in a national cemetery having grave space is available to any veteran of wartime or peacetime service. Reservists and National Guard personnel who die while performing active-duty training also are eligible. So are the wives, husbands, widows, widowers, minor children, and certain unmarried adult children of eligible veterans.

Special provisions apply to Arlington National Cemetery near Washington, D.C. Burial in Arlington is limited to persons who die while on active duty in the armed forces, retired members of the armed forces who are receiving retired pay, Medal of Honor recipients, high-ranking federal officials such as members of Congress and Supreme Court justices who have had active-duty military service, and the spouses or minor children of persons eligible or already buried there.

The VA provides without charge a headstone or grave marker for deceased veterans in national and private cemeteries. The inscribed marker or headstone is shipped to a specified location. In private cemeteries, the next of kin of the deceased or a person designated by the next of kin must accept responsibility for receiving and erecting the headstone or marker. Memorial markers also are provided for members of the armed forces who die in the service and whose remains are not recovered or are buried at sea.

How to apply: Applications for the burial allowance (VA Form 21-530) can be obtained from any VA office and submitted to a regional office. Applications for headstones or markers (VA Form 40-1330) can be obtained from any VA office and should be submitted to the Director, National Cemetery System (42), Veterans Administration, Washington, D.C. 20420. Application for burial in a national cemetery should be made only at the time of death and should be directed to the superintendent of the national cemetery in which interment is desired.

CHAPTER 8

If You Are a Rural Resident

Federal farm programs have for long been among the most controversial of government benefits. The furor usually has been created by huge payments to individual farmers for not growing certain crops. But in recent years subsidies of this type have been curtailed or eliminated and the controversy has ebbed somewhat.

There remains, however, a wide range of noncontroversial programs of benefit not only to farmers but to residents of rural and outlying areas who are not farmers.

Among the benefits offered by these programs are loans for housing purchases and improvements, farm ownership and operation, conservation of natural resources, and recreation facilities. There is even a program under which the government stocks fish—free of charge—in thousands of farm and ranch ponds.

Rural housing

Several federal programs are aimed at helping farmers and

other residents of rural or outlying areas meet their housing needs. Here are the details:

• *Loans for Homes in Outlying Areas.* Operated by the U.S. Department of Housing and Urban Development (HUD), this program offers guaranteed and insured loans to finance the purchase of proposed, under construction, or existing one-family nonfarm housing or new farm housing on five or more acres adjacent to a highway. All families—not just farmers—are eligible to apply. For most families, the maximum loan is 97 percent of the estimated value of the property. In recent years the size of the loans has averaged $13,400.

Prospective applicants are encouraged to contact their nearest HUD or Federal Housing Administration office.

• *Rural Housing Loans.* This program, administered by the Farmers Home Administration of the Department of Agriculture, is intended to help rural families with low to moderate incomes. The guaranteed and insured loans may be used for construction, repair, or purchase of housing; necessary sewage disposal facilities; purchase or installation of essential equipment which becomes part of the real estate; or to buy a home site. Under certain circumstances, housing debts may be refinanced. To qualify, an applicant must own a farm or nonfarm tract in a rural area, or become the owner when the loan is granted. In recent years these loans averaged about $20,000.

Applications are filed with the office of the Farmers Home Administration serving the county where the property is located.

• *Rural Housing Site Loans.* Nonprofit private and public organizations are eligible for direct and guaranteed loans to acquire and develop land in rural areas to be subdivided as building sites for low- and moderate-income families or for rural housing cooperatives. These loans averaged more than $175,000 during several recent years.

Applications should be made to the county supervisor of the Farmers Home Administration.

• *Rural Rental Housing Loans.* These guaranteed and insured loans can be used to construct, purchase, improve, or repair rental or cooperative housing for rural residents. The housing may be apartment buildings, duplex units, or individual detached houses. Funds may also be used to buy and improve the land on which the buildings are to be located and to provide appropriate recreational and service facilities. Applicants may be individuals or organizations operating on a profit basis, including those that agree to operate on a limited profit basis; cooperatives owned and managed by eligible low-to-moderate-income families or senior citizens; and private nonprofit corporations, consumer cooperatives, and state or local public agencies. In a typical year, a total of 1,200 loans were made, averaging more than $210,000.

Applications are made in the form of a letter to the county supervisor of the Farmers Home Administration.

• *Rural Housing Repair Loans.* This program is aimed at rural homeowners with very low incomes. It is intended to help them repair or improve their homes to make them safe and sanitary and to remove hazards, including repairs to roofs and foundations and the installation of water and waste disposal systems. The maximum loan for improvement of a farm or other rural home is $5,000. These loans cannot be used for construction of new dwellings or farm buildings.

Application forms can be obtained from the local Farmers Home Administration office.

Farm ownership and operating loans

Active farmers or ranchers are eligible for several loan programs designed to help them make more efficient use of their land, labor, and other resources and to carry on sound and successful operations. The details follow:

• *Ownership Loans.* The Farmers Home Administration has a major program of guaranteed and insured loans to assist eligible farmers and ranchers to become owner-operators of family farms. The loans, with up to forty years to repay, can be used for any of the following purposes:

• Enlarge, improve, and buy family farms.
• Refinance debts so as to place the farming operation on a sound basis.
• Provide necessary water and water facilities.
• Provide basic soil treatment and land conservation measures.
• Construct, repair, and improve buildings needed in operation of a family farm.
• Construct or repair farmhouses.
• Improve, establish, or buy a farm-forest enterprise.
• Produce fish under controlled conditions.

• Finance nonfarm enterprises, including recreation on all or part of the farm.

• Buy and develop land to be used for forestry purposes.

To qualify, an applicant must be unable to obtain adequate credit from other sources at reasonable terms; must have the necessary experience, training, and managerial ability to operate a family farm or a nonfarm enterprise; and must agree to refinance the balance due on the loan as soon as he or she is able to obtain adequate credit from another lender.

The maximum farm ownership loan may not exceed $100,000 and the combination of all debts against the security property may not be more than $225,000. The repayment period is forty years.

In recent years the average loan was about $42,500. Applications are filed with the local county office of the Farmers Home Administration.

• *Operating Loans.* Another Farmers Home Administration program offers guaranteed and insured loans to help operators of family farms obtain what might be described as working capital. Loans are scheduled for repayment over periods of up to seven years, with renewals of up to five years when justified. The loans can be used for the following purposes:

• Purchase livestock, poultry, fur-bearing and other farm animals, fish, and bees.

• Purchase farm, forestry, recreation, or nonfarm enterprise equipment.

• Provide operating expenses for farm, forestry, and nonfarm enterprise.

• Meet family subsistence needs and purchase essential home equipment.

• Make minor real estate improvements.

• Refinance secured and unsecured debts.

• Pay property taxes or insurance premiums on real estate and personal property.

An applicant must have a farm background and the experience and training needed, and must be unable to obtain sufficient credit elsewhere on reasonable terms. After the loan is made, he or she must conduct an operation no larger than a family farm as an owner or tenant. A borrower's total indebtedness for these farm operating loans may not exceed $50,000.

There is a special clause that makes loans available for farm youth. To qualify, a youth must be not more than twenty-one years of age, reside in a rural area or a town of less than 10,000 population, and need the funds to finance projects in connection with the 4-H, Future Farmers, Future Homemakers, or a similar organization.

About 40,000 loans, averaging about $11,000, were made in recent years. Application forms are available at any Farmers Home Administration office.

• *Storage Facilities Loans.* The Agricultural Stabilization and Conservation Service (ASCS) of the Agriculture Department extends direct loans to help farmers finance storage facilities and drying equipment on their farms. To be eligible the farmer must produce one of these commodities: barley, corn, grain sorghum, oats, rye, wheat, soybeans, sunflower seed, rice, dry edible beans, flaxseed, or peanuts. The loans have ranged up to $25,000 in recent years and have averaged about $4,000.

Applications are made to the ASCS county office.

• *Grazing Association Loans.* Neighboring farmers and ranchers who join together in forming a nonprofit grazing association can obtain guaranteed loans from the Farmers Home Administration. Loans made to the associations can be used to acquire and develop land for seasonal grazing for livestock owned by association members. The repayment period is forty years. In past years the loans averaged about $330,000.

Applications are made to the county Farmers Home Administration office.

Conservation and recreation aid

Owners of rural land and operators of farms and ranches are eligible for federal programs intended to increase land and water conservation and promote recreational opportunities.

For example, the Agricultural Stabilization and Conservation Service has made payments of up to $2,500 to individual landowners and tenants who sign agreements pledging to carry out approved soil, water, woodland, and wildlife conservation practices for periods ranging from three to ten years. Similar agreements are made with associations. The grants usually are on a cost-sharing basis, with the landowner, tenant, or association bearing a portion of the cost.

Public agencies and local nonprofit corporations also are eligible for a wide range of loan and grant programs intended to promote conservation of soil and water. Farmers and rural residents are the ultimate beneficiaries of these programs.

A series of separate programs is designed to aid in the construction and operation of recreational facilities in rural areas.

Under a program of guaranteed and insured loans supervised by the Farmers Home Administration, farm and ranch owners or tenants can convert all or part of their farms to income-producing outdoor recreational enterprises.

The funds can be used to develop land and water resources; repair and construct buildings; purchase land, equipment, livestock, and related recreation items; and pay necessary operating expenses.

Examples of the recreation enterprises that may be financed include campgrounds, riding stables, swimming facilities, tennis courts, shooting preserves, vacation cottages, lodges and rooms for visitors, lakes and ponds for boating and fishing, docks, nature trails, hunting facilities, and winter sports areas.

An applicant for this type of loan must be unable to obtain adequate credit from other sources at reasonable terms, must be engaged in farming when the loan is made, must have enough experience or training to be successful in the proposed recreational enterprise, and must agree to refinance the balance due on the loan as soon as he or she is able to obtain adequate credit at reasonable terms from another lender.

The loans, which carry repayment periods of up to forty years, have averaged about $52,000. Applications are filed with the county Farmers Home Administration office.

Under a program operated by the Department of the Interior's Fish and Wildlife Service, owners of farm and ranch ponds can receive free fish.

In addition to municipalities and organizations, eligible applicants include individual owners, usually those with ponds created with the assistance of the Agriculture Department.

Fish are supplied to stock new and reclaimed farm and ranch ponds, but are not available for ponds that are less than one-quarter of an acre in size, or subject to any form of commercialization, or biologically incapable of sustaining fish life. Trout and channel catfish are stocked on a one-time basis only. Each applicant is urged to permit controlled public fishing in stocked ponds.

About 20,000 farm ponds are stocked each year, with the value of the donated fish ranging from $2 to $87 and averaging about $17.

Application forms can be obtained from regional offices of the Fish and Wildlife Service or from the headquarters office, Department of Interior, Washington, D.C. 20240. Applicants are notified by postcard of the time and date for fish deliveries. In some areas, applications received after July 1 cannot be filled until the following year because of hatchery production schedules.

9

If
You
Want to
Buy
Real Estate

If you are thinking of purchasing a house, the federal government has a wide range of programs to help you save money by keeping interest rates lower and making mortgage funds more readily available.

If you are considering real estate investments, the government stands ready to help you through programs aimed directly at the investor, builder, and developer.

If you want to make major improvements on your present home, the government can assist you in obtaining financing.

If you want to live in a mobile home, a condominium, or a cooperative, government assistance is available.

And if you are interested in the development of experimental housing, you may be eligible for assistance from the federal government.

There are many federal housing programs that a citizen can take advantage of—and save money in the process.

The Increase in Homeowners

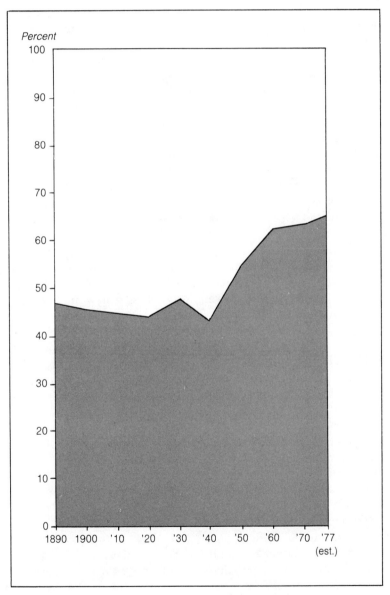

Sources: Bureau of the Census, United States League of Savings Associations

With few exceptions, the programs do not involve direct federal loans to the borrower. Rather, the government insures a lender against loss on a mortgage. This helps bring down the rate of interest charged the borrower.

The concept of government-insured loans was pioneered four decades ago with the creation of the Federal Housing Administration. In subsequent years the FHA became part of the Department of Housing and Urban Development and the government's involvement in the housing market increased dramatically.

In this chapter we review a number of FHA-HUD programs, describing the benefits of each and telling how you can apply. Some specialized housing programs are described in other chapters. For example, housing assistance available to veterans is reviewed in chapter 7; programs aimed directly at farmers and rural residents are discussed in chapter 8. If you fit any of these categories, you should carefully examine details of the special programs. But keep in mind that you are also eligible for most of the broad-gauge programs discussed here.

Home mortgages

The basic and most commonly used FHA program is known as Section 203(b) of the National Housing Act. It provides mortgage insurance to assist home buyers in purchasing new and existing one- to four-family dwellings. This is probably the program involved when someone says, "I got an FHA loan."

Under this program the home buyer makes a down payment and obtains a mortgage for the rest of the purchase price. The mortgage loan is made by a bank, savings and loan association, mortgage company, insurance company, or other FHA-approved lender. It is not a government loan. The FHA does not lend money to build or buy homes. But because FHA mortgage insurance protects a lender against loss on the mortgage, the lender can allow more liberal mortgage terms than the home buyer might otherwise be able to afford.

To qualify for an FHA-insured mortgage, the borrower must have a good credit record, the cash needed at closing of the mortgage, and enough steady income to make monthly mortgage payments without difficulty.

FHA sets no upper age limit for the borrower. Nor does it say he or she must have a certain income to buy a home at a certain price. But age and income are among the factors considered by FHA in judging whether or not the prospective borrower can repay the mortgage.

The wife's salary is taken into account by FHA when there is confirmation of employment with a good possibility for its continuation. "This confirmation may be based on the length of her employment or on her use of special training and skills in a particular position," says a government guide to home mortgage insurance. The allowable income of the wife is treated the same as that of the husband.

Before it can qualify for an FHA-insured mortgage, the property must meet FHA minimum standards. These require, in general, that the house be livable, soundly built, and suitably located as to site and neighborhood.

Through the years Congress has steadily increased the maximum mortgage that can be insured by the FHA under the Section 203(b) program. Amendments adopted in 1977 established these limits:

Single-family home	$60,000
Two- or three-family home	$65,000
Four-family home	$75,000

Within the above limits, the FHA also sets a loan-to-value ratio to determine the minimum down payment. In 1977 the loan-to-value ratios on a single-family home were 97 percent on the first $25,000 of value and 95 percent on the value between $25,000 and the $60,000 limit.

In other words, if you buy a house appraised by the FHA at $25,000, you could obtain an FHA-insured mortgage for 97 percent of the value, or $24,250. Your down payment would be $750, or 3 percent of the value. If the house is appraised at $50,000, you could obtain a mortgage for $48,000. Your down payment would be calculated this way: On the first $25,000, the down payment would be 3 percent, or $750. On the amount between $25,000 and $50,000, only 95 percent of the value counts for your mortgage, meaning you have to pay 5 percent down on this portion of the value, or $1,250. Thus your down payment would be $2,000 and your mortgage amount $48,000.

The table on page 114 shows the minimum down payment required for an FHA-insured mortgage. It also shows the monthly principal and interest for such a transaction.

FHA-Insured Mortgage Payments

Value of House	Down Payment	Mortgage Amount	Monthly Payment*
$25,000	$ 750	$24,250	$194
$30,000	$1,000	$29,000	$233
$35,000	$1,250	$33,750	$273
$40,000	$1,500	$38,500	$309
$45,000	$1,750	$43,250	$346
$50,000	$2,000	$48,000	$386
$55,000	$2,250	$52,750	$425
$60,000	$2,500	$57,500	$463

* This is the approximate monthly principal and interest for a 30-year mortgage at 9 percent interest. It does not include such other monthly items as property insurance, taxes, and the FHA mortgage insurance premium.

Note: The down payment figures in the table do not include closing costs and any other sums which must be paid before you move in.

The FHA sets a ceiling on interest rates that can be charged for FHA-insured mortgages. This maximum allowable rate changes from time to time, depending on the supply of and demand for mortgage money. For a number of years the rate was 6 percent or lower, but in more recent years it has risen to higher levels, with periodic small declines. Although the maximum FHA rate may go up or down, the interest rate on an individual's home mortgage does not change after it is insured.

In addition to the interest charged by the lending institution, the FHA charges a mortgage insurance premium of ½ percent a year on the average outstanding balance of the mortgage during the year. The FHA uses the income from this premium to pay its expenses and insurance losses and to maintain its insurance reserves. The premium is collected with the monthly mortgage payment and is in addition to the amount collected from the borrower for payment of interest and repayment of principal.

The FHA appraises the property to determine the maximum amount of mortgage it is willing to insure. The appraisal is made to estimate the value of the property solely for mortgage insurance purposes; it is not an inspection of the construction, nor does it imply approval, certify as to the condition of the house, or set a sales price. Different procedures apply to existing homes and to those which are yet to be built or are under construction.

A Break for Military Personnel

The FHA offers a special program to military personnel on active duty for two or more years. Under the program, known as Section 222, the Department of Defense pays the FHA mortgage insurance premium of $\frac{1}{2}$ percent for as long as the mortgagor is on active duty status while owning the home. Otherwise, the program is identical to Section 203(b).

For an existing home, the FHA appraisal is based upon the merits and apparent defects of the site and the structure. If the obvious defects are serious, the agency requires repairs before it will insure a mortgage on the property. This is a measure of protection for the buyer, but it is possible that defects may still exist, covered by walls or otherwise hidden, and may not appear until months after the deal is closed. For these reasons, prospective buyers should carefully examine the house and satisfy themselves of its soundness. Existing houses generally are sold "as is" unless repairs are agreed to by the seller and buyer, usually in writing. The FHA does not require a seller to give the buyer a warranty of the condition of an existing home.

For proposed construction, the appraisal is based upon the value of the site and the plans and specifications approved by the FHA. The appraisal takes into consideration the neighborhood in which the home is to be built. After the FHA approves a subdivision project and the plans and specifications of the houses to be built there, it inspects the construction at several stages of progress. To protect the buyer, the FHA requires the builder or seller to give a one-year warranty covering construction of the home. The FHA is not a party to the warranty, however, and has no legal authority to enforce it.

You apply for an FHA appraisal through an FHA-approved lender. The appraisal usually is completed within about a week after the FHA receives the application from the lender.

The fee for an appraisal is subject to change, but in late 1977 it was $50 for an existing home and $65 for a proposed home. The FHA collects this fee from the lender, who in turn collects it from the buyer or seller.

To obtain mortgage insurance you apply to any lender that the FHA has approved to make insured loans. If the lender is willing

FHA Interest Rate Ceilings
On Home Mortgages

Effective Date	Rate
November 27, 1934	5 %
August 1, 1939	$4\frac{1}{2}$
April 24, 1950	$4\frac{1}{4}$
May 2, 1953	$4\frac{1}{2}$
December 4, 1956	5
August 6, 1957	$5\frac{1}{4}$
September 24, 1959	$5\frac{3}{4}$
February 2, 1961	$5\frac{1}{2}$
May 29, 1961	$5\frac{1}{4}$
February 7, 1966	$5\frac{1}{2}$
April 2, 1966	$5\frac{3}{4}$
October 3, 1966	6
May 7, 1968	$6\frac{3}{4}$
January 24, 1969	$7\frac{1}{2}$
January 5, 1970	$8\frac{1}{2}$
December 1, 1970	8
January 12, 1971	$7\frac{1}{2}$
February 18, 1971	7
August 10, 1973	$7\frac{3}{4}$
August 25, 1973	$8\frac{1}{2}$
January 21, 1974	$8\frac{1}{4}$
April 15, 1974	$8\frac{1}{2}$
May 13, 1974	$8\frac{3}{4}$
July 8, 1974	9
August 14, 1974	$9\frac{1}{2}$
November 25, 1974	9
January 21, 1975	$8\frac{1}{2}$
March 3, 1975	0
April 27, 1975	$8\frac{1}{2}$
August 29, 1975	9
March 30, 1976	$8\frac{1}{2}$
October 15, 1976	8

Note: Rates do not include insurance premium charges.

Source: Federal Housing Administration

to make the loan, it provides the proper forms and helps you complete them. Then it forwards the papers to the FHA insuring office that serves the area in which the property is located.

The FHA office reviews the applicant's credit history to judge whether the loan would be reasonable for the borrower. At the same time, the property is appraised to determine the amount of the mortgage that the FHA will insure.

The FHA tells the lender what it has decided. The lender informs the borrower. If the FHA approves the application, the lender arranges with the borrower for the closing of the loan. The borrower deals directly with the lender. The lender handles the transaction with the FHA. Usually, the borrower has no direct contact with the FHA.

Before the house is listed for sale, an owner can obtain a statement of the mortgage amount that the FHA will insure for an acceptable buyer. To do this, the owner applies through an FHA-approved mortgage lender for a conditional commitment from the FHA. An appraisal is made and paid for before the conditional commitment is issued. This conditional commitment remains in effect for six months. If the owner decides not to sell the house or to sell it without FHA financing, he or she has no obligation to the FHA.

Financing condominiums

As the condominium method of ownership increased in popularity the government developed mortgage insurance programs to assist in financing this type of purchase.

In a condominium, an individual owns a dwelling unit in a multi-unit project. All the owners of the units have an undivided interest in such common areas as land, roofs, floors, stairways, lobbies, halls, and parking spaces.

The owner of a condominium unit can obtain a mortgage on his or her own unit. Each unit owner is also taxed separately, and thus can claim basically the same income tax deduction that is available to a conventional homeowner.

In 1961, the National Housing Act was amended to provide mortgage insurance for condominiums. First, the FHA insures mortgages obtained by investors to finance construction or rehabilitation of condominium projects. Later, the individual units in such projects are released from the blanket mortgage, sold to individual owners, and financed separately. These single units, when sold, may be financed with FHA-insured mortgages, with conventional mortgages, or with VA-guaranteed mortgages.

An individual investor, a partnership, a corporation, or another legal entity approved by HUD can be eligible for the blanket mortgage. To qualify, a project must contain four or more units. These may be detached, semidetached, or row units in either a walk-up or elevator type of building. The projects may vary widely in layout, size, and design, depending on the type of market to be served. They may include commercial space, but they must be predominantly residential. The buildings may be new or rehabilitated structures.

There are per-unit maximum amounts that limit the size of the blanket, or project, mortgage. These limitations range from $19,500 for efficiency units to $36,000 for units with four or more bedrooms. In high-cost areas, these amounts may be increased up to 50 percent. The mortgage cannot exceed 90 percent of the FHA estimate of cost, and it cannot exceed the sum of the mortgages which individual owners can obtain when they buy separate units.

Sales of individual condominium units can be made only after the FHA has found the plan of condominium ownership acceptable.

The FHA's commitment to insure the individual mortgages is based on three conditions: all planned construction must be completed; units amounting to 80 percent of the value of all units must have been sold to FHA-approved buyers; and the mortgage on a family unit must be a first mortgage.

One person may own as many as four units financed with FHA-insured mortgages, provided that he or she lives in one of them. It is not required that all of the unit mortgages be FHA-insured. Some of the unit mortgages may be FHA-insured, some may be VA-guaranteed, some may be financed conventionally, and other units may be purchased for cash.

The terms of FHA-insured mortgages on the individual condominium units are similar to those for single-family houses: The mortgage cannot exceed $60,000. Based on the FHA valuation of the unit, including common areas and facilities the mortgage can equal 97 percent of the first $25,000; and 95 percent of the amount between $25,000 and $60,000.

For a unit owned by a person who does not live in it, the mortgage amount cannot exceed 85 percent of the amount computed for an owner-occupant.

The mortgage term for any unit can be no less than ten years nor more than thirty years (thirty-five years in some cases, with FHA approval) and the interest rate cannot exceed the current FHA maximum.

How to apply: The sponsor of the condominium project usually provides the application forms for mortgage insurance and helps the prospective individual owner obtain a mortgage. If you need assistance, contact your nearest HUD area office or HUD-FHA insuring office.

Financing for cooperatives

As it does for condominiums, the FHA insures mortgages on cooperative housing projects. But there are differences in the programs, just as there are differences in the forms of ownership.

In a cooperative, an individual purchases a membership certificate or stock in the cooperative corporation and has the right to live in one of the units. The mortgage for the cooperative covers all the units and the members are not free to exclude their units from this blanket mortgage.

The board of directors of the cooperative makes the management and maintenance decisions, but the management must meet the standards of the lender and the FHA. Each member of the cooperative signs an occupancy agreement similar to a lease. In signing, a member agrees to pay the cooperative a monthly carrying charge equal to his or her share of the sum required by the cooperative to meet its expenses.

The cooperative usually has a thirty-day option to purchase the membership of any member who wishes to withdraw. If the cooperative does not act on the option, the outgoing member may sell the membership on the open market. The new member must, in any event, be approved by the cooperative.

There are several types of cooperatives. Let us look at the procedures followed by the most common, the "management type."

As a rule, the cooperative is formed by a sponsoring group that has done the groundwork required to develop the proposed housing project. The cooperative either buys the land and arranges for the construction of the project or buys a completed project from an existing owner. The money for this can come from an FHA-insured mortgage loan and from the down payments made by cooperative members. The down payments of the individual members are based on the difference between the total cost of the project and the FHA-insured mortgage. The amount of the down payment varies with the cost of the project and the size and type of living unit chosen.

The mortgage amount cannot exceed the least of the following:

• An amount equal to 98 percent of the FHA-estimated replacement cost of the project. If the project is to be rehabilitated, further limits apply.

• An amount representing a limit of $19,500 for each unit with no bedroom; $21,600 for each unit with one bedroom; $25,800 with two bedrooms; $31,800 with three bedrooms; and $36,000 with four or more bedrooms. In a structure with one or more elevators slightly higher limits apply. And in some "high cost" areas the per-unit limits may be increased up to 50 percent.

The term of the mortgage cannot exceed forty years. The maximum interest rate is subject to periodic revision by the FHA.

The FHA has other rules applying to cooperatives. Projects must have five or more dwelling units. No solicitation of prospective cooperative members can be made before the FHA has approved these documents: the basic organizational papers, including the bylaws and occupancy agreement; the subscription agreements used to obtain members; and a bulletin containing basic information that must be given to prospective members.

How to apply: The sponsor of a proposed cooperative housing project should discuss the project with the local FHA insuring office. If the FHA feasibility findings are favorable, the sponsor then submits an application, along with the required fee and exhibits, through an approved lender. The application is for insurance of a blanket mortgage to cover the entire project. The sponsor makes applications for individual membership in the cooperative available to prospective members.

Mortgages for modest incomes

The FHA offers mortgage insurance especially for low- and moderate-income families who want to purchase homes. The largest program, known as Section 221(d)(2), also is intended to help families who are displaced by government action.

FHA Mortgage Limits
For Lower-Income Families

	Standard Limit	High-Cost Area
Single-family home	$31,000	$36,000
Single family of 5 or more persons	$36,000	$42,000
Two-family home	$38,000	$45,000
Three-family home	$48,600	$57,600
Four-family home	$59,400	$68,400

The limits for high-cost areas are only for those areas in which construction costs are such that suitable housing cannot be constructed within the standard limits. This determination is made by the FHA and limits are established separately for each area. Your local FHA insuring office can advise you whether the high-cost limits apply in your area. The limits in your area may be less than the listed high-cost limits but will never be lower than the standard limits.

Although there are no specific income requirements for eligibility, the lower mortgage amounts under this program generally limit its use to families with lower incomes. The maximum mortgage amounts that the FHA insures under the program are shown in the table on this page.

The maximum amount of the mortgage is based on a loan-to-value ratio, subject to the limits discussed previously. It is a rather complex formula, with several categories:

• For a one-unit dwelling completed more than one year prior to the application or for a one-unit dwelling for which the plans were approved prior to construction, the maximum mortgage can be the appraised value and the closing costs, or 97 percent of the appraised value, closing costs, and prepaid expenses, whichever is less. For a two- to four-unit dwelling in this category, the maximum mortgage can be 97 percent of the first $15,000 of appraised value and closing costs, 90 percent of the next $10,000, and 80 percent of the amount over $25,000.

• For a dwelling for which plans were not approved prior to construction and which has been completed less than a year prior to the application, the maximum mortgage is 90 percent of the first $25,000 of the appraised value and closing costs, and 80 percent of the appraised value and closing costs in excess of $25,000.

• For families displaced by government action, the maximum mortgage can equal the appraised value and closing costs or the appraised value, closing costs, and prepaid expenses minus $200 per unit, whichever is less.

• For an approved builder, the maximum mortgage can be 85 percent of the appraised value and closing costs. Under this program, a builder can qualify for a mortgage in the full amount available to an owner-occupant under an approved lease-option agreement that provides for equity accumulation.

This program also can be used to finance rehabilitation of substandard housing. The same overall mortgage limits apply, but there is a difference in the method of calculating the loan-to-value ratios and thus the down payment.

Subject to the overall limit, the maximum mortgage can equal the appraised value before rehabilitation, closing costs, and estimated cost of rehabilitation; or the appraised value after rehabilitation and closing costs; or 97 percent of the appraised value after rehabilitation, closing costs, and prepaid expenses, whichever is less.

For displaced families, the maximum mortgage can be the appraised value before rehabilitation, closing costs, and estimated cost of rehabilitation; or the appraised value after rehabilitation, closing costs, and prepaid expenses minus $200, whichever is less.

For qualified builders, the maximum mortgage can be the least of 85 percent of the appraised value after rehabilitation and closing costs; or five times the estimated cost of rehabilitation; or 85 percent of the sum of the purchase price or appraised value before rehabilitation (whichever is less), the estimated cost of rehabilitation, and closing costs. The special provision cited previously applies to sales under lease-option plans.

How to apply: As with the regular home mortgage insurance program, applications are handled through an approved lender.

Housing subsidies

The federal government, under HUD's Section 235 program, offers subsidies to make homeownership more readily available to lower-income families. The subsidies do not go to the families directly. Rather, the monthly subsidy payments go to lenders of FHA-insured mortgages and are used to reduce the interest rate

Units Started Under HUD Interest
And Rent Subsidy Programs

Year	Section 235 Interest Subsidy	Section 236 Rent Subsidy	Total
1969	28,127	10,168	38,295
1970	116,073	105,160	221,233
1971	133,222	107,604	240,826
1972	82,807	80,688	163,495
1973	26,333	47,494	73,827
1974	26,101	40,477	66,578
1975	9,614	19,401	29,015
1976	2,615	15,535	18,150

Source: Department of Housing and Urban Development

and thus the monthly mortgage payments of the lower-income families. The average annual subsidy has been about $1,000 per dwelling unit.

The maximum insurable loan per unit is $25,000, or up to $29,000 in high-cost areas. For duplex units, the maximum insurable loan ranges from $28,000 to $36,000. An additional amount up to $4,000 is available to large families when the property contains four or more bedrooms and cost levels so require.

Families are eligible if their income is within specified limits as determined by the locality on a case-by-case basis. Handicapped persons and single persons sixty-two years of age or older also are eligible if they fall within the income criteria. Successful applicants are required to allocate at least 20 percent of their adjusted income (gross income after certain allowable deductions) for mortgage payments. The purchaser is required to recertify income and family status annually.

In addition to these subsidies for homeowners, the government offers a rent-supplement program in an effort to make good-quality rental housing available to low-income families at a cost they can afford.

The rent supplements do not go directly to the low-income families. Rather, HUD makes payments to owners of approved multifamily rental housing projects to supplement the partial rental payments of eligible tenants. The assistance covers the difference between the tenant's payment and the market rental but it cannot exceed 70 percent of the market rental. Assisted tenants usually must pay at least 25 percent of their adjusted monthly income (after certain deductions) for rent.

To qualify, tenants must have income that would qualify them for low-income housing, in addition to meeting certain criteria such as being at least sixty-two years of age or physically handicapped, or living in substandard housing or in a unit destroyed or damaged by natural disaster.

How to apply: Prospective homeowners seeking interest subsidies under Section 235 should contact approved mortgage lenders, who will assist in submitting the applications. Sponsors of multifamily housing projects should arrange a conference with their local HUD office to determine the need for rent-supplement assistance before a formal application is submitted.

Mobile home loans

One of the more recent innovations in federal housing assistance is government insurance for mobile home loans. As in the case of most other loan insurance programs, the government does not lend the money. Instead, it insures qualified financial institutions against loss on loans made from their own funds to finance mobile homes. The aim of the program is to make lenders more willing to provide loans for mobile homes. The insurance is provided by the FHA under Title I of the National Housing Act.

To qualify for a government-insured mobile home loan, you must have sufficient funds to make a specified small down payment and sufficient income to make payments on the loan; you must intend to make the mobile home your principal residence; and you must have an acceptable site on which the mobile home is to be placed. Such a site may be a rented space in a mobile home park or it may be your own land. The site must meet government standards, and both buyer and seller must certify that there will be no violation of zoning requirements and other regulations applicable to mobile homes.

The mobile home must be at least ten feet wide and forty feet long and meet HUD construction standards for mobile homes. (Virtually all mobile homes produced today meet these standards and many exceed them.) To qualify, the mobile home must be new or it must have been financed with a government-insured loan when it was new.

Following are additional details on this insured-loan program:
- *Maximum Dollar Amount:* $16,000 for a single-unit mobile home; $24,000 for a double-wide mobile home.
- *Maximum Term of Loan:* twelve years for a single-unit home; twenty-three years for a double-wide mobile home.
- *Maximum Financing Charge:* annual interest rates set at 12 percent in late 1977 but this ceiling is subject to revision.
- *Cash Down Payment:* 5 percent of the total price of a mobile home up to $3,000; 10 percent on the amount, if any, over $3,000. The "total price" of a mobile home may include furnishings, appliances, and tie-downs as well as the cost of setting up the mobile home at the site where it will be occupied and the initial premium for mobile home insurance.
- *Loan Repayment:* loans repaid in equal monthly installments.
- *Loan Security:* these personal loans are secured by conditional sales contracts or chattel mortgages on the mobile homes.

A prospective mobile home buyer may apply for a loan at any HUD-FHA approved lender (bank, savings and loan association, credit union, or finance company). There is no application fee.

Aid for experimental housing

Builders and other real estate investors may qualify for a federal mortgage insurance program intended to finance the development of homes and multifamily rental housing that incorporate new or untried construction concepts. The objective is to reduce housing costs, raise living standards, and improve neighborhood design.

As with most other housing programs, the federal government does not make the loans. Rather, it insures lenders against losses on mortgage loans and thus makes it easier for the individual to obtain a mortgage.

Loans insured under this program generally must meet the same requirements as other FHA programs, except that the use of advanced technology or experimental neighborhood design is required. The FHA explains: "The program is intended to speed the development of new concepts by reducing the risks involved in underwriting mortgages on housing incorporating experimental materials, designs, and techniques."

Applicants must be able to prove that the property proposed for mortgage insurance is an acceptable risk for testing advanced housing design or experimental property standards. Applications, which are submitted to area offices and forwarded to HUD headquarters in Washington, should include the purpose of the experiment, a complete description of the project, and the plans for its use. On larger, multifamily housing projects, those interested should contact their nearest HUD office for a conference and feasibility study before submitting an application.

In addition to single-family and multifamily housing, a companion program provides mortgage insurance to help finance the development of group medical facilities or subdivisions of new communities. Again, to qualify, the projects must incorporate new or untried construction concepts intended to reduce costs, raise standards, or improve design.

Each year HUD's Office of Policy Development and Research awards approximately $60 million in contracts or grants to promote experiments, demonstrations, and pilot programs in the search for solutions to housing and community problems. Research has related to energy conservation, neighborhood preservation and revitalization, and similar areas. Applicants should contact HUD's Assistant Secretary for Policy Development and Research, 451 Seventh Street, S.W., Washington, D.C. 20410.

Home-improvement loans

If you are seeking a way to finance improvements in your home, the answer may be an FHA Title I Loan. Banks and other qualified lenders make these loans and the Federal Housing Administration insures the lenders against possible loss.

This loan insurance program, authorized by Title I of the National Housing Act, is similar in principle to FHA mortgage insurance programs for the purchase of homes.

FHA-insured Title I loans may be used for any improvements that will make your home more livable and useful. You can use the loans even for dishwashers, freezers, and ovens that are built into the house and not free-standing. You cannot use the loans for such luxury items as a swimming pool or an outdoor fireplace or to pay for work already done.

These are examples of eligible improvements:

• Additions and alterations to increase the usefulness of an existing home, such as rooms, porches, stairways, closets, bathrooms, and entrances.

FHA-Insured Mortgages And Other Loans

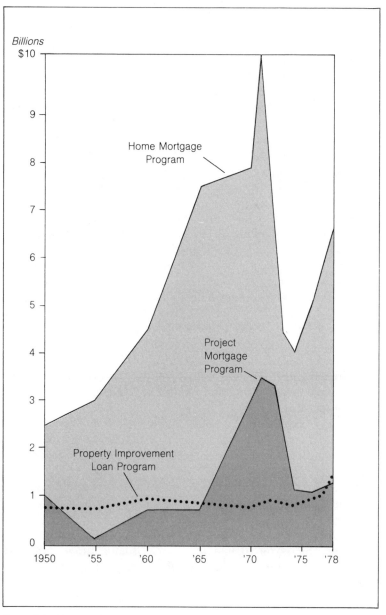

Billions

Source: Federal Housing Administration

- Exterior work to help preserve and protect a home, such as painting, roofing, and siding.
- Interior work to make a home more livable, such as painting, papering, plastering, new flooring, and tile work.
- Repairs, restoration, or replacement of important parts of a home, such as the heating system, plumbing system, septic tank, electrical wiring, and built-in kitchen appliances.
- Commercial structures such as stores, office buildings, warehouses, and factories, or agricultural buildings such as barns, granaries, and other service buildings may likewise be improved with FHA loans, provided the improvements substantially protect or increase the basic utility of the structure.

Improvements can be handled on a do-it-yourself basis or through a contractor or dealer. Your loan can be used to pay for materials and labor, architectural and engineering fees, and building permit fees.

Dealers or contractors participating in the FHA program cannot use improper selling tactics such as overpricing, debt consolidation, false guarantees, or falsified credit.

The maximum loan amount that can be insured is $15,000. The maximum maturity is fifteen years. Interest rates vary, depending on the amount and term of the loan.

To qualify, you must own the property to be improved. If you are not a holder of the title, then you must have an equitable interest in the property under an instrument of trust or purchase contract or a lease having a fixed term expiring not less than six calendar months after the loan is paid off. You also must have a satisfactory credit rating and enough income to repay the loan during its term.

The law requires that a house be completed and occupied before a loan is made. To obtain larger loans, the house must have been completed and occupied as a residence for at least ninety days.

If you are undertaking the project on a do-it-yourself basis, you will deal directly with the lender—such as your bank. If you are arranging to have the work done by a contractor or dealer, the contractor or dealer will help you with the paperwork and probably also help you to find a lender. Usually, three forms are required: the credit application, the note, and the completion certificate.

After you fill out the credit application, it will be delivered to the lending institution along with a copy of the contract you will have signed with the contractor or dealer. The lender will determine if your credit rating is satisfactory and then will contact you and the dealer. Work can then begin on the home improvements.

When the work has been completed to your satisfaction, you will sign the completion certificate. The dealer or contractor will deliver this certificate to the lender and be paid the net proceeds of the loan.

Never sign a completion certificate until all the work called for in the contract has been completed to your satisfaction. Be careful not to sign a completion certificate along with a sales order.

You should proceed cautiously if the lender or contractor demands a lien on your property. The FHA does not require a lien in the case of a Title I loan, but a few lenders take this precaution on their own initiative.

The loan is repaid to the lending institution in installments. For most loans, installments come due each month. For certain farm loans, seasonal payments can be arranged. If you repay the loan ahead of schedule, you receive a refund for unearned interest.

Aid for real estate investors

Federal housing assistance is not restricted to homeowners. In fact, there are several programs aimed directly at investors, developers, builders, and what one government handbook calls "profit-motivated sponsors." Each year, the government insures or guarantees millions of dollars in loans and mortgages under these programs. Here is a rundown of what is available:

• *Land Development.* Under Title X of the National Housing Act, HUD insures mortgages to help finance the purchase of land and the development of building sites for subdivisions or new communities. Water and sewer systems, streets and lighting, and other installations needed for residential communities can be included. But nonresidential buildings, such as schools and commercial facilities, cannot be included, with the exception of clubhouses, parking garages, and similar buildings owned and maintained jointly by property owners.

Prospective developers, subject to the approval of the FHA, are eligible. Land development must meet statutory and FHA requirements and receive all governmental approvals required by state and local law. New communities may require the approval of local governing boards and the governor of the state.

The maximum amount insurable is $25 million for a single project. In recent years the average insured project loan was slightly over $1 million, but program activity has dwindled.

The loan guarantee cannot exceed 80 percent of the estimated value of the land before development, plus 90 percent of the estimated cost of development or 75 percent of the estimated value upon completion, whichever is less. The mortgage term is ten years, except that longer terms are available for separate mortgages for water and sewer systems or for development of a new community.

How to apply: A sponsor must have a conference with officials at the local HUD insuring or area office to determine the feasibility of the project before submission of the formal application through an FHA-approved lender.

• *Rental Housing.* HUD has five programs intended to help provide good-quality rental housing by insuring lenders against losses on mortgages covering multifamily buildings or projects.

Several of the programs are specifically aimed at aiding sponsors of projects for low- and moderate-income families, the elderly, and the handicapped, and projects in urban renewal areas.

In each program, investors, builders, and developers are eligible for government-insured mortgages. In most cases the loan cannot exceed 90 percent of the estimated value. The loan term usually is forty years.

How to apply: As with the land development program, a conference with HUD or FHA officials is required to determine the feasibility before a formal application is submitted through an approved lender.

• *Mobile Home Parks.* A special HUD program, known as Section 207, aids in the financing of construction or rehabilitation of mobile home parks. Like other federal housing programs, the FHA insures lenders against losses on mortgages, thus making it easier for the investor, builder, or developer to obtain financing.

The maximum mortgage limits are $3,900 per space, but in areas where cost levels so require, limits may be increased up to $5,850 per space. In most cases the loan may not exceed 90 percent of the estimated value and the term cannot exceed forty years.

How to apply: The application is submitted through an FHA-approved lender to the HUD insuring or area office, but only after feasibility is established at a pre-application conference with federal housing officials.

• *Medical Facilities.* HUD has loan insurance programs for group medical facilities, hospitals, and nursing homes.

Under Title XI of the National Housing Act, mortgage insurance is available to help finance the construction or rehabilitation of facilities for a medical, dental, optometric, or osteopathic group. The facilities can include major movable equipment and must be used for preventive, diagnostic, and treatment services.

The sponsors of the project must be organized on a nonprofit basis, but may make the facility available to a practicing group through a lease. The loans have averaged about $1.5 million. In most cases it cannot exceed 90 percent of the estimated replacement cost of the facility, including movable equipment. The mortgage term may extend for twenty-five years.

Under Section 242 of the National Housing Act, mortgage insurance is available to finance the construction of private nonprofit and proprietary hospitals, including major movable equipment. Applicants can be either a proprietary facility or a private nonprofit corporation licensed by the state or local government. The loans, which have averaged $11 million, may not exceed 90 percent of the estimated replacement cost. The mortgage term is up to twenty-five years.

Under Section 232 of the National Housing Act, mortgage insurance is provided for nursing homes and other long-term care facilities. Eligible applicants include investors, builders, developers, and private nonprofit corporations. Insured mortgages may be used to finance construction or renovation of facilities to accommodate twenty or more patients. Major equipment for operation of the facility may be included in the mortgage. The average loan has been $1.5 million. Loans cannot exceed 90 percent of the estimated value of the physical improvements and major movable equipment. The mortgage term can be as long as forty years.

How to apply: In these three programs, conferences with HUD officials must be held to establish preliminary feasibility before the application is submitted through an FHA-approved lender.

10

If
You Want
Government
Land or
Minerals

Since the United States became a nation, more than one billion acres of government land have been transferred for homesteads, state grants, military land bounties, railroad grants, and for various other purposes. Despite this massive transfer, the government still owns more than 450 million acres of land often called the "public domain." More than half of this land is in Alaska, and the bulk of the remainder is in ten western states.

In recent years some advertisements may have led you to believe that the federal government still offered homesteads or was selling land for as little as $1 per acre. Here are the facts: There is no free government land, so there no longer is any "homesteading." And within the last few years the government has halted its periodic sales of isolated parcels of public land in the western states. Those parcels of land usually had no legal access and no water and therefore were almost worthless.

But there still are ways you can possibly benefit from these public lands. And it still is possible to obtain government assistance in developing mineral deposits.

Oil and gas leases

The Mineral Leasing Act of 1920 provides for competitive and noncompetitive oil and gas leasing on federal land except for those areas that have been withdrawn from mineral leasing by the Secretary of the Interior.

The Bureau of Land Management (BLM) administers the leasing program on public domain lands as well as on lands held by many other federal agencies. Almost all of the public domain land is in the West—Alaska, Arizona, California, Colorado, Idaho, Montana, Nevada, New Mexico, Oregon, Utah, and Wyoming. However, oil and gas leases are not necessarily available in all of these states.

Whether a lease is awarded competitively or noncompetitively is determined by the geological structure underlying the tract. If the geological structure is known to produce oil and gas, the lease must be offered on a competitive basis. All other lands, except those withdrawn, are available for leasing on a noncompetitive basis.

In competitive bidding, potential lessees offer sealed bids for the right to develop the land's resources. The bidder offering the highest bonus payment is usually awarded the lease. Bonuses offered for a promising lease often run into the millions of dollars, since the probability of striking oil, gas, or both is relatively high. Therefore, the big oil companies dominate the bidding for these leases. The individual rarely has the resources or the expertise to compete.

In contrast, the noncompetitive leases are dominated by individuals because they are awarded through what amounts to a lottery system. Here's how the system works:

On the third Monday of every month, officials in the regional offices of the Bureau of Land Management post a list and description of hundreds of land parcels—ranging in size from forty acres to several thousand acres—which are up for lease.

You can obtain a copy of these lists in any state by paying a fee to cover the cost of reproduction and handling—usually $2 to $4—to the appropriate regional office. These offices are listed on page 135.

Once you've examined the list and decided which parcel or parcels you are interested in, you mail in a form and a $10 filing fee for each parcel. Under the BLM's "simultaneous filing" system, all forms received before each month's deadline are considered to be filed at the same time. If more than one bid is received for a parcel, as is almost always the case, then all bids for that parcel are placed in a large, rotating drum and one bid is drawn. The winner is notified by mail, and has fifteen days in which to pay an advance yearly rental of $1 per acre to take over the lease. The lease expires after ten years if no oil or gas is discovered on the land.

Corporations as well as individuals can enter bids, but because the law limits each entrant to one bid per parcel, the individual has as good a chance as a corporation to win a lease. This fact is promoted by private "leasing services" which, for a fee, handle the paperwork to file entries for individuals. Some of these leasing services have been a subject of controversy and official investigation for such claims as "citizens strike it rich" and "winners frequently sell their lease rights to large oil companies for fortunes."

Records show that, in some cases, persons holding noncompetitive oil and gas leases have made substantial profits and, in a few cases, have become wealthy. But before you decide whether to enter the lottery, there are some facts you should remember:

• The leases are for wildcat land that has an unknown potential for the production of oil and gas.

• In accepting an offer to lease, the federal government makes absolutely no claim regarding the potential of the tract offered.

• Most of the public land does not have oil and gas deposits, and a great majority of the leases turn out to be worthless.

• Drilling for oil and gas requires extensive equipment and technical know-how, and the person acquiring a noncompetitive lease seldom has either of these essentials.

To develop the resources that may or may not be in the land, the leaseholder must find a company willing to risk capital on the chance that there is oil or gas beneath the surface. A company willing to take the risk will usually pay a lump sum for a lease. In some cases it will also agree to pay an additional royalty if it strikes oil or gas.

But remember that this is selling on a buyer's market. The

Bureau of Land Management
Field Offices

Alaska
555 Cordova Street
Anchorage, Alaska 99501
(907) 277-1561

Arizona
Federal Building, Room 3022
Phoenix, Arizona 85025
(602) 261-3873

California
2800 Cottage Way, Room E-2841
Sacramento, California 95825
(916) 484-4676

Colorado
Colorado State Bank Building
Room 700
Denver, Colorado 80202
(303) 837-4325

Idaho
Federal Building, Room 398
550 West Fort Street
Boise, Idaho 83724
(208) 342-2711

Montana (North Dakota, South Dakota)
Federal Building
222 East 32nd Street
Billings, Montana 59107
(406) 245-6711

Nevada
Federal Building
Room 3008
300 Booth Street
Reno, Nevada 89502
(702) 784-5451

New Mexico (Oklahoma)
South Federal Place
P.O. Box 1449
Santa Fe, New Mexico 87501
(505) 988-6217

Oregon (Washington)
729 Northeast Oregon Street
P.O. Box 2965
Portland, Oregon 97208
(503) 234-3361

Utah
136 East South Temple Street
Salt Lake City, Utah 84111
(801) 524-5311

Wyoming (Kansas, Nebraska)
2120 Capitol Avenue
P.O. Box 1828
Cheyenne, Wyoming 82001
(307) 778-2326

All other states
BLM Eastern States Office
Robin Building
7981 Eastern Avenue
Silver Spring, Maryland 20910
(301) 427-7500

Public Lands in the Western States

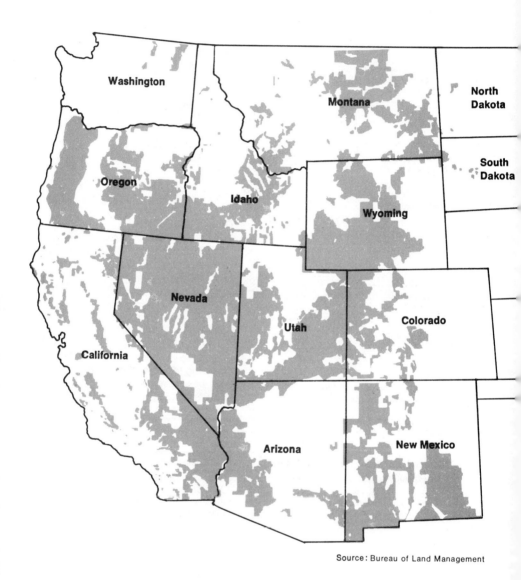

Source: Bureau of Land Management

Public Lands Managed by
the Bureau of Land Management

amount the lease will bring depends on how much value the buyer places on it. Since most oil companies consider drilling in wildcat land a high-risk venture, they seldom are willing to pay a large amount for such a lease. In fact, they may not want it at all.

In recent years most leasing interest has centered on tracts in Wyoming, New Mexico, Colorado, Montana, and Utah. In fact, in one recent eighteen-month period, nearly three million entries were received for leases in these states. In the process, the Bureau of Land Management took in about $30 million in filing fees. But the General Accounting Office (GAO), an arm of Congress, thinks the government could make even more money if it replaced the lottery with a competitive bid process. Because of the GAO's criticism, proposals to do away with the lottery system were pending before Congress in late 1977.

If, after all these warnings and words of advice, you are still interested in entering the lottery, contact one of the BLM field offices to obtain the proper forms and further instructions.

Staking a mining claim

The Bureau of Land Management has been seeking changes in a century-old law which allows individuals to prospect for minerals on federal lands not withdrawn from mining entry and to file a mining claim upon making a valid discovery of a mineral.

In late 1977 federal officials urged Congress to amend the law to curb environmental and other abuses. The outlook for congressional action was uncertain, but as you read the following description of the program, you should be aware that the law is subject to change.

Under the system that was followed for many years, to file a mining claim you must have made a discovery of a deposit of one of the locatable minerals, such as gold, silver or copper. The mineral deposit must be of such quantity that a person of ordinary prudence would be justified in the further expenditure of labor and capital, with a reasonable prospect of success, in developing a valuable mine.

If you make such a discovery, you must mark the claim so that it can be located on the ground. Driving stakes into the ground at the four corners of the claim is the usual way to mark it. A notice of the claim's location must then be filed and recorded at the appropriate county office.

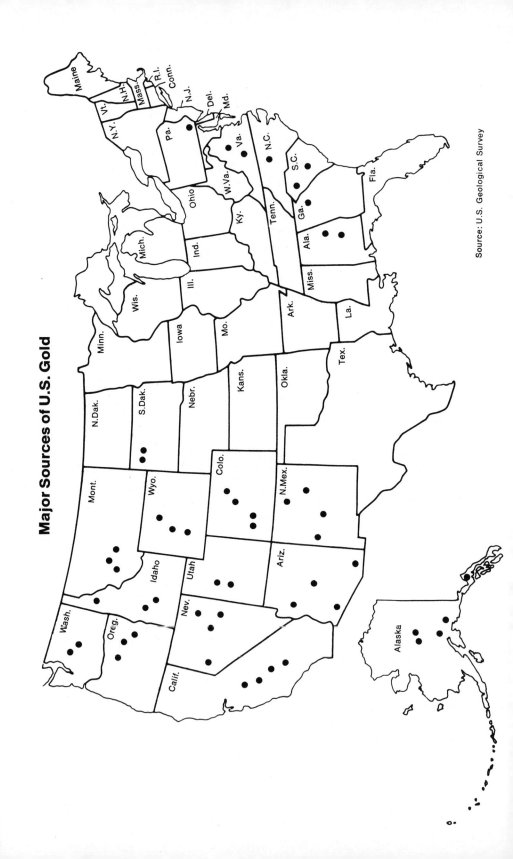

Major Sources of U.S. Gold

Source: U.S. Geological Survey

After the claim has been filed and recorded, you must perform $100 worth of assessment work each year on your claim. Assessment work is performed toward development of the mine. If you do not perform the required assessment work in any single year, other parties may file on your claim. The record of assessment work must be filed annually in the office of the county clerk or county recorder in the county where your claim is located.

A mining claim gives you the right to extract and remove locatable minerals from the land, but nothing more. Mining claims may not be used for home sites. If you erect buildings or other structures on an invalid claim, they may be subject to confiscation by the federal government.

For further information on mining claims, you should contact one of the BLM field offices.

Loans for mineral exploration

The Interior Department's Geological Survey offers loans to individuals and private firms to encourage exploration for thirty-three types of minerals within the United States.

To qualify, applicants must:

• Have sufficient interest in property which can qualify for exploration of one or more minerals.

• Furnish evidence that funds for exploration are not available from banks or other commercial sources of credit on reasonable terms.

• Certify that they would not ordinarily undertake the proposed exploration under current conditions at their sole expense.

• Have sufficient funds to meet their share of the cost of the exploration work.

As these requirements indicate, these loans cover only a portion of the exploration costs—usually 50 to 75 percent. The government contribution cannot exceed $250,000, and in most cases is much smaller. In fact, loans in the past have averaged only $20,000. The loans are repaid from royalties on the minerals discovered. However, before any money is advanced, government experts make an investigation to determine whether conditions "are favorable for the occurrence of deposits of ore."

Further information and application forms can be obtained from the U.S. Geological Survey, 12201 Sunrise Valley Drive, Reston, Virginia 22092.

General Services Administration
Regional Offices

Region 1
620 Post Office
and Courthouse Building
Boston, Massachusetts 02109
(617) 223-2663

Region 6
1500 East Bannister Road
Kansas City, Missouri 64131
(816) 926-7245

Region 2
26 Federal Plaza
New York, New York 10007
(212) 264-3590

Region 7
819 Taylor Street
Fort Worth, Texas 76102
(817) 334-2516

Region 3
Seventh and D Streets, S.W.
Washington, D.C. 20407
(202) 472-1701

Region 8
Bldg. 41, Denver Federal Center
Denver, Colorado 80225
(303) 234-3921

Region 4
1776 Peachtree Street, N.W.
Atlanta, Georgia 30309
(404) 526-5628

Region 9
525 Market Street
San Francisco, California 94105
(415) 556-5743

Region 5
230 South Dearborn Street
Chicago, Illinois 60604
(312) 353-5504

Region 10
Regional Headquarters Bldg.
GSA Center
Auburn, Washington 98002
(206) 833-6500

Buying surplus federal property

Want to buy a used typewriter? An automobile? An airplane?

The General Services Administration (GSA) and the Department of Defense sell these and hundreds of other items of surplus property no longer needed by the government. The GSA acts as sales agent for most of the federal government's civil agencies; the Defense Department handles sales for the military services.

These sales, open to the public, are made by competitive bids. They are held periodically at government offices and installations in all parts of the country. However, state and local governments may purchase the surplus personal property by negotiation before it is advertised for competitive bid sales to the general public.

In describing the property available for sale, one government publication listed "automotive and other vehicles, aircraft, hardware, plumbing and heating equipment, paper products, office supplies and equipment, and many other items." This publication added: "The government also generates a substantial quantity of scrap which is made available for public sale. Normally, there is no use restriction on property purchased from the government." In recent years more than $25 million worth of property has been sold annually under this program.

If you are interested, you can have your name placed on mailing lists maintained by GSA regional offices so that you can be notified when the types of property you wish to purchase become available. The addresses and telephone numbers of the ten regional offices are on page 140. You can also obtain a free pamphlet, *Buying Government Surplus Personal Property*, from those offices or from the GSA headquarters, Washington, D.C. 20406.

For further information on sales of Defense Department surplus personal property, you can write to the Defense Logistics Services Center, Federal Center Building, Battle Creek, Michigan 49016.

CHAPTER 11

If
You Want
Recreation
Bargains

If you owned a park stretching for more than a quarter-billion acres, you could certainly find enough recreational activities to occupy all your leisure time.

Well, as a taxpayer, you are co-owner of that much recreation land administered by a variety of federal agencies.

You have perhaps used some of these lands already, but you may not know about all the different kinds of facilities that are available across the country. Everyone has heard of Yellowstone National Park, but can you name the national historical park that extends for nearly 200 miles from Washington, D.C.? Or have you hiked one of the two long-distance national scenic trails or any of the over fifty short, urban-oriented national recreation trails?

In addition to its myriad of recreation land sites, the government can also make your leisure time more enjoyable—and safer—with a variety of free and low-cost services ranging from maps to movies. A rundown of key facilities and services follows.

National parks

Yellowstone, Yosemite, Grand Canyon, Great Smoky Mountains.

These names of famous national parks create vivid pictures of billowing geysers, tumbling waterfalls, breathtaking dropoffs, mountain lookouts.

The government's National Park Service operates these and many other historic, natural, and recreational areas throughout the country.

They range in scope from the massive parks of the West to the homes of famous people such as Franklin D. Roosevelt and Carl Sandburg; from volcanoes in Hawaii to a center for the performing arts at Wolf Trap Farm Park near Washington, D.C. And that long park stretching from Washington is Chesapeake and Ohio Canal National Historical Park, which encompasses 184 miles of an important commercial waterway abandoned in 1924 after nearly a century of use.

Because major national parks are perhaps the best-known of U.S. recreation areas, they can be the most crowded. So if you are vacationing at a seasonal peak time, you might consider exploring some of the less well-known locations in the park system. To help you find some of these less crowded spots, the National Park Service has published a booklet, available through the Government Printing Office, called *Visit a Lesser Used Park.* Attempts to devise a reservation system that would help curb disappointment over "Full" signs at campgrounds have not yet been succcessful. National Park officials say that except for a few local programs, there will be no reservation system tried again until 1978. Thus, a telephone call or letter to the park of your destination or check with your auto club is advised so that you can learn what time of day you should get to the park in order to secure space.

Information stations at each national park can provide detailed maps and information on that park and normally will have listings of other National Park Service facilities, too. Or you can contact regional National Park Service offices in Atlanta, Boston, Denver, Omaha, Philadelphia, San Francisco, Santa Fe, Seattle, or Washington, D.C., or write to the Information Office, National Park Service, Department of the Interior, Washington, D.C.

20240. The Government Printing Office, Washington, D.C. 20402, also has available at nominal prices a map of park facilities across the country with a list of facilities available at each, and a booklet, *Camping in the National Park System.*

In addition to the 37 national parks, the national park system comprises more than 250 other areas. These include more than 80 national monuments, more than 50 national historical sites, a number of national battlefields and battlefield parks, plus national seashores, lakeshores, rivers, and recreation areas.

Some of the facilities charge an entrance fee, but others are free. There usually are special fees for such recreational uses as camping. And, in some areas, you must obtain a permit to hike on back-country trails.

A variety of facilities have been designed to help blind and handicapped visitors enjoy the national parks. There are several "braille trails" with "touch-and-smell" exhibits for blind visitors. Ramps and graduated paths have been constructed with the handicapped in mind.

The national park system also features dozens of "living history" programs. These demonstrations offer insights into the past, ranging from the carving of totem poles at Sitka National Historical Park in Alaska to the operation of a moonshine still at Catoctin Mountain Park in Maryland. At other sites, visitors get a glimpse of what life was like on farms in colonial or homestead days. Some living history programs are given throughout the year, but most are concentrated during the summer months.

If you are a regular visitor to national park system facilities that charge an entrance fee, you can save money with a Golden Eagle Passport. This passport costs $10 and is valid for one calendar year. It covers all entrance fees, but not recreation fees.

If you are sixty-two years of age or older, you can get a free Golden Age Passport. This passport is valid for your entire lifetime, covers entrance fees, and entitles you to a 50 percent discount on recreation use fees, including camping fees, at recreation areas administered by several federal agencies.

Golden Eagle and Golden Age passports are available at offices of the National Park Service and U.S. Forest Service, and at areas of the national park system where entrance fees are charged. Golden Age passports are also available at a number of recreation areas and regional offices administered by other federal agencies.

National Parks

Name and Location	Year Established	Acreage
Acadia (Maine)	1919	36,980
Arches (Utah)	1971	73,388
Big Bend (Texas)	1935	709,088
Bryce Canyon (Utah)	1924	36,010
Canyonlands (Utah)	1964	337,559
Capitol Reef (Utah)	1971	241,865
Carlsbad Caverns (New Mexico)	1930	46,755
Crater Lake (Oregon)	1902	160,290
Everglades (Florida)	1934	1,400,533
Glacier (Montana)	1910	1,013,598
Grand Canyon (Arizona)	1919	1,218,375
Grand Teton (Wyoming)	1929	310,418
Great Smoky Mountains (North Carolina-Tennessee)	1926	517,014
Guadalupe Mountains (Texas)	1966	79,972
Haleakala (Hawaii)	1960	27,823
Hawaii Volcanoes (Hawaii)	1916	229,177
Hot Springs (Arkansas)	1921	5,764
Isle Royale (Michigan)	1931	539,279
Kings Canyon (California)	1940	460,122
Lassen Volcanic (California)	1916	106,372
Mammoth Cave (Kentucky)	1926	51,310
Mesa Verde (Colorado)	1906	52,036
Mount McKinley (Alaska)	1917	1,939,492
Mount Rainier (Washington)	1899	235,404
North Cascades (Washington)	1968	504,785
Olympic (Washington)	1938	897,884
Petrified Forest (Arizona)	1962	94,189
Redwood (California)	1968	62,304
Rocky Mountain (Colorado)	1915	263,791
Sequoia (California)	1890	386,823
Shenandoah (Virginia)	1926	190,420
Virgin Islands (U.S. Virgin Islands)	1956	14,470
Voyageurs (Minnesota)	1971	219,128
Wind Cave (South Dakota)	1903	28,060
Yellowstone (Wyoming-Montana-Idaho)	1872	2,219,822
Yosemite (California)	1890	761,096
Zion (Utah)	1919	146,570

An applicant for a Golden Age passport must present proof of age and apply in person.

National forests

The Forest Service, a unit of the Department of Agriculture, manages more than 187 million acres of forestland for multiple purposes, including recreation.

Campgrounds at national forests are a favorite spot for millions of Americans. Nearly 7,000 camp and picnic grounds can accommodate more than 500,000 visitors at a single time.

Entrance fees had been charged at most Forest Service recreation areas but were eliminated in 1975. Special fees are charged for such extra services as electricity, cut firewood, and boat-launching ramps.

Visitor centers at many national forests explain the botany, geology, ecology, zoology, history, geography, and archaeology of the area to add to your understanding and enjoyment.

Detailed information on national forests is available from the Regional Forester, U.S. Forest Service, in Juneau (Alaska), Portland (Oregon), San Francisco, Missoula (Montana), Ogden (Utah), Denver, Albuquerque, Milwaukee, or Atlanta, or from the Office of Information and Education, U.S. Forest Service, Department of Agriculture, Washington, D.C. 20250.

Fish and wildlife areas

The Department of the Interior's Fish and Wildlife Service administers more than 300 refuges and ranges for fish and wildlife, and has opened more than twenty-seven million acres of this land to recreational use. More than twenty million persons visit these sites annually to enjoy the wildlife trails, interpretive centers, fishing, and hunting.

Some refuges are well known as the homes of rare and endangered species. Whooping cranes make their principal winter home at Aransas Refuge in Texas. Trumpeter swans are in abundance at Red Rock Lakes Refuge in Montana. Desert bighorn sheep have special havens at two ranges in Arizona and another in Nevada.

Details on specific areas are available from the Information Office, Fish and Wildlife Service, Department of the Interior, Washington, D.C. 20240.

The service also publishes numerous pamphlets and booklets on topics such as snakes, bighorn sheep, sport fishing, and waterfowl identification. Its currently most popular publication, *Fifty Birds of Town and City,* a guide for the beginning bird watcher, is available from the Government Printing Office, Washington, D.C. 20402, stock number 2410-0332.

National fish hatcheries run by the service are located in most states. A visit to a fish hatchery is informative for children and adults alike.

Other recreation lands

Several other government agencies manage sizable amounts of land for multipurpose use, including recreation. The Bureau of Land Management and Bureau of Reclamation operate nearly 170 million acres in western states; the U.S. Army Corps of Engineers manages nearly 400 reservoirs, which have about 2,300 access areas specifically developed for recreation, including the most popular outdoor recreation facility in America—Lake Sidney Lanier in Georgia; and the Tennessee Valley Authority has developed a number of recreation areas along its power system in the South. Inquiries to regional offices of these agencies can get you more details, or you can write to their national headquarters at the following addresses: Information Office, Bureau of Land Management, Department of the Interior, Washington, D.C. 20240; Information Office, Bureau of Reclamation, Department of the Interior, Washington, D.C. 20240; Public Affairs Office, Office of the Chief of Engineers, Army Corps of Engineers, Washington, D.C. 20314; and Office of Information, Tennessee Valley Authority, New Sprankle Building, Knoxville, Tennessee 37902.

Recreation planning

The coordinating agency for recreation planning in the United States is the Department of the Interior's Bureau of Outdoor Recreation.

This bureau does not manage any facilities itself but it is helping to increase recreation opportunities for Americans by planning and coordinating recreation policy and programs at federal and state levels, and by providing technical and financial assistance.

Since the establishment of the bureau in 1962, networks of wild and scenic rivers and national scenic and recreation trails have been established for the enjoyment of all Americans.

Eleven rivers now are protected as wild, scenic, or recreational in the national rivers system: the Rio Grande in New Mexico, Saint Croix in Minnesota and Wisconsin, Wolf in Wisconsin, Eleven Point in Missouri, middle fork of the Feather in California, middle forks of the Clearwater and Salmon in Idaho, Rogue in Oregon, Allagash in Maine, Little Miami in Ohio, and the Chattooga in Georgia, South Carolina, and North Carolina.

The 2,000-mile Appalachian Trail in the East and the 2,350-mile Pacific Crest Trail in the West are the first two national scenic trails. Fourteen more routes are under study for possible trail designation by Congress.

If you are a member of a public or nonprofit organization interested in creating recreation facilities, the Bureau of Outdoor Recreation can assist you.

For the individual, the bureau publishes *A Catalog of Guides to Outdoor Recreation Areas and Facilities,* listing recreation guides available from private, state, and federal organizations. It is available from the Government Printing Office, Washington, D.C. 20402.

The bureau also publishes *Private Assistance in Outdoor Recreation,* a directory of organizations providing aid to individuals and public groups, and *Digest of Federal Outdoor Recreation Programs,* a listing of federal programs directly and indirectly related to recreation. These two are available from the Government Printing Office.

The Bureau of Outdoor Recreation has regional offices in Albuquerque, Ann Arbor, Atlanta, Denver, Philadelphia, San Francisco, and Seattle. The address of its main office is Bureau of Outdoor Recreation, Department of the Interior, Washington, D.C. 20240.

Boating services

The U.S. Coast Guard can be your best friend if boating is your recreation. Perhaps best known for its search and rescue activities, the Coast Guard helps in other ways, too. Its auxiliary and other available federal assistance also can make your pleasure boating safer and easier.

If you are a novice sailor, the Coast Guard Auxiliary offers you a choice of courses in boating safety and seamanship.

"Skipper's Outboard Special" is a one-lesson starter course presenting the basics of safe boating. "Safe Boating" is a three-lesson compact presentation of the elements of seamanship. "Principles of Safe Sailing" teaches you in seven lessons how to handle sailboats safely in all kinds of weather.

"Boating Safety and Seamanship" is the most complete course. Its twelve lessons cover ropes and rigging, seamanship, rules of the road, aids to navigation, piloting, safe motorboat operation, and boating laws.

The only charge for these courses is for materials. Contact your local Coast Guard Auxiliary flotilla or watch for information notices in your newspaper.

The auxiliary also will give your motorboat a free examination to determine if it meets federal requirements as well as additional recommended safety standards. You will receive a distinctive decal if your boat passes. If it does not, the examiner will tell you what the deficiencies are, but no report is made to any law enforcement authority.

When you are competent to handle your properly-equipped boat, the Coast Guard's radio service, publications of the National Ocean Survey, and weather data can add further to the safety of your cruise.

The Coast Guard can provide you with details about what kind of radio communications equipment you should have aboard. Strategically-placed Coast Guard stations broadcast marine information regularly. Coast Guard search and rescue stations and marine operators maintain a constant surveillance on special distress frequencies. If your craft is in trouble, you can radio for help and someone will hear.

The National Weather Service issues weather forecasts every six hours for specific coastal areas. If strong winds or hazardous sea conditions are expected, warnings are issued. Similar forecasts and warnings are issued for many inland lakes, reservoirs, and rivers throughout the country, including advice on stream flow and flood warnings as required.

These forecasts are broadcast regularly by commercial stations, marine radiotelephone broadcasters, and continuous programs which can be received on narrow-band FM equipment. The schedules of radio stations, National Weather Service telephone numbers, and locations of warning display stations are shown on marine weather service charts issued periodically for various coastal and Great Lakes areas.

These charts are available at local marinas and marine chart dealers or from Distribution Division (C44), National Ocean Survey, 6501 Lafayette Avenue, Riverdale, Maryland 20854.

The National Ocean Survey, at the same Riverdale address, also sells nautical charts, pilot books to supplement the charts, and tables of tides and currents.

Charts enable the mariner to navigate safely—or sometimes simply make an attractive wall hanging at a seaside cottage. The charts are nominally priced; catalogs of available charts are free.

Up-to-date changes in navigation aids and other navigational information are issued in the form of local notices to mariners. These are available free to subscribers upon application to your local Coast Guard district office.

Coast Guard district offices are located in Boston, Cleveland, Honolulu, Juneau, Long Beach, Miami, New Orleans, New York City, Portsmouth (Virginia), Saint Louis, San Francisco, and Seattle. Directors of Coast Guard Auxiliaries are located in each of these cities, plus Cincinnati, Gloucester (New Jersey), Milwaukee, Nashville, Saginaw (Michigan), and Saint Paul.

Coast Guard district offices can lend your organization films about historical, maritime, and boating safety subjects. A recent catalog listed films on such subjects as Arctic exploration, lighthouses, and use of safety equipment.

Flying for recreation

If you are a pleasure pilot or plan to take up flying for recreation, you will be regulated by and also assisted by services of the Federal Aviation Administration (FAA). You will be permitted to fly only after you pass medical, written, and flight examinations given under FAA auspices. Airport control towers and air traffic service facilities of the FAA will be used by you in preparing for and making your flight. Flight service specialists can brief you on weather, airport conditions, radio aids, desirable routes and other information. After you have filed your flight plan and taken off, early emergency service will be available to you if you fail to report in or become overdue at your destination.

FAA air traffic service facilities frequently hold open houses where you can become more familiar with flying if you are considering becoming a pilot.

The FAA is also a clearinghouse for much information about education in aeronautical subjects, geared to interests from elementary school age to university level.

Your organization can borrow films from the FAA library without charge. Subjects range from aerodynamics to aviation careers, from aviation history to weather. For information, write Film Library, AAC-44E, Federal Aviation Administration, P.O. Box 25082, Oklahoma City, Oklahoma 73125.

Beating the cost of ammunition

An agency of the U.S. Army called the National Board for Promotion of Rifle Practice provides free and low-cost ammunition to some 2,600 junior rifle clubs across the country and lends them rifles.

If you are working with youngsters who are interested in rifle marksmanship, they can take advantage of this program if certain qualifications are met.

They must be members of a legitimate club composed of at least ten boys or girls from twelve to nineteen years of age. The club must have three adult leaders who can pass a low-level national security check. The club must have access to a rifle range.

If criteria are met, the board will provide a modest amount of ammunition at below-retail prices. The board also will lend 22-caliber rifles to the club.

No personal assistance is provided by the board but it makes available field manuals on such subjects as small-bore shooting and weapons.

Adult rifle clubs formerly were also supplied with ammunition but this program ended several years ago. An adult group that sponsors a qualifying junior club could, however, use the weapons lent to the juniors.

An exception to the age-nineteen limit is made for college rifle clubs, where any undergraduate may participate. About 100 schools have such programs.

To apply for this program, write: National Board for Promotion of Rifle Practice, Room 1E053, West Forrestal Building, Washington, D.C. 20314.

Keeping physically fit

If your waistline is expanding or you seem out of breath after climbing a short flight of steps, you might want to find out what the President's Council on Physical Fitness and Sports can do for you.

Directly through literature and standards, and indirectly through encouragement and support of local recreation programs, the council is concerned with getting and keeping Americans in shape from school age through retirement.

The council can send you a variety of pamphlets and booklets detailing specific exercises and regimens. *An Introduction to Physical Fitness* includes self-testing activities, graded exercises, and a jogging program. *The Fitness Challenge* adapts many of the same principles into an exercise program for older persons. These publications diagram exactly how to perform the recommended exercises and tell you how long to do them.

Youth Physical Fitness details a fitness program for youngsters and suggests how schools can help keep children in shape.

To provide a carrot as well as a stick for exercises, the council sponsors presidential award programs for children and adults.

Your youngster's school, community club, scout program, recreation department, or other organization with qualified personnel can administer tests which may lead to a Presidential Physical Fitness Award. Standards and instructions are included in *Youth Physical Fitness.*

Adults can qualify for a Presidential Sports Award in more than thirty sports, including golf, tennis, skiing, handball, jogging, bowling, basketball, and softball. Qualifying standards are based more on regularity of participation than on outstanding skills.

For a small fee, winners in the youth and adult categories can get emblems signifying their achievement.

For publications and standards, write: President's Council on Physical Fitness and Sports, Washington, D.C. 20201.

CHAPTER 12

If
You Want to
Invest in
Government
Securities

The U.S. government, in addition to the hundreds of benefits and services it provides, offers Americans investment opportunities through government bonds, notes, and short-term bills.

Since they are backed by its full taxing power, securities issued by the federal government are probably as safe as any investment. They also offer a rate of return that is competitive with many other investments. It is little wonder then that in times of economic uncertainty more people take advantage of government investment opportunities.

U.S. savings bonds

The best known of the government securities are U.S. savings bonds. They generally are considered to offer a steady, though unspectacular, way to save. In the late 1970s, U.S. savings bonds have yielded an average annual return of 6 percent when held to maturity. This has been more than the annual yield on passbook savings at savings and loan institutions during the same period, but less than the yield on larger, long-term savings certificates offered by these institutions.

There are two types of U.S. savings bonds:

• *Series E.* These are bought at a 25 percent discount and increase to their full value in five years.

• *Series H.* These are "current income" bonds. The buyers pay the full face amount and receive interest payments by check twice a year.

In the case of Series E bonds, you can buy, for example, a $25 bond for $18.75 and receive $25.20 after five years, or you can pay $75 for a bond and get back $100.80 upon maturity. If you redeem the bonds earlier, you receive a lower rate of interest. And you are unable to cash them in until two months after purchase.

Series E bonds are sold in denominations of $25, $50, $75, $100, $200, $500, $1,000, and $10,000. The most you may own, purchased in any one calendar year, is $10,000 worth, but you and your spouse jointly can own up to $20,000 worth, purchased in any one year. Annual limits prior to 1974 vary.

Most employers offer payroll deduction plans for regular purchases of the bonds, and many banks offer "bond-a-month" plans. The bank deducts the cost of the bonds from your checking account at regular intervals and purchases the bonds for you. Savings bonds also can be purchased at other financial institutions.

Series E bonds offer a special attraction: income tax on interest need not be paid until the bonds are cashed in. This opens the way for several tax-saving maneuvers, as will be discussed later.

Since Series H bonds are purchased at face value, you pay, as an example, $1,000 for a $1,000 bond. And you pay federal income tax on the interest you receive twice a year. The earliest you can redeem an H bond is six months after you buy it. Like the Series E bond, the H bond has a 6 percent annual yield.

Series H bonds can be purchased in denominations of $500, $1,000, $5,000, and $10,000, with a $10,000 annual limit on the amount of purchases you can own ($20,000 if jointly owned). There is, however, no limit on the amount of H bonds received in exchange for E bonds.

Series E and Series H bonds can be purchased in the name of one person, in the names of two persons as joint owners, or in the name of one person payable on death to another designated person. For example, when John Smith buys a bond he can have it registered in one of these three ways:

- John H. Smith
  123 Main Street, Anytown, U.S.A.

- John H. Smith
  123 Main Street, Anytown, U.S.A., or Mary E. Smith

- John H. Smith,
  123 Main Street, Anytown, U.S.A.,
  Payable on death to Mary E. Smith

Under the joint-ownership option, either owner can cash in the bond without the consent of the other. If one of the owners dies, the other becomes sole owner without having to establish proof of death or transferring the bond to his or her name.

The tax-deferment feature of Series E bonds makes them an attractive vehicle for retirement planning. If you wait until you retire to cash in the bonds and pay taxes on the accrued interest, your taxes probably will be less because persons over sixty-five years old are allowed a double exemption. If you want income instead, you can convert the Series E bonds to H bonds. You will pay no tax on the E bond interest until you or your estate cashes in the H bonds. In the meantime, you will receive a check twice a year for the H bond interest, and only that is taxable. Here is an example of how this can work:

One man purchases a $100 Series E bond (for $75) each month for fifteen years before he retires. His net accumulation, assuming the present 6 percent rate: $21,397 on an investment of $13,500. When he retires, he adds $103 in cash to get a multiple of $500, and switches to $21,500 in H bonds. For the next ten years, he receives Treasury checks averaging about $110 a month, and he still keeps the $21,500 intact.

You may also be able to shift income to a lower tax bracket, and thus save on taxes, if you buy savings bonds in your child's name. In that case, you ought to file a tax return for your child and report the annual interest. After the first time that savings bond interest is declared on a child's return, he or she does not have to fill out another return until total income is large enough to require a return to be filed. It is assumed by the government for tax purposes that the interest is being declared annually, by your child, the owner of the bonds.

The Treasury Department maintains records of the ownership of bonds and will replace bonds that are lost, stolen, mutilated, or destroyed. In such a case, the bond owner should write the Bureau of the Public Debt, P.O. Box 509, Parkersburg, West Virginia 26101. Faster replacement is made if the owner reports the registration on the bond, the bond's serial number and date of issue, and the owner's Social Security number.

Other government securities

Savings bonds are sometimes called "nonmarketable" securities. You cannot sell them to another person, although you can turn them in to the government or its agent, such as a bank, at any time after a minimum holding period. There are also "marketable" government securities, which can be sold readily to other investors if you wish. These marketable securities include Treasury bills, notes, and bonds. Here are the details:

• *Treasury Bills.* These are short-term obligations, usually maturing either thirteen or twenty-six weeks after issuance but sometimes as much as one year later. They are sold on a discount basis. This means that you pay less than the face value for the bill—such as $9,820 for a $10,000 Treasury bill maturing in thirteen weeks. When the bill matures, you receive the face value. The difference between the amount you pay—$9,820—and the amount you receive—$10,000—is what you earn as interest. In this case, it is over 7 percent. If you do not want to hold the bill until maturity, you can sell it in the market at the going price.

Treasury bills obviously are short-term investments and are purchased most often by banks and trust funds rather than the average individual investor. But if you have the desire to make such an investment, purchase forms are available from Federal Reserve Banks or branches. Remember, though, that Treasury bills are in bearer form, meaning that your name does not appear on the certificate. They can be transferred easily—and they can also be stolen easily. Thus, they must be handled like cash. They should be kept in a safe-deposit box and returned for redemption by registered mail.

• *Treasury Notes.* These securities mature in from one to seven years, thus offering a medium-length investment. Usually, notes pay a higher yield than short-term bills, but this can vary according to the money market. Most issues of notes can be obtained in denominations ranging from $1,000 to $1 million. Their prices are quoted in the daily newspapers in terms of $100, with a bid and asked price, the interest rate stated on the face of the note, and the actual yield. Such a newspaper listing might look like this:

Rate	Matures	Bid	Asked	Yield
6	Nov 79	96.4	96.12	7.09

This means that if you buy this note, which bears a stated interest rate of 6 percent and matures in November 1979, you will pay about $961 for a $1,000 note, and if you hold it to maturity your yield will be 7.09 percent.

Older Treasury notes can be bought in the open market, while new ones can be purchased through almost any bank. Unlike bills, Treasury notes can be registered in your name.

• *Treasury Bonds.* These are virtually identical to Treasury notes, except that they mature in more than seven years. Their price can be determined by reading the newspaper financial pages, using the same formula outlined for Treasury notes. In fact, notes and bonds usually are listed in the same column, with an "n" denoting notes.

Like Treasury notes, bonds can be registered in your name. And like other marketable government issues, bonds can be easily sold. Older Treasury bonds can be bought and sold on the open market and new ones can be purchased through most banks.

• *Agency Securities.* There is still another classification of marketable government securities—the bonds, notes, and debentures issued by federal agencies or quasi-public agencies. These instruments include Federal Land Bank bonds, Federal Home Loan Bank notes, Federal Intermediate Credit Bank debentures, Export-Import Bank obligations, Bank for Cooperatives debentures, Federal National Mortgage Association (FNMA) issues, and Government National Mortgage Association (GNMA) issues.

These securities generally have higher yields than direct Treasury obligations. While some of these agencies have a minimum purchase level of $10,000, issues in smaller amounts may be available through bond dealers and brokers.

If you are considering investing in U.S. government securities, bear in mind that, unlike state and municipal bonds, the yield on U.S. government obligations is not exempt from federal income tax. This yield is, however, exempt from state and local taxes.

CHAPTER 13

If
You
Want a
Tax
Break

When we hear of people with big incomes paying small amounts of income tax, there is griping about the "loopholes" they seem able to exploit. We speak of these loopholes as if they were quirks or accidents of the tax law—an obscure subparagraph where someone forgot to dot the "i" or cross the "t" properly.

But so-called loopholes are not accidents at all. They are a system of rewards the tax writers of our government have devised to encourage certain behavior by taxpayers.

If you do something the government wishes to encourage, you are rewarded with a break at tax time.

The nature of our progressive tax structure is such that individuals with high incomes can save more money through tax breaks than can those with middle or low incomes.

But savings of some sort are available to all, and the more you know about what the government is encouraging, the more you will be able to cut from your tax bill.

Without getting into all the fine points of tax strategy, we will outline things you can do with substantial help from the government in the form of tax benefits.

Financing your retirement

Some of the best tax news in years for self-employed persons and even many moonlighters came when Congress passed the Employment Retirement Income Security Act of 1974.

As part of this legislation, Congress greatly increased the tax advantages of establishing your own retirement income plan. Now, self-employed persons ranging from the $50,000-a-year lawyer to the newspaper reporter who writes a few magazine articles in his or her spare time can put money aside where it will grow tax-free until retirement.

If you are self-employed, you can benefit substantially. If you are salaried, it would be well worth your while even to do a few hundred or a few thousand dollars worth of outside work where you will be paid as a consultant or private practitioner or in some way other than on a payroll.

These tax-saving devices are called Keogh plans. This is how they work:

In general, you can set aside up to 15 percent of a $50,000 maximum of your earned income for a Keogh plan fund. That is a maximum of $7,500 per year. Once in the fund, the money goes to work for you but you cannot touch it or its earnings until you reach fifty-nine and a half years of age. Then you can start drawing from the fund for your retirement income.

You get tax breaks in two ways: The money you put into the fund is deductible from your income when you figure your income tax. And the money earned by the fund each year is not subject to income tax at the time. When you retire and begin drawing the money, you will have to pay tax—but by then you will presumably be in a lower tax bracket since you will not be working. The deferment of tax for many years will have resulted in the fund growing far more than if it had been taxed each year.

Let us take an example of $1,000 put into a Keogh fund to see how this operates:

If your taxable income were $30,000, that would put you into the 39 percent tax bracket. If you put $1,000 into a Keogh plan, you would immediately save $390, since you could deduct that

$1,000 from your $30,000 taxable income. If you earmarked the $1,000 for regular savings, you would have only $610 left to put aside after paying the $390 in taxes.

Let us assume that you can earn 8 percent on the money. After a year, your $1,000 in the Keogh plan would have increased to $1,080. Your $610 in the regular investment would have increased to $658.80. But you would have to pay $19.03 in taxes on that gain, so you would be left with only $639.77. At this point, your regular investment is worth only about 59 percent of your Keogh investment. And the margin increases, so that during the seventh year your Keogh investment would be worth double your regular investment. After ten years, your Keogh money would total $2,158.92, compared to just $982.33 for the other.

If each year you put $1,000 into your Keogh plan, the total fund after ten years would be worth $15,645.47. But if you took that same $1,000 each year, paid taxes on it, and put the remainder into a regular investment at our assumed 8 percent return, you would have a nest egg of just $8,002.01. The table on page 163 shows how the differences become even greater as the years go by.

The Keogh legislation originally had a special appeal for moonlighters. As passed by Congress, the first $750 of a moonlighter's earnings could go into a Keogh plan. Prior to 1976 this meant that if you earned only $600 in outside income, all of it could go into a Keogh plan, and thus be sheltered from income taxes. Then the IRS issued a regulation saying that on outside income up to $3,000, only 25 percent could go into a Keogh plan. Finally the taxing authorities decided that the 15 percent ceiling applied to all earnings. This meant, for example, that if you had $1,000 in outside earnings, you could put $150 into a Keogh plan. Nevertheless, many moonlighters with small outside income have kept their Keogh plans in effect, even though their annual contributions are smaller than they had originally anticipated.

Keogh plans are available through a number of savings institutions, banks, securities dealers, insurance firms, and trade or professional associations. Under the old law, when the limit on annual contributions was $2,500, only an estimated 10 percent of eligible taxpayers participated. That percentage shot up sharply with the higher ceiling for the big earners and the liberalized minimum affecting moonlighters.

There are, of course, numerous details that apply to the program. For example:

• If you are self-employed but have other persons working for you, you may have to set up pension plans for them in order to take advantage of Keogh yourself.

• You will be penalized if you take money out of the plan before you are fifty-nine and a half years old, unless you are totally disabled.

• You must take money out of the plan when you reach the age of seventy and a half, even if you are still earning a large income.

• The fund must be handled by a trustee or custodian, or you may purchase special U.S. savings bonds.

A related program permits wage earners whose company does not have a retirement plan to set aside the lesser of 15 percent of their wages or $1,500 a year for retirement. These programs are called Individual Retirement Accounts, or IRA, and have tax benefits similar to Keogh plans.

An employee whose company ends its pension plan can take any money he or she has coming from that plan and put it into an IRA without paying taxes. So if you're due to get money from your pension plan but you're not retiring, check to see if it is eligible to be placed in an IRA.

Home and property ownership

The government encourages you to own your own home by providing a break that for many Americans is the biggest single deduction on their tax return.

This break lets you deduct all the interest you pay on your home mortgage. If you have purchased a home within the past several years of escalating house and financing costs, you could be paying $3,000, $4,000, or more in mortgage interest each year.

If you are in the 39 percent tax bracket, paying $3,000 as mortgage interest instead of as part of rent would be worth a $1,170 yearly tax saving.

Thus, if you are trying to decide whether to buy a house or continue as a tenant, you should take into account the effect on your income tax. The higher your tax bracket, the more help you get as a homeowner.

Another significant tax break that comes with homeownership

Keogh Plan vs. Standard Investment

If, before paying taxes, you set aside $1,000 for investing in your future retirement and if you had $30,000 in taxable income, placing you in the 39 percent tax bracket:

Under a Keogh Plan you could Invest $1,000. After one year at an 8 percent return, your $1,000 would be worth $1,080.

In a standard investment, after paying $390 in taxes, you could invest $610. After one year at an 8 percent return, your $610 would be worth $658.80, but after paying taxes on the gain, you would have only $639.77.

Here is what your original investment, assuming the same return and tax rate, would be worth after additional succeeding years:

Keogh	Years	Standard
$ 1,166.40	2	$ 670.99
1,259.71	3	703.73
1,360.49	4	738.03
1,469.33	5	774.09
1,586.87	6	811.87
1,713.82	7	851.49
1,850.93	8	893.04
1,990.00	9	936.62
2,158.92	10	982.33
3,172.17	15	1,246.58
4,660.95	20	1,581.92
6,848.47	25	2,007.46

If you added an additional amount of new investment each year on the same basis and terms as the first year, you would have this much accumulated under each system:

$15,645.47	10	$ 8,002.01
29,324.24	15	13,681.26
49,422.85	20	20,888.25
78,954.31	25	30,033.97

is the deduction for property taxes, which might cost you $500, $1,000, or even more a year.

As another encouragement to homeownership, the government will let you keep any profits you make on the sale of your house if you buy another house that costs as much or more. You can keep plowing the profits from one house into another as many times as you like, never paying tax on them unless you stop being a homeowner. Even in that event, you will get some tax relief on the final sale if you are sixty-five or older.

If you expand real estate holdings from your own home to investment property, the government will encourage you by permitting you to deduct depreciation of the property on your tax return.

Depreciation is a paper method of taking into account the theoretical fact that your building is eventually going to wear out and have to be replaced. If you figure that your building has a remaining life of forty years, you can deduct one-fortieth of its cost each year, theoretically setting aside that money so that at the end of the forty years you will have the money for a new building.

Even though you are not spending this depreciation, you can deduct it on your tax return just as if it were a cash expenditure. This is likely to lead to the phenomenon in rental property where you are pocketing profits from rents even after paying your mortgage, taxes, and other expenses, but can show a loss for your tax return after you deduct depreciation.

If you eventually sell the property, you will have to pay some of the tax you avoided earlier, but usually under more favorable terms. And as with any provision that permits you to defer tax, you have had the equivalent of an interest-free loan from the government, and you will almost certainly eventually pay with dollars that are worth less because of inflation.

The tax laws and regulations in real estate ownership are, of course, far more detailed than the highlights discussed here. But in total, they frequently can provide you with an excellent opportunity to make money by cutting your income taxes.

Securities and other investments

Capital investment ultimately spurs the economy and helps the nation grow. To encourage you to invest, the laws provide that when you receive long-term gains from your capital investment, you pay tax on these profits usually at no more than half the rate of tax you pay on ordinary income.

Let us say that you had that $30,000 in taxable income we used in an earlier example. If you received an additional $1,000 as a bonus from your employer, you would pay $390 of it in tax. But if you received an additional $1,000 as profit from the sale of stocks you had bought more than one year earlier, you would normally pay only $195 in tax.

The capital-gains rule applies not only to stocks, but to essentially all property you own and use for personal purposes, pleasure, or investment. You would get the capital-gains break if you sold a valuable painting for a profit or made money on the sale of your vacation cottage, assuming you had held these assets for longer than one year.

Local and state governments often raise money, particularly for building projects, by selling bonds to the public—a form of borrowing money. To encourage you to buy these bonds and to help the local and state governments by holding down the rate of interest they must pay, the government allows you to earn interest from these so-called municipal bonds without paying any tax on that income.

The higher your tax bracket, the more attractive are these tax-free securities. At our example 39 percent tax bracket, you would keep more money in your pocket from a municipal bond paying 6.5 percent interest than you would from a taxable-income investment paying 10 percent.

The government also encourages you to buy a number of items for business use by offering something that is even better than a tax deduction—a direct tax credit.

A deduction is something you take away from your income, reducing the amount of income on which you must pay taxes. But a tax credit is an amount you subtract dollar-for-dollar from the amount of income tax you owe.

Of course, the government mostly has in mind large corporations that build new plants and buy new equipment. But let us say that you work at home and require a typewriter. That can qualify, too, for the tax credit. Depending on the useful life of the equipment, you may deduct 7 percent of its cost directly from your tax due.

For the sophisticated investor there are also tax considerations that can add luster to investments in oil, cattle, timber, and other fields.

But news reports of bankruptcy and fraud should make it clear to all investors and potential investors that tax considerations alone are not sufficient reason to put your money into a particular investment; the deal should be sound on its own merits. If tax considerations make it an even better investment, that is fine. But bear in mind that tax breaks will not recoup all your money if it is lost in some ill-conceived scheme.

These examples are only some of the ways you can get the government to cut your tax bill. There also are various tax breaks for people over the age of sixty-five, for veterans, for people whose offices are in their homes, and for those who contribute to charities.

The Internal Revenue Service (IRS) has a number of publications that can aid taxpayers. One of the most useful for the average taxpayer is *Your Federal Income Tax,* which is published annually by the IRS.

Keep detailed records of your financial transactions and plan your family's finances with an eye on all the tax breaks that are possible. You will then be using one major means of getting your money's worth from your government.

14

If
You
Retire

When you retire, you will get back some of the tax dollars you have paid the U.S. government over the years. You may even get back many more dollars than you paid in.

Social Security is the vehicle used by the federal government to provide you with a continuing income when your family earnings are reduced because of retirement. In addition to Social Security, the government has other programs to assist retirees.

The Administration on Aging (AoA), an agency of the Department of Health, Education, and Welfare, serves as a focal point within the federal government on all matters of concern to older people. It was established to strengthen and assist state and local agencies concerned with the problems of the elderly. It administers grants to states, community organizations, and other institutions, and also serves as a central clearinghouse for information on services and opportunities available to the older generation.

The AoA does not provide funds directly to the elderly. But its grants have been used for many local programs of benefit to the elderly. For example, AoA has funded experimental housing programs in several areas of the country. And it has been involved in "meals on wheels" projects to bring nutritional meals to the homebound elderly as well as group meal services for other senior citizens. All of these programs have local sponsors. If you cannot locate the sponsor in your community, write to the Administration on Aging, U.S. Department of Health, Education, and Welfare, Washington, D.C. 20201.

Volunteer work

Volunteer opportunities for older people exist in every community, although you may have to hunt for them. Nationally, there are three federally-funded service programs predominantly for older people—the Foster Grandparent Program, the Retired Senior Volunteer Program, and SCORE (Service Corps of Retired Executives). All are administered by ACTION, a federal agency with headquarters at 806 Connecticut Avenue, N.W., Washington, D.C. 20525.

The Foster Grandparent Program offers men and women aged sixty and over who have low incomes a chance to give love and attention to institutionalized and handicapped children, receiving in return small payment but great satisfaction. They usually work twenty hours a week and usually are paid the basic minimum wage in their community.

The Retired Senior Volunteer Program (RSVP) uses the skills and experience of older people (sixty and over) in a great variety of necessary community services, aiding less mobile senior citizens as well as children and people of all ages. There is no payment for service, but out-of-pocket expenses are paid.

SCORE is made up of retired business executives who draw upon their experience to serve as volunteer consultants to small businesses in need of help.

If you cannot locate a local source of information about service in any of these programs, write to ACTION, Washington D.C. 20525.

Social Security benefits

When the Social Security program began in 1937, the idea was simple. It provided for one monthly benefit: a small payment to the wage earner who retired at age sixty-five. From that simple beginning has grown a complex, often confusing system. The program has expanded by leaps and bounds. Requirements have changed. Benefit levels have increased, and so have the taxes paid in.

And, under legislation enacted by Congress in late 1977, payroll taxes will go up even faster in the years ahead—a total of $227 billion in the decade 1977-88. The higher taxes were needed to meet growing deficits of the Social Security system.

But even with the many changes, and the higher taxes, the basic idea of the Social Security program has remained unchanged through the years. It is this: during working years, employees, their employers, and self-employed persons pay Social Security taxes which are pooled in special trust funds. When earnings stop or are reduced because the worker retires, dies, or becomes disabled, monthly cash benefits are paid to replace part of the lost earnings.

Nine out of every ten working people in the United States are covered by Social Security. Their paychecks show a deduction for "FICA." That stands for Federal Insurance Contributions Act, and the money deducted goes into the Social Security trust fund. An employee and the employer pay an equal share of Social Security taxes. A self-employed person pays at a rate somewhat lower than the combined rate for an employee and an employer.

In 1977, for instance, employees and employers each paid 5.85 percent of the employee's wages. The total rate for self-employed people was 7.90 percent. Under the 1977 amendments, the rates in both categories are scheduled to climb in the years ahead. In 1978, employees and employers were paying at a rate of 6.05 percent. This goes to 6.13 percent in 1979 and to 6.65 percent in 1981. Further increases will raise the rate to 7.15 percent in 1986 and to 7.65 percent in 1990 and later years.

The self-employed rate was 8.10 percent in 1978, with these rates scheduled in future years: 9.3 percent in 1981, 9.35 percent in 1982 through 1984, 9.9 percent in 1985, 10 percent in 1986 through 1989, and 10.75 percent in 1990 and beyond.

These rates are paid on specified amounts of annual income. In 1977, for instance, they applied to the first $16,500 of earnings. In 1978, the ceiling went to $17,700. In 1979, it was scheduled to go to $22,900, and in 1980 to $25,900. The ceiling will continue

Work Credit for Retirement Benefits

If You Reach 62 in:	Years of Credits You Need
1976	6¼
1977	6½
1978	6¾
1979	7
1981	7½
1983	8
1987	9
1991 or later	10

to rise each year, so that by 1987 it will apply to the first $42,600 of annual earnings.

Looking at it another way, the maximum annual Social Security tax paid by an employee in 1977 was $965. In 1978 this went to $1,071 and in 1979 it rises to $1,404. In future years these are the scheduled maximum taxes: $1,588 in 1980, $1,975 in 1981, $2,131 in 1982, $2,271 in 1983, $2,412 in 1984, $2,686 in 1985, $2,874 in 1986, and $3,046 in 1987.

But, looking at the brighter side, benefits also are automatically increased each year if the cost of living goes up more than 3 percent.

Further changes are possible in the future in the way the Social Security system works. You should be alert for such changes. But, in the meantime, this chapter will tell you how to determine whether you qualify for retirement benefits, how and where to apply, how to figure the size of your monthly check, and how to make certain you receive the amount to which you are entitled.

Do you qualify?

To qualify for monthly retirement benefits, you must have credit for a certain amount of time in what is called a "covered occupation." Since virtually all civilian jobs are now classified under covered occupations, the great majority of working Americans qualify for Social Security. In fact, except for a few special occupations, coverage under Social Security is compulsory—you have no choice but to participate in the system.

Your work credit is measured in calendar quarters. For each

three-month calendar quarter (January-March, April-June, July-September, October-December) that you work under Social Security and are paid wages of $50 or more, you get one Social Security quarter of coverage. If you work an entire calendar year, you get four quarters of coverage, one for each quarter worked. If you are self-employed, you receive four quarters of coverage for a year when you have a net profit of $400 or more from your self-employment.

These credits stay on your record if you stop work before you have earned enough credits for coverage under Social Security, so you can add to your record if you later return to work. Having enough credit means only that you or your family can get monthly benefit checks. The size of that check depends on your average earnings over a period of years, a subject to be taken up later. But now, examine the table on page 170 to determine how much credit you need for retirement benefits.

As this table indicates, ten years of credit is the maximum that is needed to be fully covered. In other words, if you are now thirty-five years old and have been working in a covered occupation since you were twenty-five, you already are fully insured. Even if you quit tomorrow and never work again, you would qualify for benefits when you reach retirement age. But remember, the size of your monthly check will depend on your earnings, not on your years of credit.

Figuring your retirement benefits

When it comes time for you to collect your retirement benefits, the Social Security Administration will make calculations based on your records. But you can estimate how much you will be collecting at age sixty-five by following these steps to determine your average earnings, and by consulting the tables on pages 231–239.

1. List your earnings for each year from 1951 to the present from jobs or self-employment covered by Social Security. Do not list any earnings above the Social Security tax ceilings shown in the table on page 172.

2. Estimate your expected earnings from the present through the year before you will be sixty-five. Do not list more than the ceiling for each year.

3. Select the number of years in which your earnings were the

Social Security Tax Ceilings

1951–54	$ 3,600	1974	$13,200
1955–58	$ 4,200	1975	$14,100
1959–65	$ 4,800	1976	$15,300
1966–67	$ 6,600	1977	$16,500
1968–71	$ 7,800	1978	$17,700
1972	$ 9,000	1979	$22,900
1973	$10,800	1980	$25,900

highest. If you were born in 1929 or after, you must select thirty-five of the years. If you were born prior to 1929, consult the table on page 174 to determine the number of years you must count.

4. After you have selected the appropriate number of years with the highest earnings, calculate your average annual earnings. Then divide this annual average by twelve to find your monthly average earnings.

If all this sounds too complicated, this specific example may help you: Suppose you were born in 1915 and plan to retire in 1980 at age sixty-five. To estimate your retirement benefits, list your earnings for the years 1951 through 1977, up to the ceiling amount for each year. Then list what you expect to earn from 1978 up to, but not including, 1980. Assuming that the ceiling remains the same in those years, your list might look like this:

Past Earnings

1951	$3,600	1962	$4,800	1973	$10,800
1952	$3,600	1963	$4,800	1974	$13,200
1953	$3,600	1964	$4,800	1975	$14,100
1954	$3,600	1965	$4,800	1976	$15,300
1955	$4,200	1966	$6,600	1977	$16,500
1956	$4,200	1967	$6,600		
1957	$4,200	1968	$7,800		
1958	$4,200	1969	$7,800		
1959	$4,800	1970	$7,800	**Future Earnings**	
1960	$4,800	1971	$7,800	1978	$17,700
1961	$4,800	1972	$9,000	1979	$22,900

By consulting the table on page 174, you will find that since you were born in 1915, you must count twenty-one years of earnings. Your list has earnings for twenty-nine years, so you can cross off the eight lowest years. This would be 1951 through 1958. Now add up the income for the remaining years. You come up with a total of $197,500. Now divide by twenty-one (the number of years of earnings) and you find your average annual earnings are $9,405. Now divide this by twelve to find your average monthly earnings: $784. This is the figure you use in consulting the tables on pages 231–239 showing monthly retirement benefits.

A word of caution before you study the tables: Some people think that if they have always earned the maximum amount covered by Social Security, they will get the highest benefit shown in the table. This is not so. Although retirement benefits as high as $632.90 a month are shown, payments that high cannot be paid to a worker retiring now. The maximum retirement benefit for a worker who becomes sixty-five in early 1978 is $437.10 a month.

The reason the average can be no higher now is that the maximum earnings covered by Social Security were lower in past years. Those years of lower limits must be counted in with recent years to figure your average covered yearly earnings. And this average determines the amount of your check. Survivors' and disability benefits can reach higher levels now, since fewer years and higher earnings levels are used to figure the average earnings for younger workers, as will be discussed later.

Family benefits

When you begin receiving your retirement checks, members of your family may become eligible for benefits, too. Here is a rundown on who can collect in certain circumstances:

• *Your Wife*. The wife of an insured worker is entitled to benefits equal to one-half of her husband's primary insurance if she is sixty-five or older. She can begin collecting as early as age sixty-two if she chooses to take a smaller amount, which is permanently reduced to take into account the extra years she will be receiving payments. She can collect benefits at any age if she is caring for her child under the age of eighteen or for her unmarried child aged eighteen or over who was totally disabled before the age of twenty-two.

• *A Divorced Wife*. A divorced woman who is sixty-two or over can collect a wife's benefit if she had been married to a retired

Years of Earnings to Count
For Social Security Benefits

Year of Birth	Number of Years to Count	
	Men	Women
1909	18	15
1910	19	16
1911	19	17
1912	19	18

Beginning with 1913, the number of
years to count are the same for men and women:

Year of Birth	Number of Years to Count
1913	19
1914	20
1915	21
1916	22
1917	23
1918	24
1919	25
1920	26
1921	27
1922	28
1923	29
1924	30
1925	31
1926	32
1927	33
1928	34
1929 on	35

worker at least ten years. If a divorced woman remarries, she is no longer eligible for benefits based on her first husband's Social Security coverage. But her remarriage would not halt benefits payable to her first husband's dependent children for whom she is caring.

• *A Husband.* The husband of a woman who is collecting her own monthly retirement benefits can be eligible for a husband's benefit based on his wife's work. To qualify, he must be sixty-two or older.

• *Dependent Children.* A retired worker's unmarried children can collect benefits until they are eighteen or until age twenty-two if they are full-time students. Disabled children aged eighteen or over whose disabilities began before age twenty-two are eligible. Each child's benefits are equal to one-half of the retired worker's primary insurance amount.

You will see that the tables list a "maximum family benefit." That is the most you and members of your family can collect, no matter how many members are entitled to benefits. When benefits paid to a retired worker, his wife, and children add up to more than the allowable family maximum, benefits except those paid to the worker are reduced proportionally to bring the total down to the maximum set by law.

Should you retire early?

You can retire and begin collecting benefits as early as age sixty-two. But your monthly checks will be smaller than if you had waited until age sixty-five. This is to take into account the longer period of time you will be collecting them.

The size of the reduction depends on the number of months you receive benefits between the ages of sixty-two and sixty-five. If you retire on your sixty-second birthday, your monthly benefits are 80 percent of what you would get if you were sixty-five. If you retire at sixty-three, the benefits are 86⅔ percent of the full amount. At age sixty-four, they are 93⅓ percent of the full amount. If you retire early, the benefits are permanently reduced—they will stay at the reduced level even after you are sixty-five.

Your personal situation obviously must govern your decision on whether to retire early. But this illustration may help when you are considering the possibilities:

Joe and John Smith are the same age and through the years their earnings under Social Security have been the same. At age sixty-five, each of them would be entitled to benefits totaling $2,000 a year. Joe decides to retire at age sixty-two and John waits until age sixty-five.

Because he retires early, Joe's benefits are reduced. He gets 80 percent of the amount he would have been entitled to at age sixty-five—or $1,600 instead of $2,000 a year. By the time he is seventy, Joe will have collected a total of $12,800 in benefits, while John, who did not retire until sixty-five, will have collected a total of $10,000. John's total benefits will equal Joe's when the two men are seventy-seven years old.

When early retiree Joe reaches age eighty, his benefits will have totaled $28,800, while regular retiree John will have collected benefits totaling $30,000.

If you stay on the job or go back to work after you retire, your earnings may affect your Social Security benefits. But you do not have to stop working completely to get Social Security checks.

In 1977, for example, you could earn as much as $3,000 a year without losing any benefits. If your annual earnings went above this level, Social Security withheld $1 in benefits for each $2 in earnings above the specified level.

The amount of allowable earnings is scheduled to increase. It was set at $4,000 for 1978, $4,500 for 1979, $5,000 for 1980, $5,500 for 1981, and $6,000 for 1982.

Prior to 1978 there was a provision in the law that allowed benefits to be paid for months of low earnings, regardless of annual earnings. This provision was repealed by the 1977 amendments.

The 1977 amendments also require restaurant owners and other employers to pay Social Security taxes on employee tips up to the amount that, combined with the employee's salary, equals the federal minimum wage. Previously, only the employee paid Social Security taxes on tip income, and then only if the tips exceeded $20 a month.

For most individuals, total wages, not just take-home pay, and all net self-employment earnings must be added together in figuring what income may affect your Social Security checks.

But income from savings, investments, pensions, insurance, and royalties will not affect your checks. And after you reach the age of seventy-two, there is no limit on the amount without affecting your Social Security benefits.

Different rules apply to work performed by persons receiving benefits because they are disabled. Those rules are discussed in chapter 15.

If you work after you begin receiving retirement checks, your added earnings will often result in higher benefits. Social Security will automatically refigure your benefit after the additional earnings are credited to your record.

In addition, the Social Security law provides you with a "bonus" if you work past age sixty-five without collecting retirement benefits.

Under the formula in effect for many years, if you did not receive retirement benefits before age sixty-five and continued to work without getting Social Security checks, your eventual monthly retirement benefits were increased by 1 percent for each year (1/12 of 1 percent for each month) you worked beyond age sixty-five, until you reached age seventy-two.

Thus, if you had a basic monthly benefit of $200 at age sixty-five but did not receive retirement benefits until age seventy, you would get a 5 percent bonus, of $10 a month, added to your check. The bonus applied only to the worker's check and not to those of dependents or survivors.

Under the 1977 amendments, this "delayed retirement credit" was increased from 1 percent to 3 percent, effective in 1982.

Check your work record now

Even if you are many years away from retirement, you should check to make certain that the Social Security Administration has accurately recorded your work record. This can be especially important if you have changed employers frequently or if you have in the past been self-employed. Here is how to do it:

Call or stop by your local Social Security office. (It may be listed in the telephone book under "U.S. Government, Department of Health, Education, and Welfare, Social Security Administration.") Ask for SSA (postcard) Form 7004, Request for Statement of Earnings, and fill it out. All you have to list is your name and address, Social Security number, and date of birth. The card is pre-addressed.

Within a few weeks, you will receive a Statement of Earnings, which will show your posted earnings. If you specifically request this information, you will also be told how many quarters of coverage have been credited to your work record. The statement may not include the last two or three calendar quarters if you are still working or have worked until recently. And if you are self-employed, the statement may be a year or so behind. If you think the information listed is incorrect, take it to your Social Security office and ask that it be corrected.

Applying for retirement benefits

When you apply for Social Security retirement benefits, you must prove your age. You may say, "I'm a long way from retirement. I won't worry about it now." That attitude could cause a great deal of trouble and could also cost you money. It is best to start now to assemble written evidence establishing your date of birth. The longer you wait, the more difficulty you may have in proving your age. Records too often are destroyed or misplaced.

The best evidence of your date of birth is a record made at the time of birth—in other words, an original birth certificate or a hospital birth record. If neither of these is available, the next best evidence is a physician's record or an infant religious record.

If these preferred types of evidence are not available, you may be able to establish your age through school records, census records, draft registration or military records, driver's license applications, old insurances policies, or immigration records. Keep in mind that the Social Security Administration may require more than one of these latter forms of evidence to establish your date of birth.

In addition to proving your own age, you may need to prove your spouse's age and relationship to you. A marriage certificate is adequate for proof of marriage. If your children are eligible for benefits, their birth certificates are also needed.

Other documents that you may need are a copy of your latest income tax withholding statement (Form W-2), your last income tax return if you are self-employed, an adoption certificate for an adopted child, death certificate, or divorce papers.

You should get in touch with your Social Security office if you are within two or three months of your sixty-fifth birthday—even if you do not plan to retire. This is important, not only to discuss your retirement benefits, but to take steps toward obtaining

Medicare benefits, which are available to you at age sixty-five whether or not you retire.

If you plan to retire, bear in mind that retirement checks do not begin automatically. Before you or your family can receive benefits, you must apply for them.

The Social Security Administration has about 1,300 offices in cities and towns throughout the country. In addition, representatives of these offices make regular visits to neighboring communities. Do not hesitate to call, visit, or write any Social Security office. The people there will have the answers to your questions and can help you with any problems involving Social Security. Remember, they are there to serve you. After all, your tax dollars pay their salaries.

15

If You Are Handicapped or Disabled

Millions of Americans who are handicapped or disabled have found the federal government a major source of assistance. Cash benefits and a variety of other forms of assistance are provided by the government to help the recipients and their families lead as normal a life as possible.

What follows is first an outline of aid for the handicapped, then a report on assistance for the disabled.

Aid for the handicapped

Much of the federal aid for the handicapped is channeled through states, public or nonprofit private agencies and organizations, and such institutions as universities. These bodies then provide aid or services for the handicapped. For example, the U.S. Office of Education awards funds for the establishment and operation of model centers across the country to improve the education of children with specific learning disabilities.

But there are programs of direct assistance for the handicapped. Here are the details:

• *Books for the Blind and Physically Handicapped.* This program operated by the Library of Congress provides talking books, books in braille, and talking-book machines to blind and physically handicapped residents of the United States and its territories. In a typical year, about 480,000 blind and physically handicapped persons are served by fifty-three regional libraries in the United States with a collection of about 20,000 books in recorded and braille form and 37,000 music scores in braille. Applications for this service can be made through the regional libraries or to the Division for the Blind and Physically Handicapped, Library of Congress, 1291 Taylor Street, N.W., Washington, D.C. 20542.

• *Captioned Films for the Deaf.* The U.S. Office of Education supervises a free loan service of captioned films and instructional material for the deaf. The films are distributed to state and local public agencies and schools, as well as to organizations and groups of deaf persons. It is estimated that about three million persons benefit each year from the captioned films. More information can be obtained from the Media Services and Captioned Films Branch, Division of Educational Services, Bureau of Education for the Handicapped, Office of Education, Department of Health, Education, and Welfare, Washington, D.C. 20202.

• *Employment Service.* The U.S. Employment Service and affiliated state agencies offer specialized services to the handicapped. These include special employment counseling and placement assistance intended to match the physical demands of the job with the capabilities of the worker. Information and educational activities also are directed toward employers and labor organizations to improve educational opportunities for the handicapped. To obtain this assistance, contact any of the more than 2,400 local employment service offices.

• *Federal Employment.* The Civil Service Commission has selective placement programs to help the handicapped obtain employment with the U.S. government. The services are available to the physically handicapped, including the blind and the deaf, and the mentally retarded. Included are counseling, referral, placement, and trial appointments. Under the program, each federal agency has a coordinator for selective placement, with specific responsibility for assuring that qualified handicapped applicants receive full consideration for employment. In one recent year, more than 5,750 handicapped persons were hired by federal agencies. To apply for this assistance, handicapped persons or rehabilitation personnel working in their behalf should contact the appropriate regional or local office of the Civil Service Commission or the coordinator of selective placement in any federal agency.

Aid for the disabled

Disability can have more of an impact on a family's financial security than retirement or even death of the breadwinner. Besides cutting off the family's income, disabling disease or injury is often accompanied by continuing medical bills, thus adding to a family's already strained finances.

As might be expected, there is some overlapping of benefits for the disabled and the handicapped, especially for those whose handicap resulted from work-related injury or disease. Benefits for those whose disabilities result from military service were discussed in chapter 7. What follows, then, is an outline of the disability benefits available under the Social Security system.

The Social Security law was amended in 1951 to establish disability insurance, which now provides benefits for people in all walks of life: the forty-year-old salesman who has a heart attack; the twenty-three-year-old secretary out of work for more than a year because of an automobile accident; the fifty-three-year-old widow who is crippled with advanced arthritis; the retired worker's thirty-two-year-old son who has been mentally retarded since birth.

In brief, Social Security disability benefits can be paid to:

• Disabled workers under the age of sixty-five and their families.

• Persons disabled before the age of twenty-two who continue to be disabled. These benefits are payable as early as age eighteen when a parent receives Social Security retirement or disability benefits or when an insured parent dies.

• Disabled widows, disabled widowers, and, under certain conditions, disabled divorced wives of workers who were insured at death. These benefits are payable as early as age fifty.

In addition, as will be discussed more fully in the next chapter, a disabled person, regardless of age, is eligible for Medicare after being entitled to disability payments for twenty-four consecutive months.

Before you can qualify for disability benefits, you must have worked under Social Security long enough and recently enough. The amount of work credits you will need depends on your age when you become disabled:

• *Before age twenty-four.* You will need credit for one and one-half years of work in the three-year period ending when your disability begins.

• *Ages twenty-four through thirty.* You will need credit for having worked half of the years between age twenty-one and the time you become disabled.

• *Thirty-one or older.* All workers disabled at age thirty-one or older—except the blind—need to be fully insured and have credit for at least five years of work out of the ten years ending when they become disabled. The years need not be continuous or in units of full years. For example, nine months of credit in 1976 and three months of credit in 1975 would count as one year of credit.

A blind person no longer has to meet this standard of recently covered work, but does need credit for one-fourth year of work each year since 1950, or the year the person reached twenty-one if later, up to the year when blindness began. A minimum of one and one-half years of credit is needed.

Criteria for disabled status

Under Social Security law, you are considered disabled if you have a physical or mental condition that prevents you from doing any substantial gainful work and is expected to last (or has lasted) for at least twelve months or is expected to result in your death.

Certain conditions which are ordinarily severe enough to be considered disabling under the law are described in Social Security regulations. You can examine these regulations at any Social Security office. Some examples of disabling conditions listed in the regulations are:

• Loss of major function of both arms, both legs, or a leg and an arm.

• Progressive diseases that have resulted in the loss of a leg or have caused it to become useless.

• Severe arthritis that causes recurrent inflammation, pain, swelling, and deformity in major joints so that the ability to get about or use the hands has been severely limited.

• Diseases of heart, lung, or blood vessels that have resulted in serious loss of heart or lung reserve as shown by X-ray, electrocardiogram, or other tests; and in spite of medical treatment, there is breathlessness, pain, or fatigue.

• Diseases of the digestive system that result in severe malnutrition, weakness, and anemia.

• Serious loss of function of the kidneys.

• Cancer that is progressive, and has not been controlled or cured.

• Damage to the brain or brain abnormality that has resulted in severe loss of judgment, intellect, orientation, or memory.

• Mental illness resulting in marked constriction of activities and interests, deterioration in personal habits, and seriously impaired ability to get along with other people.

• Total inability to speak.

In cases of individuals disabled before the age of twenty-two, conditions less severe than those listed in the regulations can be considered disabling. This is because their relatively less education, training, and work experience can be taken into account for these applicants.

Payments may be made to a person who meets the criteria even if expected to recover from the disability.

Estimating monthly benefits

Like retirement benefits, the amount of your monthly disability benefit is based on your average earnings under Social Security over a period of years. Your average earnings also govern the amount of monthly payments to your dependents.

The precise size of your monthly check cannot be calculated in advance. This is because all of your earnings in your Social Security record at the time of your application must be considered. But you can estimate the amount of your disability benefit by following these steps:

1. Count the number of years to be used in figuring your average earnings. (At least two years of earnings must be used to figure disability benefits.) If you were born before 1930, begin with 1956. If you were born after 1929, begin with the year you reached twenty-seven. Count your starting year and each year

until, but not including, the year in which you became disabled.

2. List your earnings for each year beginning in 1951, up to the ceiling for each year. Include the year your disability began. The ceiling amounts are:

1951-54	$3,600
1955-58	$4,200
1959-65	$4,800
1966-67	$6,600
1968-71	$7,800
1972	$9,000
1973	$10,800
1974	$13,200
1975	$14,100
1976	$15,300
1977	$16,500

3. Cross off your list the years of lowest earnings until the number of years remaining is the same as your answer to the first step. It may be necessary to leave in years during which you had no earnings.

4. Add up the earnings for the years left on your list. Divide by the number of years you used. This will give you your average annual earnings. To calculate your average monthly earnings, divide the annual figure by twelve. Now look at the tables on pages 231–239 to estimate your monthly benefits.

Limitations are placed on the amount you receive if you are a disabled worker under the age of sixty-two and are entitled to both Social Security disability benefits and worker's compensation. The total monthly payments to you and your family cannot be more than 80 percent of your average monthly earnings before you were disabled.

In computing your average earnings for this purpose, your *full* earnings, including any amounts above the maximum creditable for Social Security, may be considered. If combined benefits from Social Security and worker's compensation are over this 80 percent limit, Social Security benefits must be reduced.

Your dependents

If you are eligible for benefits as a disabled worker, payments can also be made to certain members of your family. They include:

- Your unmarried children who are under the age of eighteen.
- Your children aged eighteen to twenty-two if they are unmarried and attending school full time.
- Your unmarried children aged eighteen or older who were disabled before reaching twenty-two and continue to be disabled.
- Your wife at any age if she has in her care a child who is receiving benefits based on your Social Security record because he or she is under eighteen or became disabled before twenty-two.
- Your wife aged sixty-two or older even if there are no children entitled to benefits. And if you are a woman, your husband aged sixty-two or older is eligible.

Stepchildren and adopted children also may qualify for benefits on your record. A child may be eligible on a grandparent's Social Security record only if the child's parents are disabled or deceased and the child was living with and dependent upon the grandparent at the time the grandparent qualified for benefits.

Disabled widow or widower

If you are disabled and are the widow or widower of a worker who worked long enough under Social Security, you may be able to receive monthly benefits as early as age fifty. The benefits will be permanently reduced, with the amount of the reduction depending on the age when benefits begin. You need no work credits of your own to get benefits based on the earnings of your deceased spouse.

Under this section of the law, you may be considered disabled only if your impairment is so severe that it would ordinarily prevent a person from working and it is expected to last at least twelve months. Vocational factors, such as age, education, and previous work experience, are not considered in deciding whether a widow or widower is disabled.

As a general rule, you cannot receive these benefits unless your disability begins before your spouse's death or within seven years after the death. But if you receive benefits as a widow with children, you can be eligible if you become disabled before those payments end or within seven years after they end. This seven-year period is intended to provide coverage for the widow until she has a chance to earn enough work credits for disability protection on her own Social Security record.

A disabled divorced wife may get benefits based on the earnings of her deceased former husband only if their marriage lasted ten years or more.

Disabled since childhood

If you have an unmarried son or daughter eighteen years old or older who became disabled before the age of twenty-two and is still disabled, he or she may be eligible for benefits. These can begin at the same time as your disability benefits.

A person disabled before the age of twenty-two needs no Social Security work credits to qualify for benefits. This is because the payments are based on the earnings of the parent. The payments may continue for as long as the person is disabled and the parent's eligibility continues. Whether a person has been disabled since childhood is decided by the same rules that apply to a disabled worker.

If a child with a severe medical condition is now receiving child's insurance benefits under other Social Security provisions and these benefits are scheduled to stop when he or she reaches eighteen, someone in the family should contact a Social Security office a few months before the child's eighteenth birthday to find out if benefits can be continued beyond the age of eighteen on the basis of the disability.

The mother of a disabled son or daughter who is entitled to childhood disability payments may also qualify for benefits regardless of her age if she has the child in her care.

Provisions for the blind

Under Social Security law, a person whose vision is no better than 20/200 even with glasses, or who has a limited visual field of twenty degrees or less, is considered blind.

If you meet this test of blindness, and if you have worked long enough under Social Security, you are eligible for a disability "freeze" even though you are actually working. This means that the amount of your future benefits, which are figured from your average earnings, will not be reduced because you had low earnings or no earnings in years in which you were disabled.

If you are between the ages of fifty-five and sixty-five, meet the test of blindness, and have worked long enough under Social Security, you can receive disability benefits if you are unable to perform work requiring skills or abilities comparable to those required by the work you did regularly before you reached fifty-five or became blind, whichever is later. But benefits will not be paid for any months in which you perform substantial gainful work.

If you are blind and under fifty-five, you can become entitled to cash benefits only if you are unable to engage in any substantial gainful work.

The waiting period

Disability benefits cannot begin until after you have been disabled for five full calendar months. No benefits can be paid for these first five months of disability. Your first payment is for the sixth full month.

If you were disabled for more than six full months before applying, back benefits may be payable—but not for the period before the sixth full month of disability. Social Security officials stress the importance of applying soon after the disability begins, since back payments are limited to the twelve months preceding the month you apply.

If you have recovered from a disability that lasted twelve months or more but have not yet applied for benefits, you may still be eligible for some back payments. But if you wait longer than fourteen months after you recover to apply, you will not be eligible for any back benefits.

Under recent amendments in the law, an application for disability benefits can now be filed after the death of a disabled worker. If the claim is approved, back payments may be made for some months preceding the worker's death. The application for back payments must be filed within three months after the death of the worker. In addition, survivors' benefits may be payable, beginning with the month the worker died.

The five-month waiting period does not apply to a person disabled before age twenty-two. He or she may receive benefits beginning with the month the parent's retirement or disability payments begin or the month the insured parent dies.

Benefit payments may continue as long as you remain unable to work. As a general rule, the benefits will stop if you marry while you are receiving benefits as a person disabled in childhood or as a disabled widow or widower. In some cases, however, they

can be continued. You can get more information on these exceptions from your Social Security office.

Disability vs. retirement benefits

You cannot collect disability benefits while you are receiving
benefits from other Social Security programs. If you become entitled to more than one monthly benefit at the same time, the
amount you receive ordinarily will be equal to the larger of the
benefits.

If you become disabled after you begin receiving Social Security benefits (such as for early retirement), it may be to your advantage to switch to benefits based on your disability. If, for example,
you begin receiving reduced retirement benefits at age sixty-two,
and then become disabled at age sixty-three, your payments
probably would be higher if you switched to the disability program.

You should know, however, that if the payments you were
receiving before you became disabled were for a reduced retirement benefit or a reduced widow's benefit, your disability benefits also will be reduced to take into account the number of
months you received the other benefits. But even with this reduction, your disability payments may be higher than the other
benefits you were receiving.

The tables on pages 231–247 can give you a comparison of the
monthly payments in different categories. Your local Social Security office also can give you specific amounts of benefits in your
particular situation.

Returning to work

If you are receiving disability benefits, you are required by law
to notify the Social Security Administration if your condition im-
proves or if you return to work, no matter how little you earn.
This can be done by sending in a postcard form which you will be
given when your claim for disability benefits is approved. Or you
can write, visit, or telephone your Social Security office.

Be assured, however, that you will not automatically be cut off
from further benefits. If medical evidence shows that your condition has improved so much that you are no longer disabled, you
still will receive benefits for a three-month period of adjustment.
This period includes the month in which your condition im-

proved and two additional months. Only then will benefits be stopped.

If you return to work in spite of a severe condition, you will continue to be paid during a trial work period of up to nine months, which need not be consecutive months. This period will give you a chance to test your ability to work. If, after nine months, it is decided that you are able to do substantial gainful work, your benefits will be paid for an adjustment period of three additional months.

Thus, if you go back to work in spite of your disability, you may continue to receive disability benefits for up to twelve months, even though the work is substantial gainful work. If it is decided that the work you are able to do is not substantial and gainful, you would continue to receive your regular benefits. Should your condition improve so that it is no longer disabling, your benefits would be stopped after a three-month adjustment period even though your trial work period might not be over.

This trial work provision does not apply to a disabled widow, disabled widower, or disabled surviving divorced wife. If persons in these categories begin to do substantial gainful work, benefits will stop three months after the work begins.

What happens if you go back to work, and become disabled for a second time?

If this occurs within five years after your benefits as a disabled worker had stopped because you returned to work or recovered, then your benefits can begin with the first full month in which you are disabled.

The period allowed is seven years for a disabled widow, disabled widower, disabled surviving divorced wife, or a person disabled before age twenty-two. Another five-month waiting period is not required for disabled workers, disabled widows, or disabled widowers. Thus the payment of benefits for these categories can begin right away. But you are not eligible for a trial work period.

You are not subject to the general rule (such as for the retirement program) under which some benefits are withheld if you have substantial earnings. This is because of the special rules for determining how any work you do might affect your disability payments.

But if you are a disabled worker and one of your dependents, who is not disabled, works and has earnings above a certain level, some of that dependent's benefits may be withheld. This level of earnings varies from year to year, so for the latest information you should contact your nearest Social Security office.

The number of persons receiving disability payments pushed toward the five-million mark in 1978, and the annual payments reached about $11.5 billion, causing some members of Congress to express concern about "runaway expansion" of the program. This concern could lead to tougher eligibility requirements in the years ahead.

How to apply for disability benefits

If you think you are entitled to disability benefits, contact your local Social Security office. You will be given a four-page form to fill out, and you will be asked to provide medical evidence to support your claim. This usually is a report from your doctor, hospital, or clinic giving the medical history of your condition: what the doctors have found wrong with you, how severe it is, what medical tests have shown, and what treatment you have received. Your doctors are not asked to decide whether you are disabled under the Social Security law.

After all the forms have been completed and the medical evidence collected, the Social Security office will send the full record to an agency in your state—usually the vocational rehabilitation agency.

All the facts in your file will be considered by a team of trained people in the state agency—including a physician and a disability evaluation specialist. Additional medical information may be needed to determine whether you are disabled under the law. If this information is not available in the records of your family physician or from a hospital or clinic where you have been treated, you may be asked to undergo additional medical examinations and tests at government expense.

Based on all the information, the state agency will make a decision on whether you are disabled under the Social Security law. As soon as a decision is reached in your case, the Social Security Administration will advise you.

The Social Security Administration's rules for deciding whether you are disabled are different from the rules of some other government and private disability programs. For instance, you may be considered disabled under Veterans Administration regulations, but still not meet Social Security criteria. However, the report of any examination made for another agency as well as the decision of that agency may be considered in deciding your eligibility for disability benefits under Social Security.

Other assistance

Even if you are ruled ineligible for Social Security disability benefits, you may be offered help in improving your condition and in preparing for and finding work.

When you submit an application for Social Security disability benefits, you will be considered for vocational rehabilitation services by your state agency. Information in your file is made available to help the specialists in that agency decide whether you can benefit from rehabilitation services and, if so, what kinds of services will be most useful in helping you to return to work.

These counseling, training, and other services usually are financed by a combination of federal and state funds. But in some cases, Social Security will pay the costs of rehabilitating individuals receiving disability benefits, acting on the theory that, in the long run, the cost of rehabilitation is less than the expense of paying benefits. In addition, you may also receive employment counseling and special placement services from your state employment service.

Persons entitled to benefits because of disability will not be paid those benefits if, without good cause, they refuse counseling, training, or other services offered by their state vocational rehabilitation agencies.

If your claim is rejected

If your application for Social Security benefits is turned down, you may appeal the decision through the following steps.

1. *Reconsideration.* This is a complete review of your claim by officials other than those who made the original decision. You may submit new evidence, which will be considered along with the evidence you originally submitted. The request for reconsideration must be filed within sixty days from the date you receive the notice of the first decision.

2. *A Hearing.* If, after reconsideration, your claim is rejected again you may ask for a hearing before an administrative law

judge, who is an attorney in the Bureau of Hearings and Appeals of the Social Security Administration. This hearing, which has the atmosphere of an informal court proceeding, usually is held in the city where the Social Security office that processed your claim is located. The administrative law judge (who formerly was called a hearing examiner) will review evidence previously submitted and examine any new evidence. Witnesses may be called to testify under oath. You can represent yourself or be represented by a person of your choice. A request for a hearing must be filed within sixty days from the date you receive the notice of the reconsideration decision.

3. *Appeals Council Review.* If your claim remains rejected after a hearing, you have sixty days in which to ask for a review by the Appeals Council, located in Washington, D.C. The council will decide whether or not to review the decision of the administrative law judge. If the council accepts your case, you can present new evidence and file a written statement. When the case is decided, a copy of the written decision will be mailed to you.

4. *Court Action.* If the Appeals Council refuses to review your case or if it makes a review and decides against you, then you may bring suit in a federal district court. That is your last resort. Your complaint must be filed in a district court of the United States within sixty days from the date of the mailing of the notice of the Appeals Council decision or denial of review.

CHAPTER 16

If
You Need
Medical
Care

The U.S. Congress in 1965 enacted a broad program of health insurance, known as Medicare, for people sixty-five years of age and older, and in 1972 provided this protection for some people under the age of sixty-five who are disabled.

A decade after Medicare was introduced, Congress was debating whether it should enact a national health insurance program for all Americans.

We will first discuss how the Medicare program can help you save on medical and hospital costs, and how you can make sure that you receive the full benefits. Then we will review the major proposals for national health insurance to give you an indication of what might be available in the years ahead.

Medicare—the basics

Medicare has two parts. One is hospital insurance and is known as Part A. The other is medical insurance, known as Part B.

In general, all persons eligible for Social Security or railroad retirement cash benefits are eligible for free coverage under Part A of Medicare when they reach age sixty-five, regardless of past or present income.

Part B, which is optional coverage, involves a monthly premium. This premium is $7.70 a month, but it can increase as medical costs rise.

Part A coverage also can be purchased by those who do not qualify under Social Security eligibility. The premium through June 30, 1978, is $54 a month. This sum also may go up as costs of hospital care increase.

The vast majority of Americans over the age of sixty-five are automatically eligible for the program.

Persons who are retired because of disability also are considered eligible. And there is a special provision for individuals who need certain kidney therapy.

Unlike Social Security retirement benefits, there is no provision for scaled-down benefits before the age of sixty-five.

Hospital insurance can help pay for inpatient care in a hospital, and, after a hospital stay, for inpatient care in a skilled nursing facility and for care in your home by a home health agency.

Medical insurance can help pay for necessary doctor's services, outpatient hospital services, outpatient physical therapy, and a number of other medical services and supplies not covered by the hospital insurance portion of Medicare.

Medicare does not cover all costs. The amounts or the share of the costs for which you are responsible will be discussed in the following pages.

If you cannot pay these amounts or for other health services, you may be able to receive assistance from the Medicaid program in your state.

The Social Security Administration operates the Medicare program. The actual payments are handled by private insurance companies under contract with the government. For that reason, claims are filed with these private companies—not with the Social Security Administration.

When you enroll in Medicare, you will receive a card in the mail. This card shows the Medicare protection that you have (hospital insurance, medical insurance, or both) and the date your protection began. The card also shows your health insurance

Government Outlays for Health

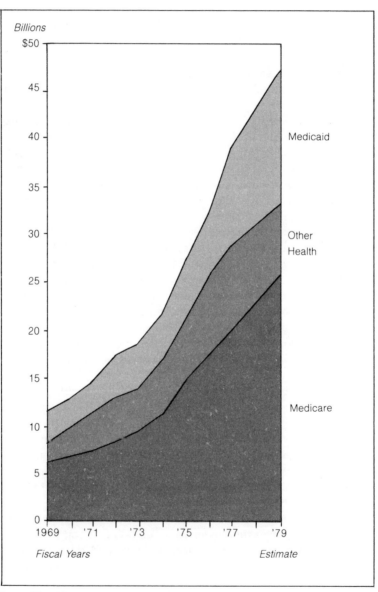

Billions

Medicaid

Other
Health

Medicare

1969   '71   '73   '75   '77   '79

Fiscal Years   *Estimate*

Source: Office of Management and Budget

claim number. Be sure to put this claim number on all Medicare claims and correspondence. If a husband and wife both have Medicare, they receive separate cards and different claim numbers. Each must use the exact claim number shown on his or her card.

What is not covered

There are two important rules to bear in mind: Medicare does not cover care that is not "reasonable and necessary" for the treatment of an illness or injury; and it does not cover care that is "custodial."

The Social Security Administration explains the first rule this way:

"If a doctor places you in a hospital or skilled nursing facility when the kind of care you need could be provided elsewhere, your stay would not be considered reasonable and necessary. So Medicare could not cover your stay. If you stay in a hospital or skilled nursing facility longer than you need to be there, Medicare payments would end at the time further inpatient care is no longer reasonable and necessary."

Each hospital and skilled nursing facility has a utilization review committee, composed of at least two doctors, to help Medicare decide whether inpatient care is reasonable and necessary.

As for the second rule, Social Security offers this explanation:

"Care is considered custodial when it is primarily for the purpose of meeting personal needs and could be provided by persons without professional skills and training; for example, help in walking, getting in and out of bed, bathing, dressing, eating, and taking medicine. Even if you are in a participating hospital or skilled nursing facility or you are receiving care from a participating home health agency, Medicare does not cover your care if it is mainly custodial."

Hospital insurance

Medicare hospital insurance will pay for most—but not all—of the services you receive in a hospital or skilled nursing facility or from a home health agency. There is, however, a limit on how many days of care qualify in each "benefit period." A benefit period is a way of measuring your use of services under Medicare's hospital insurance. Your first benefit period commences the first time you enter a hospital after your hospital insurance begins. When you have been out of a hospital (or other facility primarily providing skilled nursing or rehabilitation services) for at least sixty consecutive days, a new benefit period begins the next time you are admitted as a hospital patient. There is no limit to the number of benefit periods you can have.

When you are in the hospital, Medicare can help pay for your care if all of these four conditions are met:

1. A doctor prescribes inpatient hospital care for treatment of an illness or injury.

2. You require the kind of care that can be provided only in a hospital.

3. The hospital is participating in Medicare.

4. The utilization review committee of the hospital does not disapprove your stay.

If these four conditions are met, then your stay in a hospital is covered by Medicare. But you still are responsible in 1978 for the first $144 of hospital charges in each benefit period. This is known as the "hospital insurance deductible." Once that deductible is exceeded, Medicare will pay for all other covered services for up to sixty days if your medical condition requires that you remain in the hospital that long. From the sixty-first through the ninetieth day, hospital insurance pays for all covered services except for $36 a day.

If you need more than ninety days of inpatient hospital care in a benefit period, you may use what are called "reserve days." Everyone participating in the Medicare program has sixty reserve days. You are responsible for no more than $72 a day for each reserve day you use. But once you use a reserve day it is permanently subtracted from your original total of sixty. Reserve days are not renewable like your ninety hospital days in each benefit period.

Here are some examples of the major services covered by Medicare while you are in a hospital:

- A semiprivate room (two to four beds in a room)
- All your meals, including special diets
- Regular nursing services
- Intensive-care unit costs
- Drugs furnished by the hospital during your stay
- Laboratory tests included in your hospital bill

- X-rays and other radiology services, including radiation therapy, billed by the hospital
  - Medical supplies such as casts, surgical dressings, and splints
  - Use of appliances such as a wheelchair
  - Operating and recovery room costs
  - Rehabilitation services, such as physical therapy, occupational therapy, and speech pathology services

Medicare will not pay for personal convenience items such as a television set, radio, or telephone that you request for your hospital room. Nor will it pay for private-duty nurses; nor for any extra charges for a private room, unless you need it for medical reasons.

After you leave the hospital, Medicare can help pay for your inpatient care in a participating skilled nursing facility. But all five of these conditions must be met:

1. You have been in a hospital at least three consecutive days before you transfer to the skilled nursing facility.

2. You are transferred to a skilled nursing facility because you require care for a condition that was treated in the hospital.

3. You are admitted to the facility within a short time (usually fourteen days) after you leave the hospital.

4. A doctor certifies that you need, and you actually receive, skilled nursing or skilled rehabilitation services on a daily basis.

5. The facility's utilization review committee does not disapprove your stay.

Skilled nursing care means services that can be performed only by, or under the supervision of, licensed nursing personnel. Skilled rehabilitation services may include, for example, physical therapy performed by, or under the supervision of, a professional therapist. The skilled nursing care and skilled rehabilitation services you receive must be under the general direction of a doctor.

As noted earlier, Medicare will not pay for your stay if you are in a skilled nursing facility mainly because you need custodial care. And it will not pay for your stay if you need skilled nursing or rehabilitation services on an occasional basis, such as once or twice a week.

Medicare will help pay for your care in a skilled nursing facility for up to 100 days in each benefit period. During the first twenty days of your stay, Medicare pays for all covered services. For the twenty-first through the hundredth day, it pays the cost of all covered services except for $18 a day.

If you leave a skilled nursing facility but are readmitted within fourteen days, you do not have to have a new three-day stay in the hospital for your care to be covered, so long as you have some of your hundred days left.

Hospital insurance does not cover your doctor's services while you are in a hospital or skilled nursing facility. But those expenses can be covered by Medicare's medical insurance.

Medical insurance

Medicare's medical insurance (also known as Part B) can help pay for doctors' services, outpatient hospital care, outpatient physical therapy and speech pathology services, home health care, and many other health services and supplies which are not covered by Medicare's hospital insurance.

As a general rule, after you have $60 of covered medical expenses in a calendar year, your medical insurance will pay 80 percent of the reasonable charges for any additional covered services you receive during the rest of that year. You need to meet the $60 medical insurance deductible only once in a calendar year, and you can do so with any combination of covered expenses. You do not need to meet a separate deductible for each kind of covered service you might receive.

There also is a "carryover rule," which the Social Security Administration explains this way: "If you have covered medical expenses in the last three months of a year that can be counted toward your $60 deductible for that year, they can also be counted toward your $60 deductible for the next year." Your local Social Security office can give you more information if you think the carryover rule might apply in your case.

Medical insurance can help pay for covered services you receive from your doctor in his or her office, in a hospital, in a skilled nursing facility, in your home, or in any other location in the United States. Payment can be made either to you or to your doctor.

Here are some examples of doctors' services for which your medical insurance will pay 80 percent of the reasonable charges after you meet the $60 annual deductible:

- Medical and surgical services

• Diagnostic tests and procedures that are part of your treatment

• Other services which are ordinarily furnished in the doctor's office and included in the bill, such as X-rays you receive as part of your treatment, services of your doctor's office nurse, drugs and biologicals that cannot be self-administered, medical supplies, physical therapy, and speech pathology services

Some of the doctor's services that are *not* covered by medical insurance include routine physical examinations, eye or hearing examinations for prescibing or fitting eyeglasses or hearing aids, immunizations unless required because of an injury or immediate risk of infection, and cosmetic surgery unless it is needed because of accidental injury or to improve the functioning of a malformed part of the body.

Medicare law also has some special clauses you should be aware of. They include:

• *Radiology and Pathology Services by Doctors.* While you are an inpatient in a hospital, medical insurance pays 100 percent of the reasonable charges for services by doctors in the fields of radiology and pathology, even if you have not met your $60 deductible for the year.

• *Outpatient Treatment of Mental Illness.* Doctors' services you receive for outpatient treatment of mental illness are covered, but medical insurance can pay no more than $250 in any one year for these services.

• *Chiropractors' Services.* Medical insurance helps pay for only one kind of treatment furnished by a licensed and Medicare-certified chiropractor. The only treatment that can be covered is manual manipulation of the spine to correct a subluxation that can be demonstrated by X-ray. Medical insurance does not pay for the X-ray or for any other diagnostic or therapeutic services furnished by a chiropractor.

• *Podiatrists' Services.* Medical insurance can help pay for any covered services for a licensed podiatrist, except for routine foot care. Routine foot care includes hygienic care; teatment for flat feet or other structural misalignments of the feet; and removal of corns, warts, and calluses. However, medical insurance can help pay for routine foot care if you have a medical condition affecting the lower limbs, such as severe diabetes, which requires that such care be performed by a podiatrist or a doctor.

• *Dental Care.* Medical insurance can help pay for dental care only if it involves surgery of the jaw or related structures or setting fractures of the jaw or facial bones. Care in connection with the treatment, filling, removing, or replacing of teeth, root-canal therapy, surgery for impacted teeth, and other surgical procedures involving the teeth or structures directly supporting teeth are not covered.

If you are treated at a participating hospital as an outpatient, Medicare helps pay for such expenses as emergency-room services, laboratory tests billed by the hospital, X-rays and other radiology services billed by the hospital, medical supplies such as splints and casts, and drugs which cannot be self-administered.

Medicare also will help you pay for other services and supplies. They include:

• *Independent Laboratory Services.* Diagnostic tests, including X-rays, provided by independent laboratories may be covered. The laboratory must be certified by Medicare for the services you receive. Not all laboratories are certified by Medicare, and some labs are certified only for certain kinds of tests. Your doctor can usually tell you what laboratories are certified and whether the tests being prescribed are covered by Medicare.

• *Ambulance Transportation.* Medicare can help pay for ambulance transportation only if two requirements are met: first, that the ambulance, equipment, and personnel meet Medicare standards; and second, transportation in any other vehicle could endanger the patient's health. Usually, ambulance transportation is covered only in your local area. But if there are no facilities in your area equipped to provide the care you need, Medicare will help pay for necessary ambulance transportation to the closest facility outside your local area that can provide the necessary care.

• *Prosthetic Devices.* Medical insurance helps pay for prosthetic devices needed to substitute for an internal body organ. Examples are heart pacemakers, corrective lenses needed after cataract operation, and colostomy or ileostomy bags and certain related supplies. Medical insurance can also help pay for artificial limbs and eyes, and for arm, leg, back, and neck braces. Dental plates and other dental devices are not covered.

• *Durable Medical Equipment.* Medicare will help pay for durable medical equipment such as oxygen equipment, wheelchairs, home dialysis systems, and other medically necessary equipment that your doctor prescribes for use in your home. You can rent or buy this equipment. In either case, Medicare usually makes its payments monthly. If you rent, the medical insurance will help pay the reasonable rental charges for as long as the equipment is medically necessary. If you buy, regardless of whether you pay for the equipment in a lump sum or in installments, Medicare will make monthly payments until its share of the reasonable purchase price is paid or until the equipment is no longer medically necessary, whichever comes first.

• *Medical Supplies.* Medical insurance can help pay for surgical dressings, splints, casts, and similar supplies ordered by a doctor in connection with your medical treatment. This does not include adhesive tape, antiseptics, or other first-aid supplies.

Home health care

Sometimes people are confined to their homes because of an illness or injury and need skilled health services only on a part-time basis. In such cases, either hospital insurance or medical insurance can help pay for covered services furnished by home health agencies. The Social Security Administration defines home health agencies this way: "A public or private agency that specializes in giving skilled nursing services and other therapeutic services, such as physical therapy, in your home."

Medicare does not cover home services furnished primarily to assist people in meeting personal, family, and domestic needs. For instance, it would not pay for such services as general housekeeping, preparing meals, shopping, or assistance in bathing.

It does, however, cover part-time skilled nursing care, physical therapy, speech therapy, occupational therapy, and medical supplies and equipment provided by the home health agency.

When care in your home is covered by Medicare, the services you receive are counted in "visits." For example, if you receive one home health service twice in the same day, or two different home health services in the same day, two visits would be counted.

The hospital insurance portion of Medicare can pay for home health visits if all six of these conditions are met:

1. You were in a participating hospital for at least three consecutive days.

2. The home health care is for further treatment of a condition that was treated in a hospital or skilled nursing facility.

3. The care you need includes part-time skilled nursing care, physical therapy, or speech therapy.

4. You are confined to your home.

5. A doctor determines that you need home health care and sets up a home health plan for you within fourteen days after your discharge from a hospital or skilled nursing facility.

6. The home health agency providing services is participating in Medicare.

If these six conditions are met, hospital insurance can pay for the full cost of up to 100 home health visits during the twelve months after your discharge from a hospital or participating skilled nursing facility.

If you do not meet the first two conditions, but meet the other four, you still may be eligible for assistance under the medical insurance portion of Medicare. And medical insurance also can pay for up to 100 home health care visits in a calendar year if this care is still needed after you have used up the 100 visits covered under hospital insurance. After you meet the $60 yearly deductible, medical insurance pays the full costs for covered home services in each calendar year.

Methods of payment

There are two ways that payments are made under Medicare's medical insurance. One way is to pay you directly. The other way is for the payment to go to the doctor or the supplier of services. This latter payment method is called "assignment," and you should be aware of special rules concerning it.

When a doctor or supplier accepts an assignment of the medical insurance payment, he or she also agrees to accept what Medicare calls the "reasonable charge" as the total charge to you for covered services. Medicare pays your doctor or supplier 80 percent of the reasonable charges, after subtracting any part of the $60 deductible you have not met. The doctor or supplier using the "assignment" method cannot charge you more than the remaining 20 percent of the reasonable charges, plus any part of the $60 deductible you have not met and the costs of non-covered services.

Because of the way in which Medicare calculates the "reasonable charges," the doctor's bill may be higher than what Medicare will pay. This might be the case, for example, if the doctor recently raised the charge and it has not been in effect long enough to be included in Medicare's annual review. For this reason, you may want to find out in advance whether the doctor or supplier will accept assignment. If he or she will not, Medicare will make direct payment to you covering 80 percent of the reasonable charges, after subtracting any part of the $60 deductible you have not met. You are responsible for the balance of the doctor's or supplier's bill.

How to submit a bill

To file a claim, you must fill out a "Request for Medicare Payment" form, also called Form 1490. All Social Security offices and most doctors' offices have copies of the form. Instructions on how to fill it out are on the back of the form.

If the doctor or supplier is willing to use the assignment method of payment, he or she submits the claim. You complete and sign Part I of the form. The doctor or supplier completes Part II and sends in the form.

If the doctor or supplier does not accept assignment, you submit the form so that payment will be made directly to you. Complete and sign Part I of the form. Ask the person who provided the services either to complete Part II of the form or to give you an itemized bill to send in with the form. An itemized bill must show:

1. The date you received the services.
2. The place where you received the services.
3. A description of the services.
4. The nature of your illness or injury (diagnosis).
5. The charge for each service.
6. Your name and your health insurance claim number, including the letter at the end of the number.

If the bill does not include all of this information, your payment may be delayed.

You may submit a number of itemized bills with a single "Request for Medicare Payment" form. It does not matter whether all the bills are from one doctor or supplier or from several.

Before the Medicare payment can be made, your record must show that you have met the annual $60 deductible. So, as soon as

Public Health Expenditures Increase

Fiscal Year 1965
$38.9 Billion

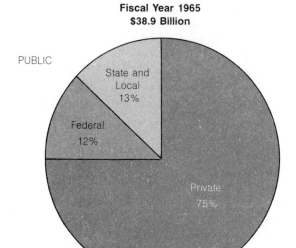

PUBLIC

State and
Local
13%

Federal
12%

Private
75%

Fiscal Year 1976
$139.3 Billion

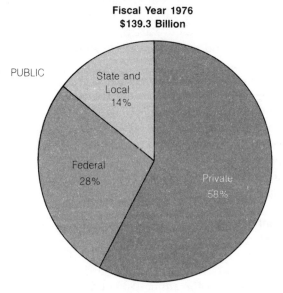

PUBLIC

State and
Local
14%

Federal
28%

Private
58%

Source: Office of Management and Budget

your bills total $60, send them to the private company that handles your medical insurance claims with a "Request for Medicare Payment" form. After you have met the $60 deductible, it is a good idea to send in bills for covered services as soon as you receive them so that the Medicare payment can be made promptly.

After you or the doctor or supplier sends in a claim, Medicare will send you an "Explanation of Medicare Benefits Notice." This notice shows what expenses were covered, what charges were approved, how much was credited toward your $60 deductible, and the amount Medicare paid. If there is anything you do not understand, you can get an explanation from your local Social Security office.

If you disagree with a decision on the amount Medicare will pay on a claim or whether services you received are covered by Medicare, you have the right to ask for a review of the decision. Any Social Security office can help you request such a review.

Medicaid

A companion to the Medicare program is Medicaid, a grant-in-aid program under which the federal government pays part of the costs incurred by states in providing medical services to persons who are unable to pay for such care. The federal government pays from 50 to 81 percent of the costs, depending on the per-capita income in the state.

Each state has the primary responsibility for administering its Medicaid program, although federal officials must approve each state's plan. The services provided to Medicaid recipients vary among states. So do eligibility requirements. But generally, Medicaid is intended to pay the health care costs for persons who are receiving public assistance. And, as a minimum, all states must provide inpatient and outpatient hospital services, laboratory and X-ray services, skilled nursing services, home health services, early and periodic screening of those under age twelve, family planning services, and physician services.

Your state or local public assistance office can give you more details on your state's Medicaid program.

National health insurance

A decade after Congress enacted the Medicare program, its

members were debating whether there should be a comprehensive national health insurance program. The debate was likely to continue for the years ahead—it was under way more than thirty years previously when President Harry S Truman promoted the idea.

Congress has examined the national health insurance issue extensively in recent years, but no legislative agreement emerged. Most of the advocates seemed to accept the idea of making uniform health insurance coverage available to all U.S. citizens, but the debate centered on the role of the federal government—a subject closely tied to the cost and administration of any national plan.

In general, liberal Democrats and organized labor favored a comprehensive, federally operated program financed in part from payroll taxes. Groups representing doctors, hospitals, and insurance companies, supported by such Republicans as Gerald Ford, preferred private financing and administration of the basic portion of a national plan. Some conservatives objected to any further federal encroachment into the health care field. The eventual outcome of the debate remains muddled.

17

If
a Member
of Your
Family
Dies

Through several programs, the U.S. government pays billions of dollars in benefits to the dependents and survivors of American citizens who die.

If the deceased was a veteran, cash aid may be paid by the Veterans Administration, as was discussed in chapter 7. If the deceased was a worker covered by Social Security, the benefits are paid by monthly checks from the Social Security Administration.

The life insurance aspects of government programs can be especially important to a young worker who has a growing family. If he dies, the monthly benefit checks could mean the difference between his family struggling in poverty or having an adequate standard of living. In fact, some families may be able to collect a quarter of a million dollars or more in Social Security survivors' benefits.

Young parents generally do not like to think about the possibili-

ty of their children becoming orphans. Yet they should be aware
of these stark statistics:

• There are an estimated 3.4 million orphans under the age of
eighteen in the United States—or about 5 percent of the total
child population.

• Since women usually outlive their husbands, the financial
burdens often fall hardest on widows. Of all orphans in this country, about 70 percent have lost only their fathers. About 26
percent have lost only their mothers. About 2.5 percent—or approximately 85,000 children—have lost both parents.

According to statistics, the chances are 46 in 1,000 that a child
born to a father who is twenty-five years of age will be orphaned
by the time he or she is eighteen. If the father is thirty-five when
the child is born, the chances are twice as great. And nearly one
of every four children born to fathers forty-five years old will be
orphans before they reach their eighteenth birthday.

Because of statistics like these, the concept of Social Security
was expanded many years ago from a simple retirement program
to one providing for dependents of a worker who dies. Now
about twenty cents of every dollar collected in Social Security
taxes is paid out as protection for survivors.

Like the retirement program, you must have a certain amount
of work credit before benefits can be paid to your survivors. As
the table on page 211 shows, the minimum needed to qualify is
one and one-half years of work credits. The maximum required is
ten years of credits. (The credits are calculated in the same way
as for retirement benefits. This was explained in chapter 14.)

Having enough work credits to be fully insured means only
that your survivors are eligible for benefits. It does not govern the
amount of the benefits. That depends on your average earnings.

Who receives benefits?

If you die insured—in other words, if you have enough Social
Security work credits—the following members of your family
may be eligible for benefits, regardless of your age at death:

• Your widow aged sixty or older, or if disabled, aged fifty or
over.

• Your widow, regardless of her age, if she is caring for your
children under age eighteen or for an older disabled child who is
eligible for benefits.

Work Credit for Survivors' Benefits

Born After 1929, Die at Age	Born Before 1930, Die Before Age 62 in	Years of Work Credit You Need
28 or younger		1½
30		2
32		2½
34		3
36		3½
38		4
40		4½
42		5
44		5½
46		6
48	1977	6½
50	1979	7
52	1981	7½
54	1983	8
56	1985	8½
58	1987	9
60	1989	9½
62 or older	1991 or later	10

• Your unmarried, dependent children under the age of eighteen, or under twenty-two if they are full-time students.

• Your disabled child eighteen years old or over if the disability began before age twenty-two.

• Your parents, if they are sixty-two or older and were dependent upon you at the time of your death.

Checks also can go to a surviving divorced widow at age sixty, or to a disabled surviving divorced widow at age fifty—but only if the marriage lasted ten years or more. Children also may be eligible for Social Security survivors' benefits based on a grandparent's earnings under certain conditions.

Determining benefits

The monthly benefits for your survivors are geared to your "primary insurance amount." This is the equivalent of the amount you would have received if you had reached age sixty-five.

To determine your average monthly income, follow the same steps outlined in the chapter on retirement benefits. Then consult the tables on pages 240–247 to get an idea of the size of the monthly checks.

Here is how the figures in the tables are calculated:

• *Your Widow.* A widow who begins receiving benefits at age sixty-five or later is entitled to an amount equal to 100 percent of her husband's primary benefit, unless her husband already had been receiving benefits. If so, the widow's benefits are limited to the amount her husband would receive if he were still alive.

Your widow can begin receiving benefits at age sixty, but they will be reduced to take account of the longer period over which they will be paid. The benefits are reduced 19/40th of 1 percent for each month below age sixty-five. Thus, a widow at age sixty would receive 71.5 percent of the amount she would receive if she were sixty-five. At age sixty-two, her benefits would equal 82.9 percent of the primary insurance amount. At sixty-three, it would be 88.6 percent. At sixty-four, it would be 94.3 percent.

Beginning in 1978, if a widow remarries after age sixty, her benefits will not be reduced. Formerly, she could receive benefits equal to only 50 percent of her deceased spouse's primary insurance amount. If a widow who remarries is also entitled to a wife's benefit, she will receive only the larger of the two payments.

The provisions covering widows now also apply to widowers.

• *Your Widow Under Sixty-Two With Children.* If your widow is younger than sixty-two and is caring for one or more of your eligible dependent or disabled children, she is eligible for a monthly benefit equal to 75 percent of your primary benefit. This is known as the "mother's benefit."

Unless one of the children in her care is totally disabled, benefits would stop when the youngest child reaches age eighteen or marries. Then she would not be able to begin receiving benefits again before age sixty, creating what is known as "the widow's gap." Her benefits will also stop if she remarries before age sixty.

• *Your Children.* Each of your unmarried, dependent children under the age of eighteen is entitled to benefits equal to 75 percent of your primary insurance amount. A child's benefits can continue until age twenty-two if he or she is a full-time student in a public or accredited school, including a college or a vocational school. Payments also continue after age eighteen if the child is disabled before reaching the age of twenty-two.

• *Your Parents.* If your parents received at least one-half of their support from you, they are entitled to survivors' benefits at age sixty-two. Each parent who qualifies is entitled to an amount equal to 75 percent of your primary insurance amount. But if only one parent collects benefits, he or she will receive an amount equal to 82.5 percent of your primary benefit. Your parents have two years after your death to prove they were dependent on you.

A dependent parent who is entitled to retirement benefits based on his or her own work record would receive whichever is higher—the retirement benefit or the benefit as a dependent parent; he or she could not receive both.

• *Lump-Sum Death Payment.* Upon your death, your widow or widower may be eligible for a lump-sum death payment of $255. To qualify, you and your spouse must have been living in the same household when you died. Otherwise, the lump-sum benefit can be paid to the funeral home for any part of the burial expenses that have not been paid. If the funeral home has been paid in full, then the death benefit may go to reimburse whoever paid the burial expenses. Application for this benefit must be made within two years of the death.

Ceiling on family benefits

As with retirement benefits, the "maximum family benefit" places a ceiling on the amount that can be paid each month to your survivors.

The maximum family benefit is roughly equal to the amount that would be paid to a widow with two dependent children. A family with three or more dependent children would receive the same amount as a family with two.

The mother would receive two checks a month—one for her benefits and the other for her children's benefits. Both checks would be made out to her. The checks would begin arriving six to eight weeks after the application had been filed.

Higher benefits for younger families

You should be aware of the fact that younger families in some cases receive higher survivors' benefits than older families. This results from the periodic increases in the level of earnings which can be credited to your Social Security account each year.

Suppose you are a man twenty-six years old. To qualify your family for survivors' benefits you need only two years of credited work. If you had died in 1977 those two years could have been 1975 and 1976. In 1975 your earnings under Social Security could have been $14,100. In 1976 they could have been $15,300. Those were the ceilings for those two years.

Thus, for Social Security purposes, your earnings would have averaged $14,700, entitling your wife and two children to the highest possible benefit.

But suppose you are a forty-six-year-old man. To qualify your family for survivors' benefits, you would need nineteen years of earnings. If you had died in 1977 those nineteen years could have been from 1958 through 1976. For the first of those years, 1958, the maximum earnings for which you could receive credit were $4,200. The maximum was $4,800 for 1959–65; $6,600 for 1966–67; $7,800 for 1968–71; $9,000 for 1972; $10,800 for 1973; $13,200 for 1974; $14,100 for 1975; and $15,300 for 1976.

The average for the nineteen years would have been $7,610, considerably less than the $14,700 of the younger man in the previous example.

Thus, the family of the older man would not receive as much in monthly benefits as the family of the younger man.

An example

To illustrate what Social Security benefits can mean for your family, here is the hypothetical example of Joe Jones.

Mr. Jones died in June 1977 at the age of twenty-eight, leaving a wife aged twenty-seven and three children ages one, three, and five. His average earnings for Social Security purposes were $10,000.

His primary insurance amount under rates prevailing at that time was $502. His widow was entitled to three-fourths of this amount in survivor's benefits, or $376.50 per month. Since each of the three children also was entitled to benefits, the family easily qualified for a maximum family benefit of $878.50 a month.

Mrs. Jones and the children would collect this amount for fifteen years, until the two oldest children were over eighteen and off the rolls. During those fifteen years, benefits would total $158,130.

Then, during the next two years, the youngest child would collect his three-fourths of his father's primary insurance benefit which, together with his mother's equal benefit, would add up to $753 per month, or a total of $18,072 for those two years.

Mrs. Jones's benefits would then stop, but assuming the youngest child went to college, he would be entitled to his benefit of $376.50 a month for the four years until he was twenty-two years old. That amounts to $18,072.

The widow would not be entitled to more benefits until she reached age sixty. For Mrs. Jones, that "widow's gap" would be sixteen years—from the time she was forty-four and the youngest child turned eighteen until she was sixty when she could qualify for widow's benefits of $359 a month.

Assuming that she lived until age eighty-one (a woman's life expectancy at age sixty is twenty-one years), she would receive a total of $90,468.

That means that through the years, based on benefits being paid at the time of Mr. Jones's death, the family would receive, including the lump-sum death payment, a total of almost $285,000 in benefits.

Because of the cost-of-living clause, Social Security survivors' benefits are to be raised automatically each year if the cost of living increases by 3 percent or more. So the Jones family in all likelihood would collect even more than $285,000.

How to apply

Like retirement benefits, survivors' benefits are not automatic. You have to apply for them so that the checks can begin arriving every month.

If your town lacks a Social Security office, someone at your local post office can provide the address of the nearest one or can tell you when a Social Security representative will be in your area.

Social Security representatives will assist you in filling out the applications and help you gather the necessary documents to submit with the applications. They also will answer any questions you might have.

18

If
Disaster
Strikes

If a natural disaster—a hurricane, tornado, earthquake, or flood—strikes your home or business, the federal government has scores of programs to help you recover from the damage. These programs offer low-cost loans and such other assistance as temporary housing.

In addition to after-the-fact aid, the government offers programs such as flood insurance which are intended to ease the financial blow if disaster strikes. There also is low-cost crime insurance for businesses in certain areas.

Physical disaster loans

Individuals, business concerns, churches, private schools, colleges, and universities are eligible to apply for physical disaster loans administered by the Small Business Administration. The loans are intended to restore, repair, or replace damaged or destroyed household and other personal property as well as realty, machinery, and equipment. These loans are not available to persons engaged in agriculture and no part of the funds can be used for agricultural purposes. There are other loan programs, however, especially designed to help farmers recover from natural disasters, as will be discussed later.

To qualify for physical disaster loans, applicants must have suffered property loss as a result of a disaster that occurred in an area designated as eligible for assistance by the government. In addition to floods and other natural disasters, such occurrences as riots and civil disturbances can result in a disaster declaration.

An applicant must provide proof of the loss, to the extent possible, and a list of realty and personal property to be repaired or replaced. Financial statements and, in some cases, copies of the applicant's latest income tax returns also must be presented.

For direct home loans, there is a $55,000 limit. But in some cases, an additional $50,000 can be lent to refinance existing liens. Direct business loans cannot exceed $500,000. In addition to direct loans, additional amounts are available as guaranteed loans made by financial institutions. In most cases, the loans are made for thirty years. Interest rates vary, but for direct loans they generally are less than the market rate.

How to apply: Applications are made on a standard form, regardless of whether it is a home or business loan, and are submitted to the nearest SBA office or special disaster office. Eligibility to file ends two months from the date of the disaster declaration, unless this deadline is extended.

Economic injury disaster loans

The economic injury disaster loan program, also administered by the SBA, is intended to help business concerns that suffer economic damage as a result of disasters.

To qualify, the applicant must be a small business concern as described in SBA rules and regulations, and must furnish evidence of the extent of economic injury claimed.

The loans, with a thirty-year repayment term, can be made to a single firm or to a group of affiliated companies. The funds can be used to pay current liabilities which could have been paid if the disaster had not occurred, and can be used for working capital for a limited period to keep the business operating. Funds cannot be used for realty or the acquisition or repair of equipment.

The interest rate may vary according to the date of the disaster and governing legislation. SBA loans are usually under $350,000, but additional amounts are available as guaranteed loans from other financial institutions, such as banks.

How to apply: Applications are filed with the nearest SBA field office. Prior to application, interviews generally are held to acquaint the applicant with procedures and to discuss what assistance may be available.

Mortgage insurance for disaster victims

Families who are victims of an officially proclaimed disaster are eligible for guaranteed or insured mortgage loans under a section of the National Housing Act, administered by the Department of Housing and Urban Development.

As with other HUD programs, the agency insures lenders against loss on the mortgage loans. The funds may be used to finance the purchase of proposed, under construction, or existing single family homes by an occupant-mortgagor who is the victim of a major disaster.

No down payment is required for these loans and the interest rate is based on current market rates. The mortgage term usually is thirty years.

How to apply: The application is submitted through a lender approved by the Federal Housing Administration.

Help for farmers

Farmers and ranchers are eligible for emergency loans to cover losses resulting from designated disasters. Oyster breeders also are eligible for these loans, which are guaranteed or insured by the Agriculture Department's Farmers Home Administration.

These loans are not made to finance new farming or ranching operations. Rather, they are made to cover expenses that went into damaged or destroyed crops, to replace equipment and livestock, to make real estate repairs, and under certain conditions to refinance debts made necessary by the disaster.

In recent years, these loans have ranged upward from $500, and have averaged about $16,000. The repayment periods and interest rates vary. Application forms are provided by the Farmers Home Administration and must be submitted through the agency's county offices.

The government also sponsors an all-risk insurance program to protect individual farmers against losses because of droughts, freezes, insects, and other natural disasters. In recent years, coverage has exceeded the $2 billion mark.

Insurance is offered on the following crops: apples, barley, beans, citrus, combined crops, corn, cotton, flax, grain sorghum, grapes, oats, peaches, peanuts, peas, raisins, rice, soybeans, sugar beets, sugarcane, sunflowers, tobacco, tomatoes, and wheat.

Producers are not indemnified for losses resulting from negligence or failure to observe good farming practices. Payments to farmers who have suffered losses have ranged up to $250,000, but have averaged only about $750.

Producers interested in applying should contact their local Federal Crop Insurance Corporation district office. Applications must be filed before the normal planting date of the crop.

There are other, more specialized programs. One is intended to indemnify dairy farmers and manufacturers of dairy products who are forced to remove their milk or dairy products from the market because of contamination with pesticide residues. A similar program helps beekeepers who, through no fault of their own, suffer losses of honey bees as a result of the use of pesticides near, or adjacent to, the property on which the beehives are located.

Another program is intended to aid livestock owners whose normal supplies of feed have been interrupted by severe drought, flood, hurricane, blizzard, or other uncontrollable catastrophe. Under this program, the Commodity Credit Corporation makes stocks of feed grains available at reduced prices. To qualify, livestock owners must establish that they do not have sufficient feed, have suffered serious loss of feed, require feed purchases larger than usual because of emergency, and would suffer undue hardship in obtaining sufficient feed through normal channels. The Secretary of Agriculture designates areas eligible for the program. Applications are made to the county offices of the Agricultural Stabilization and Conservation Service.

Flood insurance

For many years, property owners in coastal and inland communities who faced the threat of floods were virtually unable to obtain flood insurance coverage. In 1968, however, Congress enacted the National Flood Insurance Program, a federally-subsidized cooperative effort between the government and the private insurance industry. Within a few years, hundreds of thousands of property owners had obtained the low-cost flood insurance.

To qualify for the program, communities must adopt and enforce land use and control measures that guide land development in flood-prone areas. These measures are intended to avoid or reduce future flood damage. Once a community has qualified, its property owners may purchase flood insurance policies from any property and casualty insurance agent or broker licensed to do business within the state.

All buildings used for residential, business, religious, or agricultural purposes, buildings occupied by nonprofit organizations, and buildings owned by state or local governments or agencies are eligible for flood insurance coverage.

The maximum amounts of coverage under the original program are $35,000 for a single-family home, $100,000 for all other residential buildings, $10,000 per dwelling unit for the contents, $100,000 for nonresidential buildings, and $100,000 per occupant (such as a business firm) for contents of the nonresidential building.

In communities where actuarial rates have been determined, a second layer of coverage equal to those set out in the initial program may be obtained at the actuarial rate, which is usually higher.

The premiums for flood insurance vary according to the location, but a typical homeowner can purchase $10,000 of flood insurance for about $25 a year.

Flood loss claims are processed in the same way as loss claims for other types of property insurance. Claims may be filed either with the local insurance agent or broker who sold the policy or with the local insurance company that issued the policy.

The policy covers losses resulting from a flood, which is defined as "a general and temporary condition of partial or complete inundation of normally dry land areas from (1) the overflow of inland or tidal waters, (2) the unusual and rapid accumulation or runoff of surface waters from any source, or (3) mudslides which are caused or precipitated by accumulations of water on or under the ground."

How to apply: Contact a local insurance agent or broker.

Crime insurance

The federal government offers low-cost, noncancellable burglary and robbery insurance to small business people and residential property owners and tenants in states that have been
declared eligible for the Federal Crime Insurance Program.

The insurance was available in 1977 in Arkansas, Colorado,
Connecticut, Delaware, the District of Columbia, Florida, Georgia, Illinois, Kansas, Maryland, Massachusetts, Minnesota, Missouri, New Jersey, New York, Ohio, Pennsylvania, Rhode Island,
Tennessee, and Virginia.

Coverage is available to all residents in an eligible state, regardless of their occupations or the crime rate in their neighborhood,
at rates that are uniform within the metropolitan area of each
city. Thus, inner-city business people and residents are able to
obtain crime insurance at rates no higher than those charged in
the suburbs of their city.

Under the program, commercial losses from burglary or robbery or combined burglary-robbery can be insured in amounts
from $1,000 to $15,000 and residential losses from $1,000 to
$10,000. The policies cover burglary and larceny by means of
forcible entry, as well as robbery and "observed theft" when an
insured victim is held up or observes the taking of his or her
property. Property damage caused by these crimes or by attempts to commit these crimes is also covered.

Residential policies, besides protecting against loss resulting
from robbery or burglary of your home or apartment, also insure
up to $500 of the contents of a locked car trunk. There is a $100
limit on the loss of cash and a $500 limit on the loss of securities
but no claim limit on jewelry or furs.

Both types of policies have deductible clauses. For residential
policies, the deductible is $75 or 5 percent of the gross amount of
the loss, whichever is greater. For commercial policies, the deductible varies from $50 to $200 depending upon the gross annual receipts of the business or 5 percent of the gross amount of the
loss, whichever is greater.

Premiums range upward from $20 a year for residential poli-
cies and from $50 a year for business policies. The size of the
premium for a business policy depends upon the class of business,
the annual amount of gross receipts, and the city or town in
which the business is located.

Crimes Against Property

Year	Robbery	Burglary	Larceny-Theft
1964	129,860	1,201,600	2,489,300
1965	138,130	1,270,200	2,546,900
1966	157,350	1,396,500	2,793,700
1967	202,100	1,616,500	3,080,500
1968	261,780	1,841,100	3,447,800
1969	297,650	1,962,900	3,849,700
1970	348,460	2,183,800	4,183,500
1971	386,150	2,376,300	4,379,900
1972	374,790	2,352,800	4,109,600
1973	382,680	2,540,900	4,304,400
1974	436,000	2,973,000	5,165,000
1975	464,970	3,252,100	5,977,700
1976	420,210	3,089,800	6,270,800

Source: Federal Bureau of Investigation

For example, a Boston drugstore owner with annual gross receipts under $100,000 would pay $260 a year for $5,000 of burglary insurance and $1,000 of robbery insurance.

Commercial applicants for burglary or combined burglary-robbery policies must have protective equipment that meets certain standards. These standards vary widely according to types of businesses.

Under a residential burglary policy, claims will not be paid unless a few basic protective-device requirements have been met. These include a requirement that exterior doors have a dead bolt or a self-locking dead latch, and that sliding doors and windows at basement or ground level have some type of locking device.

How to apply: Applications can be made to local insurance agents or brokers.

Urban property insurance

The federal government has a program to assure availability of essential insurance coverage for urban property, particularly property located in areas subject to riots and civil disorders. Under the program, the government provides reinsurance to insurers against catastrophic losses due to such causes.

Insurance Provided by FAIR Plans

State	Insurance in Force (000 omitted)
California	$4,061,233
Connecticut	319,827
Delaware	70,740
District of Columbia	554,632
Georgia	173,066
Illinois	1,654,062
Indiana	103,249
Iowa	29,034
Kansas	77,239
Kentucky	156,000
Louisiana	242,487
Maryland	659,530
Massachusetts	2,116,930
Michigan	2,910,397
Minnesota	51,266
Missouri	533,672
New Jersey	1,732,221
New Mexico	2,501
New York	3,360,552
North Carolina	228,211
Ohio	477,527
Oregon	25,347
Pennsylvania	1,576,978
Puerto Rico	2,204
Rhode Island	424,332
Virginia	281,257
Washington	59,146
Wisconsin	160,212
Total	$22,043,852

Sources: Property Insurance Plans Service Office, Insurance Information Institute

The federal reinsurance is available only to companies participating as risk-bearing members of the FAIR plan (for Fair Access to Insurance Requirements). Policies written by these companies offer fire, extended coverage, vandalism, and malicious mischief insurance for eligible urban properties.

When you apply for a policy, the insurer will inspect the property to determine if it meets minimum safety standards and is structurally sound. If your property is found to be insurable, a policy will be issued upon payment of a one-year premium. If your property is found ineligible for coverage, you will be advised what changes are necessary to make it eligible. You may qualify for federal grants or loans to make repairs necessary to meet safety standards.

How to apply: Not all states have a FAIR plan. You can learn about FAIR from your state insurance department or your local insurance agent or broker, or by writing to the Federal Insurance Administration, Department of Housing and Urban Development, Washington, D.C. 20410.

CHAPTER 19

If You Want More Information

If you need information on any subject, chances are good that your government can help you find it or at least steer you in the right direction.

The secret to finding the information you want is knowing where to go and whom to ask. What follows are clues to help in your search for the information you seek.

Federal Information Centers

Beginning in 1966 the government began establishing Federal Information Centers in major metropolitan areas. Now, there are more than three dozen of these centers receiving the public's questions about federal agencies and providing the desired information or an accurate referral to the office that can be of assistance.

During a typical week, these centers provide information and assistance to 125,000 people. In addition to verbal answers, the centers distribute free literature supplied by a number of government departments and agencies on a variety of subjects.

In each of the cities listed on page 228 the Federal Information Center is located in a federal building, U.S. post office, or U.S. courthouse. You can find the address in the "U.S. Government" section of the telephone book. If your city does not have a Federal Information Center, it may have a toll-free telephone tie-line. For example, residents of four cities in Ohio—Akron, Columbus, Dayton, and Toledo—are able to use the telephone tie-line to call the centers in Cleveland and Cincinnati free of charge. These tie-line numbers may also be listed in the "U.S. Government" section of your local telephone book.

Still another source of information is the home district office of your member of Congress. His or her staff assistants frequently can point you in the right direction.

Government Printing Office

The Government Printing Office (GPO) is one of the world's largest publishers. About twenty-four thousand titles, covering nearly every field of interest, are available for purchase at nominal fees. Each year, about five million sales orders are received, processed, and filled by the GPO. Total sales exceed seventy million copies a year.

The GPO will send you a monthly list of selected new and older U.S. government publications. You can obtain more detailed lists on specific areas, such as "Energy Conservation," "The Home," and "Veterans' Affairs and Benefits," by writing to the Superintendent of Documents, U.S. Government Printing Office, Washington, D.C. 20402.

A complete monthly listing of new government publications is compiled by the GPO for use by libraries and the public. If your local public library does not have these lists, you might suggest to your librarian that a subscription be entered.

If you visit a Government Printing Office bookstore, you may find helpful publications simply by browsing. The main bookstore is in Washington, but there are others with a good selection of titles in Atlanta, Birmingham, Boston, Canton, Chicago, Cleveland, Dallas, Denver, Detroit, Jacksonville, Kansas City, Los Angeles, Milwaukee, New York, Philadelphia, Pueblo, San Francisco, and Seattle. All are in federal buildings.

Locations of Federal Information Centers

Arizona—Phoenix	**Minnesota**—Minneapolis
California—Los Angeles, Sacramento, San Diego, San Francisco	**Missouri**—Kansas City, Saint Louis
	Nebraska—Omaha
Colorado—Denver	**New Jersey**—Newark
District of Columbia	**New Mexico**—Albuquerque
Florida—Miami, Saint Petersburg	**New York**—Buffalo, New York City
Georgia—Atlanta	**Ohio**—Cincinnati, Cleveland
Hawaii—Honolulu	**Oklahoma**—Oklahoma City
Illinois—Chicago	**Oregon**—Portland
Indiana—Indianapolis	**Pennsylvania**—Philadelphia, Pittsburgh
Kentucky—Louisville	
Louisiana—New Orleans	**Tennessee**—Memphis
Maryland—Baltimore	**Texas**—Fort Worth, Houston
Massachusetts—Boston	**Utah**—Salt Lake City
Michigan—Detroit	**Washington**—Seattle

If you order by mail from the Government Printing Office, it may take six to eight weeks to process your order, and your check may clear the bank long before you get your publications. Eliminating that time lag is one advantage of browsing at a GPO bookstore if one is near you.

Here is another cost- and time-saving tip: the government agency or department that prepared the publication in the first place may give you a single copy free if you write or telephone.

These examples illustrate the breadth and detail of government publications you can obtain:

Produced by the Department of Agriculture's Research Service: *Home Care of Purchased Frozen Foods* and *Equipment for Cooling Your Home.*

Produced by the Department of Agriculture's Consumer and Marketing Service: a number of "How to Buy . . ." publications on products ranging from steak to fruit, from cheese to beans.

Produced by the National Bureau of Standards: *Adhesives for Everyday Use,* including how to select and use adhesives.

Produced by the Interstate Commerce Commission: *Summary of Information for Shippers of Household Goods.*

Government maps

If your travels take you to mountains, lakes, or rivers, you can add to your enjoyment and knowledge—and even your safety— with maps available at little charge from the government.

Of course, service stations or your state highway department can provide you with road maps, but for real detail, you might wish to obtain topographic maps published by the Department of the Interior's Geological Survey.

In addition to roads and highways, these topographic maps show ground elevations, woods, clearings, and streams. Even the locations of buildings are shown. More recent maps depict features such as trails, fence lines, and fire lanes—those strips of forest cleared of timber and brush to prevent fires spreading.

On the most detailed of the Geological Survey maps, an inch of the map is equal to only about two-fifths of a mile, providing plenty of detail for hikers and other lovers of the outdoors.

The National Topographic Map Series has been designed so that maps of adjacent areas can generally be combined to form a single large map.

Indexes of topographic maps published for each state are available from the U.S. Geological Survey, Washington, D.C. 20242, or the U.S. Geological Survey, Federal Center, Denver, Colorado 80225. These indexes list special maps, addresses of local map reference libraries, local map dealers, and federal map distribution centers.

The Geological Survey can also send you a complete list of types of maps published by other government agencies ranging from a Tennessee Valley Authority map of the Tennessee River to U.S. Forest Service maps of national forest regions.

And for the fisherman who would like to know where it is deep and where it is shallow in that big lake behind the dam, the Geological Survey might provide the answer. Survey officials will check old maps and other data to determine for you the bottom conditions of man-made bodies of water. Send the name of the lake or reservoir, the state and county or township where it is located, and, if the lake or reservoir is new or under construction, the name of the creek or river being impounded. Write to: Map

Information Office, U.S. Geological Survey National Center, Sunrise Valley Drive, Reston, Virginia 22092.

Government libraries

Perhaps the best known of all government libraries is the Library of Congress. It is, in effect, a national library of the United States. The library's extensive collections include millions of books on every subject and in many languages, volumes relating to science and the law, manuscript collections including the papers of many Presidents, newspapers and periodicals, motion pictures, microfilms, and many other kinds of materials.

The use of the Library of Congress is free to adults, but for certain materials, credentials are required, depending on the value and rarity of the materials. As time permits, the library provides reference service in answer to written requests for information from individuals who have exhausted local, state, and regional resources. Write to the Library of Congress, Washington, D.C. 20540.

The National Archives and Records Service also provides reference assistance to the general public through its headquarters in Washington, six presidential libraries, and fifteen Federal Archives and Records Centers.

There also are more than 1,100 "depository libraries" across the country which receive selected government publications for use by the general public. These libraries, designated by members of Congress, usually include those of land-grant colleges. During a typical year, these libraries receive more than thirteen million government publications.

Monthly Social Security Benefits
For Retired or Disabled Workers
(In effect December 1977, subject to future revision)

	Retired Worker Aged 65 at Time Of Retirement or Disabled Worker				Retired Worker Aged 62 At Time of Retirement			
		Worker With Spouse Claiming Benefit at				Worker With Spouse Claiming Benefit at		
Average Monthly Wage	Worker Alone	Age 65 or Over	Age 62	With Spouse & Child	Worker Alone	Age 65 or Over	Age 62	With Spouse & Child
$ 0-76	$114.30	$171.50	$157.20	$171.50	$ 91.50	$148.70	$134.40	$148.70
77-78	116.10	174.50	159.70	174.30	92.90	151.00	136.50	151.10
79-80	118.80	178.20	163.40	178.40	95.10	154.50	139.70	154.70
81-81	121.00	181.50	166.40	181.60	96.80	157.30	142.20	157.40
82-83	123.10	184.70	169.30	184.70	98.50	160.10	144.70	160.10
84-85	125.80	188.70	173.00	188.80	100.70	163.60	147.90	163.70
86-87	128.10	192.20	176.20	192.30	102.50	166.60	150.60	166.70
88-89	130.10	195.20	179.00	195.30	104.10	169.20	153.00	169.30
90-90	132.70	199.10	182.50	199.10	106.20	172.60	156.00	172.60
91-92	135.00	202.50	185.70	202.60	108.00	175.50	158.70	175.60
93-94	137.20	205.80	188.70	205.80	109.80	178.40	161.30	178.40
95-96	139.40	209.10	191.70	209.20	111.60	181.30	163.90	181.40
97-97	142.00	213.00	195.30	213.00	113.60	184.60	166.90	184.60
98-99	144.30	216.50	198.50	216.50	115.50	187.70	169.70	187.70
100-101	147.10	220.70	202.30	220.70	117.70	191.30	172.90	191.30
102-102	149.20	223.80	205.20	224.00	119.40	194.00	175.40	194.20
103-104	151.70	227.60	208.70	227.70	121.40	197.30	178.40	197.40
105-106	154.50	231.80	212.50	231.80	123.60	200.90	181.60	201.00
107-107	157.00	235.50	215.90	235.60	125.60	204.10	184.50	204.20
108-109	159.40	239.10	219.20	239.20	127.60	207.30	187.40	207.40
110-113	161.90	242.90	222.70	242.90	129.60	210.60	190.40	210.60
114-118	164.20	246.30	225.80	246.40	131.40	213.50	193.00	213.60
119-122	166.70	250.10	229.30	250.30	133.40	216.80	196.00	217.00
123-127	169.30	254.00	232.90	254.10	135.50	220.20	199.10	220.30
128-132	171.80	257.70	236.30	257.80	137.50	223.40	202.00	223.50
133-136	174.10	261.20	239.50	261.30	139.30	226.40	204.70	226.50
137-141	176.50	264.80	243.80	264.90	141.20	229.50	207.50	229.60
142-146	179.10	268.70	246.30	268.70	143.30	232.90	210.50	232.90
147-150	181.70	272.60	249.90	272.70	145.40	236.30	213.60	236.40
151-155	183.90	275.90	252.90	275.90	147.20	239.20	216.50	239.20

| | Retired Worker Aged 65 at Time Of Retirement or Disabled Worker | | | | Retired Worker Aged 62 At Time of Retirement | | | |
| | Worker With Spouse Claiming Benefit at | | | | Worker With Spouse Claiming Benefit at | | |
Average Monthly Wage	Worker Alone	Age 65 or Over	Age 62	With Spouse & Child	Worker Alone	Age 65 or Over	Age 62	With Spouse & Child
$156-160	$186.50	$279.80	$256.50	$279.90	$149.20	$242.50	$219.20	$242.60
161-164	189.00	283.50	259.90	283.60	151.20	245.70	222.10	245.80
165-169	191.40	287.10	263.20	287.20	153.20	248.90	225.00	249.00
170-174	194.00	291.00	266.80	291.00	155.00	252.20	228.00	252.20
175-178	196.30	294.50	270.00	294.50	157.10	255.30	230.80	255.30
179-183	198.90	298.40	273.60	298.50	159.20	258.70	233.90	258.80
184-188	201.30	302.00	276.90	302.10	161.10	261.80	236.70	261.90
189-193	203.90	305.90	280.40	306.10	163.20	265.20	239.70	265.40
194-197	206.40	309.60	283.80	309.80	165.20	268.40	242.60	268.60
198-202	208.80	313.20	287.10	313.20	167.10	271.50	245.40	271.50
203-207	211.50	317.30	290.90	317.30	169.20	275.00	248.60	275.00
208-211	214.00	321.10	294.30	321.00	171.20	278.20	251.50	278.20
212-216	216.00	324.00	297.00	324.00	172.80	280.80	253.80	280.80
217-221	218.70	328.10	300.80	328.10	175.00	284.40	257.10	284.40
222-225	221.20	331.80	304.20	331.80	177.00	287.60	260.00	287.60
226-230	223.90	335.90	307.90	335.90	179.20	291.20	263.20	291.20
231-235	226.30	339.50	311.20	339.50	181.10	294.30	266.00	294.30
236-239	229.10	343.70	315.10	343.70	183.30	297.90	269.30	297.90
240-244	231.20	346.80	317.90	348.40	185.00	300.60	271.70	302.20
245-249	233.50	350.30	321.10	355.70	186.80	303.60	274.40	309.00
250-253	236.40	354.60	325.10	361.40	189.20	307.40	277.90	314.50
254-258	238.70	358.10	328.30	368.50	191.00	310.40	280.60	320.80
259-263	240.80	361.20	331.10	375.60	192.70	313.10	283.00	327.50
264-267	243.70	365.60	335.20	381.30	195.00	316.90	286.50	332.60
268-272	246.10	369.20	338.50	388.50	196.90	320.00	289.30	339.30
273-277	248.70	373.10	342.00	395.50	199.00	323.40	292.30	345.80
278-281	251.00	376.50	345.20	401.20	200.80	326.30	295.00	351.00
282-286	253.50	380.30	348.60	408.30	202.80	329.60	297.90	357.60
287-291	256.20	384.30	352.30	415.60	205.00	333.10	301.10	364.40
292-295	258.30	387.50	355.20	421.10	206.70	335.90	303.60	369.50
296-300	261.10	391.70	359.10	428.30	208.90	339.50	306.90	376.10
301-305	263.50	395.30	362.40	435.50	210.80	342.60	309.70	382.80
306-309	265.80	398.70	365.50	441.20	212.70	345.60	312.40	388.10
310-314	268.50	402.80	369.30	448.30	214.80	349.10	315.60	394.60
315-319	270.70	406.10	372.30	455.50	216.60	352.00	318.20	401.40
320-323	273.20	409.80	375.70	461.20	218.60	355.20	321.10	406.60

	Retired Worker Aged 65 at Time Of Retirement or Disabled Worker				Retired Worker Aged 62 At Time of Retirement			
		Worker With Spouse Claiming Benefit at				Worker With Spouse Claiming Benefit at		
Average Monthly Wage	Worker Alone	Age 65 or Over	Age 62	With Spouse & Child	Worker Alone	Age 65 or Over	Age 62	With Spouse & Child
$324-328	$275.80	$413.70	$379.30	$468.20	$220.70	$358.60	$324.20	$413.10
329-333	278.10	417.20	382.50	475.30	222.50	361.60	326.90	419.70
334-337	281.00	421.50	386.40	481.20	224.80	365.30	330.20	425.00
338-342	283.00	424.50	389.20	488.20	226.40	367.90	332.60	431.60
343-347	285.60	428.40	392.70	495.40	228.50	371.30	316.80	438.30
348-351	288.30	432.50	396.50	501.10	230.70	374.90	338.90	443.50
352-356	290.50	435.80	398.50	508.10	232.40	377.70	341.40	450.00
357-361	293.30	440.00	403.40	515.30	234.70	381.40	344.80	456.70
362-365	295.60	443.40	406.50	521.00	236.50	384.30	347.40	461.90
366-370	297.90	446.90	409.70	528.10	238.40	387.40	350.20	468.60
371-375	300.60	450.90	413.40	535.20	240.50	390.80	353.30	475.10
376-379	303.10	454.70	416.80	541.10	242.50	394.10	356.20	480.50
380-384	305.70	458.60	420.40	548.30	244.60	397.50	359.30	487.20
385-389	307.90	461.90	423.40	555.30	246.40	400.40	361.90	493.80
390-393	310.30	465.50	426.70	560.90	248.30	403.50	364.70	498.90
394-398	313.00	469.50	430.40	568.20	250.40	406.90	367.80	505.60
399-403	315.40	473.10	433.70	575.40	252.40	410.10	370.70	512.40
404-407	318.20	477.30	437.60	580.80	254.60	413.70	374.00	517.20
408-412	320.20	480.30	440.30	588.00	256.20	416.30	376.30	524.00
413-417	322.50	483.80	443.50	595.10	258.00	419.30	379.00	530.60
418-421	324.80	487.50	446.60	600.80	259.90	422.30	381.70	535.90
422-426	327.40	491.10	450.20	608.00	262.00	425.70	384.80	542.60
427-431	329.60	494.40	453.20	615.20	263.70	428.50	387.30	549.30
432-436	331.60	497.40	456.00	622.20	265.30	431.10	389.70	555.90
437-440	334.40	501.60	459.80	625.00	267.60	434.80	393.00	558.20
441-445	336.50	504.80	462.80	628.90	269.20	437.50	395.50	561.60
446-450	338.70	508.10	465.80	632.30	271.00	440.40	398.10	564.60
451-454	341.30	512.00	469.40	635.10	273.10	443.80	401.20	566.90
455-459	343.50	515.30	472.40	638.50	274.80	445.60	403.70	569.80
460-464	345.80	518.70	475.50	642.00	276.70	449.60	406.40	572.90
465-468	347.90	521.90	478.40	645.10	278.40	452.40	408.90	575.60
469-473	350.70	526.40	482.30	648.70	280.60	456.00	412.20	578.60
474-478	352.60	528.90	484.90	652.20	282.10	458.40	414.40	581.70
479-482	354.90	532.40	488.10	655.10	284.00	461.50	417.20	584.20
483-487	357.40	536.10	491.50	658.80	286.00	464.70	420.10	587.40
488-492	359.70	539.60	494.70	662.30	287.80	467.70	422.80	590.40

	Retired Worker Aged 65 at Time Of Retirement or Disabled Worker			Retired Worker Aged 62 At Time of Retirement			
		Worker With Spouse Claiming Benefit at		With		Worker With Spouse Claiming Benefit at	With
Average Monthly Wage	Worker Alone	Age 65 or Over	Age 62	Spouse & Child	Worker Alone	Age 65 or Over	Age 62	Spouse & Child
$493-496	$361.90	$542.90	$497.70	$665.10	$289.60	$470.60	$425.40	$592.80
497-501	364.50	546.80	501.30	668.70	291.60	473.90	428.40	595.80
502-506	366.60	549.90	504.10	672.20	293.30	476.60	430.80	598.90
507-510	368.90	553.40	507.30	675.10	295.20	479.70	433.60	601.40
511-515	371.10	556.70	510.30	678.70	296.90	482.50	436.10	604.50
516-520	373.70	560.60	513.90	682.30	299.00	485.90	439.20	607.60
521-524	375.80	563.70	516.80	685.00	300.70	488.60	441.70	609.90
525-529	378.10	567.20	520.00	688.70	302.50	491.60	444.40	613.10
530-534	381.80	571.20	523.60	692.20	304.70	495.10	447.50	616.10
535-538	382.80	574.20	526.40	695.00	306.30	497.70	449.90	618.50
539-543	385.10	577.70	529.60	698.70	308.10	500.70	452.60	621.70
544-548	387.60	581.40	533.00	702.20	310.10	503.90	455.50	624.70
549-553	389.90	584.90	536.20	705.70	312.00	507.00	458.30	627.80
554-556	392.10	588.20	539.20	707.90	313.70	509.80	460.80	629.50
557-560	393.90	590.90	541.70	710.70	315.20	512.20	463.00	632.00
561-563	396.10	594.20	544.70	712.90	316.90	515.00	465.50	633.70
564-567	398.20	597.30	547.60	715.80	318.60	517.70	468.00	636.20
568-570	400.40	600.60	550.60	717.80	320.40	520.60	470.60	637.80
571-574	402.30	603.50	553.20	720.70	321.90	523.10	472.80	640.30
575-577	404.40	606.60	556.10	723.00	323.60	525.80	475.30	642.20
578-581	406.20	609.30	558.60	725.60	325.00	528.10	477.40	644.40
582-584	408.40	612.60	561.60	727.80	326.80	531.00	480.00	646.20
585-588	410.20	615.30	564.10	730.80	328.20	533.30	482.10	648.80
589-591	412.60	618.90	567.40	732.80	330.10	536.40	484.90	650.30
592-595	414.60	621.90	570.10	735.60	331.70	539.00	487.20	652.70
596-598	416.70	625.10	573.00	737.70	333.40	541.80	489.70	654.40
599-602	418.70	628.10	575.80	740.70	335.00	544.40	492.10	657.00
603-605	420.70	631.10	578.50	742.90	336.60	547.00	494.40	658.80
606-609	422.80	634.20	581.40	745.60	338.30	549.70	496.90	661.10
610-612	424.90	637.40	584.30	747.90	340.00	552.50	499.40	663.00
613-616	426.90	640.40	587.10	750.70	341.60	555.10	501.80	665.40
617-620	428.90	643.40	589.80	753.50	343.20	557.70	504.10	667.80
621-623	431.00	646.50	592.70	755.60	344.80	560.30	506.50	669.40
624-627	433.00	649.50	595.40	758.60	346.40	562.90	508.80	672.00
628-630	435.10	652.70	598.30	761.30	348.10	565.70	511.30	674.30
631-634	437.10	655.70	601.10	764.90	349.70	568.30	513.70	677.50

| | Retired Worker Aged 65 at Time Of Retirement or Disabled Worker | | | | Retired Worker Aged 62 At Time of Retirement | | | |
| Average Monthly Wage | Worker Alone | Worker With Spouse Claiming Benefit at | | With Spouse & Child | Worker Alone | Worker With Spouse Claiming Benefit at | | With Spouse & Child |
		Age 65 or Over	Age 62			Age 65 or Over	Age 62	
$635-637	$439.20	$658.80	$603.90	$768.60	$351.40	$571.00	$516.10	$680.80
638-641	441.40	662.10	607.00	772.20	353.20	573.90	518.80	684.00
642-644	443.20	664.80	609.40	775.60	354.60	576.20	520.80	687.00
645-648	445.40	668.10	612.50	779.40	356.40	579.10	523.50	690.40
649-652	447.40	671.10	615.20	782.80	358.00	581.70	525.80	693.40
653-656	448.60	672.90	616.90	785.00	358.90	583.20	527.20	695.30
657-660	449.90	674.90	618.70	787.30	360.00	585.00	528.80	697.40
661-665	451.50	677.30	620.90	790.10	361.20	587.00	530.60	699.80
666-670	453.10	679.70	623.10	792.90	362.50	589.10	532.50	702.30
671-675	454.80	682.20	625.40	795.60	363.90	591.30	534.50	704.70
676-680	456.40	684.60	627.60	798.60	365.20	593.40	536.40	707.40
681-685	458.00	687.00	629.80	801.40	366.40	595.40	538.20	709.80
686-690	459.80	689.70	632.30	804.20	367.90	597.80	540.40	712.30
691-695	461.50	691.80	634.20	807.20	369.00	599.60	542.00	715.00
696-700	462.80	694.20	636.40	810.00	370.30	601.70	543.90	717.50
701-705	464.50	696.80	638.80	812.70	371.60	603.90	545.90	719.80
706-710	466.10	699.20	641.00	815.50	372.90	606.00	547.80	722.30
711-715	467.70	701.60	643.20	818.30	374.20	608.10	549.70	724.80
716-720	469.40	704.10	645.50	821.20	375.60	610.30	551.70	727.40
721-725	471.00	706.50	647.70	824.00	376.80	612.30	553.50	729.80
726-730	472.60	708.90	649.90	827.00	378.10	614.40	555.40	732.50
731-735	474.20	711.30	652.10	829.80	379.40	616.50	557.30	735.00
736-740	475.90	713.90	654.40	832.50	380.80	618.80	559.30	737.40
741-745	477.40	716.10	656.50	835.60	382.00	620.70	561.10	740.20
746-750	478.90	718.40	658.60	838.30	383.20	622.70	562.90	742.60
751-755	480.40	720.60	660.60	840.80	384.40	624.60	564.60	744.80
756-760	481.80	722.70	662.50	843.00	385.50	626.40	566.20	746.70
761-765	483.20	724.80	664.40	845.00	386.60	628.20	567.80	748.80
766-770	484.50	726.80	666.30	847.90	387.60	629.90	569.40	751.00
771-775	485.80	728.70	668.00	850.20	388.70	631.60	570.90	753.10
776-780	487.20	730.80	669.90	852.40	389.80	633.40	572.50	755.00
781-785	488.60	732.90	671.90	854.80	390.90	635.20	574.20	757.10
786-790	489.80	734.70	673.50	857.20	391.90	636.80	575.60	759.30
791-795	491.10	736.70	675.30	859.50	392.90	638.50	577.10	761.30
796-800	492.50	738.80	677.30	861.90	394.00	640.30	578.80	763.40
801-805	494.00	741.00	679.30	864.40	395.20	642.20	580.50	765.60

| | **Retired Worker Aged 65 at Time Of Retirement or Disabled Worker** | | | | **Retired Worker Aged 62 At Time of Retirement** | | | |
| | | Worker With Spouse Claiming Benefit at | | | | Worker With Spouse Claiming Benefit at | | |
Average Monthly Wage	Worker Alone	Age 65 or Over	Age 62	With Spouse & Child	Worker Alone	Age 65 or Over	Age 62	With Spouse & Child
$806-810	$495.30	$743.00	$681.10	$866.70	$396.30	$644.00	$582.10	$767.70
811-815	496.70	745.10	683.00	869.10	397.40	645.80	583.70	769.80
816-820	498.00	747.00	684.80	871.40	398.40	647.40	585.20	771.80
821-825	499.40	749.10	686.70	873.80	399.60	649.30	586.90	774.00
826-830	500.70	751.10	688.50	876.10	400.60	651.00	588.40	776.00
831-835	502.00	753.00	690.30	878.60	401.60	652.60	589.90	778.20
836-840	503.30	755.00	692.10	880.90	402.70	654.40	591.50	780.30
841-845	504.70	757.10	694.00	883.30	403.80	656.20	593.10	782.40
846-850	506.00	759.00	695.80	885.40	404.80	657.80	594.60	784.20
851-855	507.50	761.30	697.90	887.90	406.00	659.80	596.40	786.40
856-860	508.80	763.20	699.60	890.20	407.10	661.50	597.90	788.50
861-865	510.20	765.30	701.60	892.60	408.20	663.30	599.60	790.60
866-870	511.50	767.30	703.40	895.10	409.20	665.00	601.10	792.80
871-875	512.90	769.40	705.30	897.30	410.40	666.90	602.80	794.80
876-880	514.10	771.20	707.00	899.70	411.30	668.40	604.20	796.90
881-885	515.50	773.30	708.90	902.10	412.40	670.20	605.80	799.00
886-890	516.80	775.20	710.60	904.40	413.50	671.90	607.30	801.10
891-895	518.20	777.30	712.60	907.00	414.60	673.70	609.00	803.40
896-900	519.60	779.40	714.50	909.20	415.70	675.50	610.60	805.30
901-905	521.00	781.50	716.40	911.60	416.80	677.30	612.20	807.40
906-910	522.30	783.50	718.20	914.10	417.90	679.10	613.80	809.70
911-915	523.70	785.60	720.20	916.50	419.00	680.90	615.50	811.80
916-920	525.10	787.70	722.10	918.50	420.10	682.70	617.10	813.50
921-925	526.30	789.50	723.70	921.10	421.10	684.30	618.50	815.90
926-930	527.60	791.40	725.50	923.40	422.10	685.90	620.00	817.90
931-935	529.00	793.50	727.40	925.80	423.20	687.70	621.60	820.00
936-940	530.40	795.60	729.30	928.20	424.40	689.60	623.30	822.20
941-945	531.70	797.60	731.20	930.50	425.40	691.30	624.90	824.20
946-950	533.00	799.50	732.90	932.80	426.40	692.90	626.30	826.20
951-955	534.50	801.80	735.00	935.30	427.60	694.90	628.10	828.40
956-960	535.90	803.90	736.90	937.70	428.80	696.80	629.80	830.60
961-965	537.30	806.00	738.90	939.90	429.90	698.60	631.50	832.50
966-970	538.40	807.60	740.30	942.40	430.80	700.00	632.70	834.80
971-975	539.80	809.70	742.30	944.80	431.90	701.80	634.40	836.90
976-980	541.20	811.80	744.20	947.00	433.00	703.60	636.00	838.80
981-985	542.60	813.90	746.10	949.40	434.10	705.40	637.60	840.90

| | Retired Worker Aged 65 at Time Of Retirement or Disabled Worker | | | | Retired Worker Aged 62 At Time of Retirement | | | |
| | | Worker With Spouse Claiming Benefit at | | | | Worker With Spouse Claiming Benefit at | | |
Average Monthly Wage	Worker Alone	Age 65 or Over	Age 62	With Spouse & Child	Worker Alone	Age 65 or Over	Age 62	With Spouse & Child
$ 986-990	$543.80	$815.70	$747.80	$951.80	$435.10	$707.10	$639.10	$843.10
991-995	545.20	817.80	749.70	954.20	436.20	708.80	640.70	845.20
996-1,000	546.60	819.90	751.60	956.40	437.30	710.60	642.30	847.10
1,001-1,005	547.80	821.70	753.30	958.40	438.30	712.20	643.80	848.90
1,006-1,010	548.90	823.40	754.80	960.70	439.20	713.70	645.10	851.00
1,011-1,015	550.20	825.30	756.60	962.80	440.20	715.30	646.60	852.80
1,016-1,020	551.50	827.30	758.40	965.10	441.20	717.00	648.10	854.80
1,021-1,025	552.60	828.90	759.90	967.00	442.10	718.40	649.40	856.50
1,026-1,030	553.80	830.70	761.50	969.20	443.10	720.00	650.80	858.50
1,031-1,035	555.10	832.70	763.30	971.30	444.10	721.70	652.30	860.30
1,036-1,040	556.20	834.30	764.80	973.40	445.00	723.10	653.60	862.20
1,041-1,045	557.50	836.30	766.60	975.50	446.00	724.80	655.10	864.20
1,046-1,050	558.80	838.20	768.40	977.80	447.10	726.50	656.70	866.10
1,051-1,055	559.80	839.70	769.80	979.80	447.90	727.80	657.90	867.90
1,056-1,060	561.10	841.70	771.60	982.10	448.90	729.50	659.40	869.90
1,061-1,065	562.40	843.60	773.30	984.00	450.00	731.20	660.90	871.60
1,066-1,070	563.60	845.40	775.00	986.40	450.90	732.70	662.30	873.70
1,071-1,075	564.80	847.20	776.60	988.40	451.90	734.30	663.70	875.50
1,076-1,080	566.00	849.00	778.30	990.60	452.80	735.80	655.10	877.40
1,081-1,085	567.30	851.00	780.10	992.50	453.90	737.60	666.70	879.10
1,086-1,090	568.40	852.60	781.60	994.80	454.80	739.00	668.00	881.20
1,091-1,095	569.70	854.60	783.40	996.90	455.80	740.70	669.50	883.00
1,096-1,100	571.00	856.60	785.20	999.00	456.80	742.30	671.00	884.80
1,101-1,105	572.00	858.00	786.50	1,001.00	457.60	743.60	672.10	886.60
1,106-1,110	573.30	860.00	788.40	1,003.30	458.70	745.40	673.80	888.70
1,111-1,115	574.60	861.90	790.10	1,005.40	459.70	747.00	675.20	890.50
1,116-1,120	575.70	863.60	791.70	1,007.70	460.60	748.50	676.60	892.60
1,121-1,125	577.00	865.50	793.40	1,009.60	461.60	750.10	678.00	894.20
1,126-1,130	578.20	867.30	795.10	1,011.80	462.60	751.70	679.50	896.20
1,131-1,135	579.40	869.10	796.70	1,013.80	463.60	753.30	680.90	898.00
1,136-1,140	580.60	870.90	798.40	1,016.20	464.50	754.80	682.30	900.10
1,141-1,145	581.90	872.90	800.20	1,018.30	465.60	756.60	683.90	902.00
1,146-1,150	583.10	874.70	801.80	1,020.30	466.50	758.10	685.20	903.70
1,151-1,155	584.00	876.30	803.30	1,022.40	467.40	759.60	686.50	905.60
1,156-1,160	585.50	878.30	805.10	1,024.50	468.40	761.20	688.00	907.40
1,161-1,165	586.70	880.10	806.80	1,026.70	469.40	762.80	689.50	909.40

| | Retired Worker Aged 65 at Time Of Retirement or Disabled Worker | | | | Retired Worker Aged 62 At Time of Retirement | | | |
| | | Worker With Spouse Claiming Benefit at | | | | Worker With Spouse Claiming Benefit at | | |
Average Monthly Wage	Worker Alone	Age 65 or Over	Age 62	With Spouse & Child	Worker Alone	Age 65 or Over	Age 62	With Spouse & Child
$1,166-1,170	$587.90	$881.90	$808.40	$1,028.90	$470.40	$764.40	$690.90	$911.40
1,171-1,175	589.20	883.80	810.20	1,031.00	471,40	766.00	692.40	913.20
1,176-1,180	590.30	885.50	811.70	1,033.10	472.30	767.50	693.70	915.10
1,181-1,185	591.40	887.10	813.20	1,035.00	473.20	768.90	695.00	916.80
1,186-1,190	592.60	888.90	814.90	1,037.00	474.10	770.40	696.40	918.50
1,191-1,195	593.70	890.60	816.40	1,038.90	475.00	771.90	697.70	920.20
1,196-1,200	594.80	892.20	817.90	1,041.00	475.90	773.30	699.00	922.10
1,201-1,205	595.90	893.90	819.40	1,042.90	476.80	774.80	700.30	923.80
1,206-1,210	597.10	895.70	821.10	1,044.90	477.70	776.30	701.70	925.50
1,211-1,215	598.20	897.30	822.60	1,046.80	478.60	777.70	703.00	927.20
1,216-1,220	599.30	899.00	824.10	1,048.90	479.50	779.20	704.30	929.10
1,221-1,225	600.40	900.60	825.60	1,050.80	480.40	780.60	705.60	930.80
1,226-1,230	601.60	902.40	827.10	1,052.80	481.30	782.10	706.90	932.50
1,231-1,235	602.70	904.10	828.80	1,054.70	482.20	783.60	708.30	934.20
1,236-1,240	603.80	905.70	830.30	1,056.80	483.10	785.00	709.60	936.10
1,241-1,245	605.00	907.50	831.90	1,058.60	484.00	786.50	710.90	937.60
1,246-1,250	606.10	909.20	833.50	1,060.70	484.90	788.00	712.30	939.50
1,251-1,255	607.20	910.80	834.90	1,062.60	485.80	789.40	713.50	941.20
1,256-1,260	608.30	912.50	836.50	1,064.70	486.70	790.90	714.90	943.10
1,261-1,265	609.50	914.30	838.10	1,066.50	487.60	792.40	716.20	944.60
1,266-1,270	610.60	915.90	839.60	1,068.60	488.50	793.80	717.50	946.50
1,271-1,275	611.70	917.60	841.20	1,070.50	489.40	795.30	718.90	948.20
1,276-1,280	612.80	919.20	842.60	1,072.40	490.30	796.70	720.10	949.90
1,281-1,285	613.80	920.70	844.00	1,074.20	491.10	798.00	721.30	951.50
1,286-1,290	614.90	922.40	845.60	1,076.10	492.00	799.50	722.70	953.20
1,291-1,295	616.00	924.00	847.00	1,078.00	492.90	800.80	723.80	954.80
1,296-1,300	617.00	925.50	848.40	1,079.80	493.60	802.10	725.00	956.40
1,301-1,305	618.10	927.20	850.00	1,018.70	494.50	803.60	726.40	958.10
1,306-1,310	619.10	928.70	851.30	1,083.50	495.30	804.90	727.50	959.70
1,311-1,315	620.20	930.30	852.80	1,085.40	496.20	806.30	728.80	961.40
1,316-1,320	621.30	932.00	854.40	1,087.30	497.10	807.80	730.20	963.10
1,321-1,325	622.30	933.50	855.70	1,089.10	497.90	809.10	731.30	964.70
1,326-1,330	623.40	935.10	857.20	1,091.00	498.80	810.60	732.60	966.40
1,331-1,335	624.40	936.60	858.60	1,092.80	499.60	811.30	733.80	968.00
1,336-1,340	625.50	938.30	861.10	1,094.70	500.40	813.20	735.00	969.60
1,341-1,345	626.60	939.90	861.10	1,096.40	501.30	814.60	736.30	971.10

| Average Monthly Wage | Retired Worker Aged 65 at Time Of Retirement or Disabled Worker | | | | Retired Worker Aged 62 At Time of Retirement | | | |
| | | Worker With Spouse Claiming Benefit at | | | | Worker With Spouse Claiming Benefit at | | |
	Worker Alone	Age 65 or Over	Age 62	With Spouse & Child	Worker Alone	Age 65 or Over	Age 62	With Spouse & Child
$1,346-1,350	$627.60	$941.40	$863.00	$1,098.40	$502.10	$815.90	$737.50	$972.90
1,351-1,355	628.70	943.10	864.50	1,100.10	503.00	817.40	738.80	974.40
1,356-1,360	629.90	944.60	865.90	1,102.10	503.80	818.70	740.00	976.20
1,361-1,365	630.80	946.20	867.40	1,103.80	504.70	820.10	741.30	977.70
1,366-1,370	631.80	947.70	868.80	1,105.80	505.50	821.40	742.50	979.50
1,371-1,375	632.90	949.40	870.30	1,107.70	506.40	822.90	743.80	981.20

Monthly Social Security Benefits for Survivors
(In effect December 1977, subject to future revision)

Average Monthly Wage	Widow or Widower Claiming Benefit at Age 65 or Over	Age 60	Age 50 (Disabled)	One Child	Mother and One Child	Two Children	Maximum Family Benefit
$ 0-76	$114.30	$ 81.80	$ 57.30	$114.30	$171.60	$171.60	$171.50
77-78	116.10	83.10	58.20	114.30	174.20	174.20	174.20
79-80	118.80	85.00	59.50	114.30	178.20	178.50	178.30
81-81	121.00	86.60	60.60	114.30	181.60	181.80	181.60
82-83	123.10	88.10	61.70	114.30	187.80	184.80	184.70
84-85	125.80	90.00	63.00	114.30	188.80	188.70	188.70
86-87	128.10	91.60	64.10	114.30	192.20	192.30	192.20
88-89	130.10	93.10	65.70	114.30	195.20	195.30	195.30
90-90	132.70	94.90	66.40	114.30	199.20	199.20	199.10
91-92	135.00	96.60	67.60	114.30	202.60	202.50	202.50
93-94	137.20	98.10	68.70	114.30	205.80	205.80	205.80
95-96	139.40	99.70	69.80	114.30	209.20	209.10	209.10
97-97	142.00	101.60	71.10	114.30	213.00	213.00	213.00
98-99	144.30	103.20	72.20	114.30	216.60	216.60	216.50
100-101	147.10	105.20	73.60	114.30	220.80	220.80	220.70
102-102	149.20	106.70	74.70	114.30	223.80	224.10	223.90
103-104	151.70	108.50	75.90	114.30	227.60	227.70	227.60
105-106	154.50	110.50	77.30	115.90	231.80	231.90	231.80
107-107	157.00	112.30	78.60	117.80	235.60	235.50	235.50
108-109	159.40	114.00	79.80	119.60	239.20	239.40	239.20
110-113	161.90	115.80	81.00	121.50	243.00	243.00	242.90
114-118	164.20	117.50	82.20	123.20	246.40	246.30	246.30
119-122	166.70	119.20	83.40	125.10	250.20	250.20	250.20
123-127	169.30	121.10	84.80	127.00	254.00	254.10	254.00
128-132	171.80	122.90	86.00	128.90	257.80	258.00	257.80
133-136	174.10	124.50	87.10	130.60	261.20	261.30	261.30
137-141	176.50	126.20	88.30	132.40	264.80	264.90	264.80
142-146	170.10	128.10	89.60	134.40	268.80	268.80	268.70
147-150	181.70	130.00	91.00	136.30	272.60	272.70	272.60
151-155	183.90	131.50	92.00	138.00	276.00	276.00	275.90
156-160	186.50	133.40	93.40	139.90	279.80	279.90	279.80
161-164	189.00	135.20	94.60	141.80	283.60	283.50	283.50
165-169	191.40	136.90	95.80	143.60	287.20	287.10	287.10
170-174	194.00	138.80	97.10	145.50	291.00	291.00	291.00
175-178	196.30	140.40	98.20	147.30	294.60	294.60	294.50
179-183	198.90	142.30	99.60	149.20	298.40	298.50	298.50
184-188	201.30	144.00	100.80	151.00	302.00	302.10	302.00
189-193	203.90	145.80	102.00	153.00	306.00	306.30	306.10
194-197	206.40	147.60	103.30	154.80	309.60	309.90	309.70

Average Monthly Wage	Widow or Widower Claiming Benefit at			One Child	Mother and		Maximum Family Benefit
	Age 65 or Over	Age 60	Age 50 (Disabled)		One Child	Two Children	
$198-202	$208.80	$149.30	$104.50	$156.60	$313.20	$313.20	$313.20
203-207	211.50	151.30	105.90	158.70	317.40	317.40	317.30
208-211	214.00	153.10	107.10	160.50	321.00	321.00	321.00
212-216	216.00	154.50	108.10	162.00	324.00	324.00	324.00
217-221	218.70	156.40	109.40	164.10	328.20	328.20	328.10
222-225	221.20	158.20	110.70	165.90	331.80	331.80	331.80
226-230	223.90	160.10	112.00	168.00	336.00	336.00	335.90
231-235	226.30	161.90	113.30	169.80	339.60	339.60	339.50
236-239	229.10	163.90	114.70	171.90	343.80	343.80	343.70
240-244	231.20	165.40	115.70	173.40	346.80	348.60	348.40
245-249	233.50	167.00	116.80	175.20	350.40	355.80	355.60
250-253	236.40	169.10	118.30	177.30	354.60	361.50	361.40
254-258	238.70	170.70	119.40	179.10	358.20	368.70	368.50
259-263	240.80	172.20	120.50	180.60	361.20	375.60	375.50
264-267	243.70	174.30	122.00	182.80	365.60	381.30	381.20
268-272	246.10	176.00	123.10	184.60	369.20	388.50	388.40
273-277	248.70	177.90	124.50	186.60	373.20	395.40	395.40
278-281	251.00	179.50	125.60	188.30	376.60	401.10	401.10
282-286	253.50	181.30	126.80	190.70	380.40	408.30	408.30
287-291	256.20	183.20	128.20	192.20	384.40	415.50	415.50
292-295	258.30	184.70	129.20	193.80	387.60	421.20	421.70
296-300	261.10	186.70	130.60	195.90	391.80	428.40	428.20
301-305	263.50	188.50	131.90	197.70	395.40	435.60	435.40
306-309	265.80	190.10	133.00	199.40	398.80	441.30	441.10
310-314	268.50	192.00	134.30	201.40	402.80	448.20	448.20
315-319	270.70	193.60	135.40	203.00	406.20	455.40	455.40
320-323	273.20	195.40	136.70	204.90	409.80	461.10	461.10
324-328	275.80	197.70	138.00	206.90	413.80	468.30	468.20
329-333	278.10	198.90	139.20	208.60	417.20	475.50	475.30
334-337	281.00	201.00	140.60	210.80	421.60	481.20	481.20
338-342	283.00	202.40	141.60	212.30	424.60	488.20	488.10
343-347	285.60	204.30	142.90	214.20	428.40	495.40	495.30
348-351	288.30	206.20	144.30	216.30	432.60	501.10	501.00
352-356	290.50	207.80	145.40	217.90	435.80	508.20	508.10
357-361	293.30	209.80	146.80	220.00	440.00	515.40	515.30
362-365	295.60	211.40	147.90	221.70	443.40	521.10	521.00
366-370	297.90	213.00	149.00	223.50	447.00	528.30	528.10
371-375	300.60	215.00	150.40	225.50	451.00	535.20	535.10
376-379	303.10	216.80	151.70	227.40	454.80	541.20	541.10

Average Monthly Wage	Widow or Widower Claiming Benefit at			One Child	Mother and		Maximum Family Benefit
	Age 65 or Over	Age 60	Age 50 (Disabled)		One Child	Two Children	
$380-384	$305.70	$218.60	$152.90	$229.30	$458.60	$548.40	$548.20
385-389	307.90	220.20	154.10	231.00	462.00	555.30	555.20
390-393	310.30	221.90	155.20	232.80	465.60	561.00	560.90
394-398	313.00	223.80	156.60	234.80	469.60	568.20	568.10
399-403	315.40	225.60	157.80	336.60	473.20	575.40	575.30
404-407	318.20	227.60	159.20	238.70	477.40	580.80	580.80
408-412	320.20	229.00	160.20	240.20	480.40	588.00	588.00
413-417	322.50	230.60	161.30	241.90	483.80	595.20	595.10
418-421	324.80	232.30	162.50	243.60	487.20	600.90	600.80
422-426	327.40	234.10	163.80	245.60	491.20	608.10	607.90
427-431	329.60	235.70	164.90	247.20	494.40	615.30	615.10
432-436	331.60	237.10	165.90	248.70	497.40	622.20	622.20
437-440	334.40	239.10	167.30	250.80	501.60	625.20	625.00
441-445	336.50	240.60	168.30	252.40	504.80	628.80	628.80
446-450	338.70	242.10	169.40	254.10	508.20	632.40	632.30
451-454	341.30	244.10	170.80	256.00	512.00	635.10	635.00
455-459	343.50	245.70	171.90	257.70	515.40	638.70	638.50
460-464	345.80	247.30	173.00	259.40	518.80	642.00	642.00
465-468	347.90	248.80	174.10	261.00	522.00	645.30	645.10
469-473	350.70	250.80	175.40	263.10	526.20	648.60	648.60
474-478	352.60	252.20	176.40	264.50	529.00	652.20	652.20
479-482	354.90	253.80	177.50	266.20	532.40	655.20	655.10
483-487	357.40	255.80	178.80	268.10	536.20	658.80	658.70
488-492	359.70	257.20	179.90	269.80	539.60	662.40	662.30
493-496	361.90	258.80	181.00	271.50	543.00	665.10	665.10
497-501	364.50	260.70	182.40	273.40	546.80	668.70	668.60
502-506	366.60	262.20	183.40	275.00	550.00	672.30	672.10
507-510	368.90	263.80	184.50	276.70	553.40	675.30	675.10
511-515	071.10	265.40	185.70	278.40	556.80	678.60	678.60
516-520	373.70	267.20	186.90	280.30	560.60	682.50	682.30
521-524	375.80	268.70	188.00	281.90	563.80	684.90	684.90
525-529	378.10	270.40	189.20	283.60	567.20	688.80	688.60
530-534	380.80	272.30	190.50	285.60	571.20	692.10	692.10
535-538	382.80	273.80	191.50	287.10	574.20	695.10	695.00
539-543	385.10	275.40	192.70	288.90	577.80	698.70	698.60
544-548	387.60	277.20	193.90	290.70	581.40	702.30	702.10
549-553	389.90	278.80	195.00	292.50	585.00	705.90	705.70
554-556	392.10	280.40	196.10	294.10	588.20	708.00	707.80
557-560	393.90	281.70	197.10	295.50	591.00	710.70	710.70

Average Monthly Wage	Widow or Widower Claiming Benefit at			One Child	Mother and		Maximum Family Benefit
	Age 65 or Over	Age 60	Age 50 (Disabled)		One Child	Two Children	
$561-563	$396.10	$283.30	$198.20	$297.10	$594.20	$713.10	$712.90
564-567	398.20	284.80	199.20	298.70	597.40	715.80	715.70
568-570	400.40	286.30	200.30	300.00	600.60	717.90	717.80
571-574	402.30	287.70	201.30	301.80	603.60	720.60	720.60
575-577	404.40	289.20	202.30	303.30	606.60	723.00	722.90
578-581	406.20	290.50	203.20	304.70	609.40	725.70	725.60
582-584	408.40	292.10	204.30	306.30	612.60	727.80	727.80
585-588	410.20	293.30	205.20	307.70	615.40	730.80	730.70
589-591	412.60	295.10	206.40	309.50	619.00	732.90	732.80
592-595	414.60	296.50	207.40	311.00	622.00	735.60	735.60
596-598	416.70	298.00	208.50	312.60	625.20	737.70	737.60
599-602	418.70	299.40	209.40	314.10	628.20	740.70	740.70
603-605	420.70	300.90	210.50	315.60	631.20	742.80	742.80
606-609	422.80	302.40	211.50	317.10	634.20	745.50	745.50
610-612	424.90	303.90	212.60	318.70	637.40	747.90	747.80
613-616	426.90	305.30	213.60	320.20	640.40	750.90	750.70
617-620	428.90	306.70	214.50	321.70	643.40	753.60	753.50
621-623	431.00	308.20	215.60	323.30	646.60	755.70	755.60
624-627	433.00	309.60	216.60	324.80	649.60	758.70	758.50
628-630	435.10	311.10	217.60	326.40	652.80	761.40	761.20
631-634	437.10	312.60	218.70	327.90	655.80	765.00	764.90
635-637	439.20	314.10	219.70	329.40	658.80	768.60	768.50
638-641	441.40	315.70	220.80	331.10	662.20	772.20	772.20
642-644	443.20	316.90	221.70	332.40	664.80	775.80	775.60
645-648	445.40	318.50	222.80	334.10	668.20	779.40	779.40
649-652	447.40	319.90	223.80	335.60	671.20	783.00	782.80
653-656	448.60	320.80	224.40	336.50	673.00	785.10	785.00
657-660	449.90	321.70	225.00	337.50	675.00	787.20	787.20
661-665	451.50	322.90	225.90	338.70	677.40	790.20	790.10
666-670	453.10	324.00	226.60	339.70	679.80	792.90	792.90
671-675	454.80	325.20	227.50	341.10	682.20	795.60	795.60
676-680	456.40	326.40	228.30	342.30	684.60	798.60	798.50
681-685	458.00	327.50	229.00	343.50	687.00	801.60	801.40
686-690	459.80	328.80	230.00	344.90	689.80	804.30	804.10
691-695	461.20	329.80	230.70	345.90	691.80	807.30	807.10
696-700	462.80	331.00	231.50	347.10	694.20	810.00	809.90
701-705	464.50	332.20	232.40	348.40	696.80	812.70	812.70
706-710	466.10	333.30	233.10	349.60	699.20	815.70	815.50
711-715	467.70	334.50	234.00	350.80	701.60	818.40	818.30

Average Monthly Wage	Widow or Widower Claiming Benefit at			One Child	Mother and		Maximum Family Benefit
	Age 65 or Over	Age 60	Age 50 (Disabled)		One Child	Two Children	
$716-720	$469.40	$335.70	$234.80	$352.10	$704.20	$821.40	$821.20
721-725	471.00	336.80	235.60	353.30	706.60	824.10	824.00
726-730	472.60	338.00	236.40	354.50	709.00	827.10	826.90
731-735	474.20	339.10	237.20	355.70	711.40	829.80	829.90
736-740	475.90	340.30	238.00	357.00	714.00	832.50	832.60
741-745	477.40	341.40	238.80	358.10	716.20	835.50	835.60
746-750	478.90	342.50	239.60	359.20	718.40	838.20	838.70
751-755	480.40	343.50	240.30	360.30	720.60	840.90	840.70
756-760	481.80	344.50	241.00	361.40	722.80	843.00	843.10
761-765	483.20	345.50	241.70	362.40	724.80	845.40	845.50
766-770	484.50	346.50	242.40	363.40	726.80	847.80	847.90
771-775	485.80	347.40	243.00	364.40	728.80	850.20	850.20
776-780	487.20	348.40	243.70	365.40	730.80	852.60	852.50
781-785	488.60	349.40	244.40	366.50	733.00	855.00	854.90
786-790	489.80	350.30	245.00	367.40	734.80	857.10	857.20
791-795	491.10	351.20	245.70	368.40	736.80	859.50	859.50
796-800	492.50	352.20	246.40	369.40	738.80	861.90	861.90
801-805	494.00	353.30	247.10	370.50	741.00	864.30	864.40
806-810	495.30	354.20	247.80	371.50	743.00	866.70	866.60
811-815	469.70	355.20	248.50	372.60	745.20	869.10	869.20
816-820	498.00	356.10	249.10	373.50	747.00	871.50	871.40
821-825	499.40	357.10	249.80	374.60	749.20	873.90	873.90
826-830	500.70	358.10	250.50	375.60	751.20	876.30	876.20
831-835	502.00	359.00	251.10	376.50	753.00	878.70	878.50
836-840	503.30	359.90	251.70	377.50	755.00	880.80	880.80
841-845	504.70	360.90	252.40	378.60	757.20	883.50	883.30
846-850	506.00	361.80	253.10	379.50	759.00	885.60	885.50
851-855	507.50	362.90	253.80	380.70	761.40	888.00	888.00
856-860	508.80	363.80	254.50	381.60	763.20	890.40	890.30
861-865	510.20	364.80	255.20	382.70	765.40	892.80	892.70
866-870	511.50	365.80	255.90	383.70	767.40	895.20	895.10
871-875	512.90	366.80	256.60	384.70	769.40	897.30	897.40
876-880	514.10	367.60	257.10	385.60	771.20	899.70	899.70
881-885	515.50	363.60	257.80	386.70	773.40	902.10	902.20
886-890	516.80	369.60	258.50	387.60	775.20	904.50	904.40
891-895	518.20	370.00	259.20	388.70	777.40	907.20	906.30
896-900	519.60	371.60	259.90	389.70	779.40	909.30	909.30
901-905	521.00	372.60	260.60	390.80	781.60	911.70	911.70
906-910	522.30	373.50	261.30	391.80	783.60	914.10	914.10

Average Monthly Wage	Widow or Widower Claiming Benefit at			One Child	Mother and		Maximum Family Benefit
	Age 65 or Over	Age 60	Age 50 (Disabled)		One Child	Two Children	
$ 911-915	$523.70	$374.50	$262.00	$392.80	$785.60	$916.50	$916.40
916-920	525.10	375.50	262.70	393.90	787.80	918.60	918.50
921-925	526.30	376.40	263.30	394.80	789.60	921.20	921.10
926-930	527.60	377.30	263.90	395.70	791.40	923.30	923.30
931-935	529.00	378.30	264.60	396.80	793.60	925.80	925.70
936-940	530.40	379.30	265.30	397.80	795.60	928.20	928.10
941-945	531.70	380.20	265.90	398.80	797.60	930.50	930.50
946-950	533.00	381.10	266.60	399.80	799.60	932.80	932.80
951-955	534.50	382.20	267.30	400.90	801.80	935.40	935.30
956-960	535.90	383.20	268.00	402.00	804.00	937.70	937.60
961-965	537.30	384.20	268.70	403.00	806.00	940.00	939.90
966-970	538.40	385.00	269.30	403.80	807.60	942.20	942.30
971-975	539.80	386.00	270.00	404.90	809.80	944.80	944.70
976-980	541.20	387.00	270.70	405.90	811.80	947.00	946.90
981-985	542.60	388.00	271.40	407.00	814.00	949.40	949.30
986-990	543.80	388.90	272.00	407.90	815.80	951.60	951.70
991-995	545.20	389.90	272.70	408.90	817.80	954.10	954.10
996-1,000	546.60	390.90	273.40	410.00	820.00	956.50	956.40
1,001-1,005	547.80	391.70	274.00	410.90	821.80	958.50	958.40
1,006-1,010	548.90	392.50	274.50	411.70	823.40	960.60	960.70
1,011-1,015	550.20	393.40	275.20	412.70	825.40	962.80	962.70
1,016-1,020	551.50	394.40	275.90	413.70	827.40	965.10	965.00
1,021-1,025	552.60	395.20	276.40	414.50	829.00	967.20	967.00
1,026-1,030	553.80	396.00	277.00	415.40	830.80	969.30	969.20
1,031-1,035	555.10	396.90	277.60	416.40	832.80	971.40	971.30
1,036-1,040	556.20	397.70	278.70	417.20	834.40	973.50	973.40
1,041-1,045	557.50	398.70	278.90	418.20	836.40	975.60	975.60
1,046-1,050	558.80	399.60	279.50	419.10	838.20	977.70	977.70
1,051-1,055	559.80	400.30	280.00	419.90	839.80	979.80	979.70
1,056-1,060	561.10	401.20	280.60	420.90	841.80	982.20	982.00
1,061-1,065	562.40	402.20	281.30	421.80	843.60	984.00	984.00
1,066-1,070	563.60	403.00	281.90	422.70	845.40	986.40	986.30
1,071-1,075	564.80	403.90	282.50	423.60	847.20	988.50	988.30
1,076-1,080	566.00	404.70	283.10	424.50	849.00	990.60	990.50
1,081-1,085	567.30	405.70	283.80	425.50	851.00	992.70	992.50
1,086-1,090	568.40	406.50	284.30	426.30	852.60	994.80	994.70
1,091-1,095	569.70	407.40	285.00	427.30	854.60	996.90	996.90
1,096-1,100	571.00	408.30	285.60	428.30	856.60	999.00	999.00
1,101-1,105	572.00	409.00	286.10	429.00	858.00	1,001.10	1,001.00

Average Monthly Wage	Widow or Widower Claiming Benefit at			One Child	Mother and		Maximum Family Benefit
	Age 65 or Over	Age 60	Age 50 (Disabled)		One Child	Two Children	
$1,106-1,110	$573.30	$410.00	$286.80	$430.00	$860.00	$1,003.20	$1,003.20
1,111-1,115	574.60	410.90	287.40	431.00	862.00	1,005.30	1,005.30
1,116-1,120	575.70	411.70	288.00	431.80	863.60	1,007.70	1,007.60
1,121-1,125	577.00	412.60	288.60	432.80	865.60	1,009.80	1,009.60
1,126-1,130	578.20	413.50	289.20	433.70	867.40	1,011.90	1,011.80
1,131-1,135	579.40	414.30	289.80	434.60	869.20	1,014.00	1,013.80
1,136-1,140	580.60	415.20	290.40	435.50	871.00	1,016.10	1,016.10
1,141-1,145	581.90	416.10	291.00	436.50	873.00	1,018.20	1,018.20
1,146-1,150	583.10	417.00	291.70	437.40	874.80	1,020.30	1,020.30
1,151-1,155	584.20	417.80	292.20	438.20	876.40	1,022.40	1,022.30
1,156-1,160	585.50	418.70	292.90	439.20	878.40	1,024.50	1,024.50
1,161-1,165	586.70	419.50	293.40	440.10	880.20	1,026.60	1,026.60
1,166-1,170	587.90	420.40	294.10	441.00	882.00	1,029.00	1,028.90
1,171-1,175	589.20	421.30	294.70	441.90	883.80	1,031.10	1,030.90
1,176-1,180	590.30	422.10	295.20	442.80	885.60	1,033.20	1,033.00
1,181-1,185	591.40	422.90	295.80	443.60	887.20	1,035.00	1,034.90
1,186-1,190	592.60	423.80	296.40	444.50	889.00	1,037.10	1,036.90
1,191-1,195	593.70	424.50	296.90	445.30	890.60	1,038.90	1,038.90
1,196-1,200	594.80	425.30	297.50	446.10	892.20	1,041.00	1,040.90
1,201-1,205	595.90	426.10	298.00	447.00	894.00	1,042.80	1,042.80
1,206-1,210	597.10	427.00	298.70	447.90	895.80	1,044.90	1,044.90
1,211-1,215	598.20	427.80	299.20	448.70	897.40	1,047.00	1,046.80
1,216-1,220	599.30	428.50	299.70	449.50	899.00	1,048.80	1,048.80
1,221-1,225	600.40	429.30	300.30	450.30	900.60	1,050.90	1,050.70
1,226-1,230	601.60	430.20	300.90	451.20	902.40	1,052.70	1,052.70
1,231-1,235	602.70	431.00	301.50	452.10	904.20	1,054.80	1,054.60
1,236-1,240	603.80	431.80	302.00	452.90	905.80	1,056.90	1,056.70
1,241-1,245	605.00	432.60	302.60	453.80	907.60	1,058.70	1,058.60
1,246-1,250	606.10	433.40	303.10	454.60	909.20	1,060.60	1,060.60
1,251-1,255	607.20	434.20	303.70	455.40	910.80	1,062.60	1,062.50
1,256-1,260	608.30	435.00	304.30	456.30	912.60	1,064.70	1,064.60
1,261-1,265	609.50	435.80	304.80	457.70	914.40	1,066.50	1,066.50
1,266-1,270	610.60	436.60	305.40	458.00	916.00	1,068.60	1,068.50
1,271-1,275	611.70	437.40	305.90	458.80	917.60	1,070.40	1,070.40
1,276-1,280	612.80	438.20	306.50	459.60	919.20	1,072.50	1,072.40
1,281-1,285	613.80	438.90	307.00	460.40	920.80	1,074.30	1,074.20
1,286-1,290	614.90	439.70	307.50	461.20	922.40	1,076.10	1,076.10
1,291-1,295	616.00	440.50	308.10	462.00	924.00	1,077.90	1,077.90
1,296-1,300	617.00	441.20	308.60	462.80	925.60	1,080.00	1,079.80

Average Monthly Wage	Widow or Widower Claiming Benefit at			One Child	Mother and		Maximum Family Benefit
	Age 65 or Over	Age 60	Age 50 (Disabled)		One Child	Two Children	
$1,301-1,305	$618.10	$442.00	$309.20	$463.60	$927.20	$1,081.80	$1,081.60
1,306-1,310	619.10	442.70	309.60	464.40	928.80	1,083.60	1,083.50
1,311-1,315	620.20	443.50	310.20	465.20	930.40	1,085.40	1,085.30
1,316-1,320	621.30	444.30	310.80	466.00	932.00	1,087.30	1,087.20
1,321-1,325	622.30	445.00	311.30	466.80	933.60	1,089.10	1,089.00
1,326-1,330	623.40	445.80	311.80	467.60	935.20	1,091.00	1,090.90
1,331-1,335	624.40	446.50	312.30	468.30	936.60	1,092.70	1,092.70
1,336-1,340	625.50	447.30	312.90	469.20	938.40	1,094.70	1,094.60
1,341-1,345	626.60	448.10	313.40	470.00	940.00	1,096.50	1,096.40
1,346-1,350	627.60	448.80	313.90	470.70	941.40	1,098.30	1,098.30
1,351-1,355	628.70	449.60	314.50	471.60	943.20	1,100.20	1,100.10
1,356-1,360	629.70	450.30	315.00	472.30	944.60	1,102.00	1,102.00
1,361-1,365	630.80	451.10	315.50	473.10	946.20	1,103.90	1,103.80
1,366-1,370	631.80	451.80	316.00	473.90	947.80	1,105.70	1,105.80
1,371-1,375	632.90	452.60	316.60	474.70	949.40	1,107.60	1,107.60

Index